The Handweaver's Pattern Directory

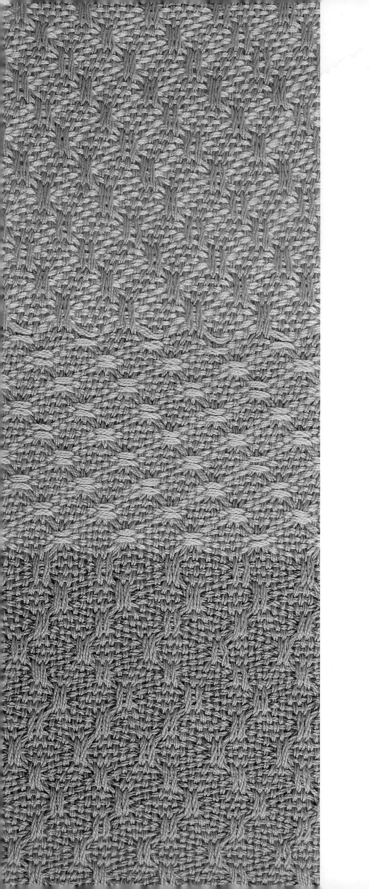

The Handweaver's Pattern Directory

Over 600 weaves for four-shaft looms

Anne Dixon

 INTERWEAVE.

interweavestore.com

A QUARTO BOOK

Copyright © 2007 Quarto Inc.

First edition for North America published
in 2007 by:

Interweave Press LLC
201 East Fourth Street
Loveland, CO 80537-5655
interweavestore.com

ISBN: 978-1-59668-040-1

Conceived, designed, and produced by
Quarto Publishing plc
The Old Brewery
6 Blundell Street
London N7 9BH

QUAR.TWE

Library of Congress Cataloging-in-Publication Data
    Dixon, Anne.
    The handweaver's pattern directory : over 600 weaves for 4-shaft
    looms / Anne Dixon.
        p. cm.
    Includes index.
    ISBN 978-1-59668-040-1
    1. Hand weaving--Patterns. 2. Weaving--Patterns.
    I. Title.
    TT848.D54 2007
    746.1'4041--dc22
    2007026351

Project editors: Mary Groom & Katie Hallam
Copy editor: Vicki Vrint
Art director: Caroline Guest
Art editor: Julie Joubinaux
Designer: Tania Field
Photographer: Philip Wilkins
Illustrator: Kate Simunek

Creative director: Moira Clinch
Publisher: Paul Carslake

Manufactured by Modern Age Repro House Ltd,
                                        Hong Kong
Printed in China by 1010 Printing International Ltd

10 9 8 7 6 5 4 3

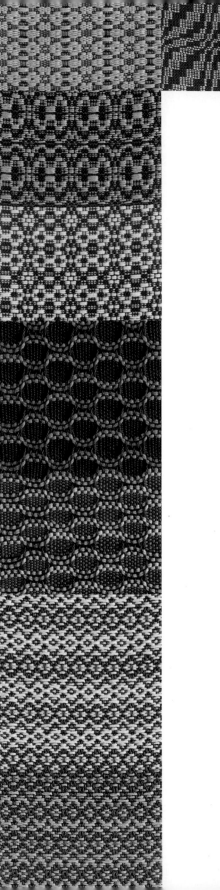

Contents

Introduction

Weaving is our inheritance from our forebears, handed down through generations for thousands of years.

I love the challenge, anticipation, and sense of achievement it brings. The controlled structure of the process provides a framework within which to experiment and to push the boundaries. There are so many techniques to try. Each piece of fabric that you weave is unique.

Throughout my weaving I have received kindness and tremendous help from others. I have been so lucky.

Thank you.

Anne

A Craftsman's Creed

All of the fine traditions and the skill
Are mine to use to raise my craft renown,
And mine to teach again with reverent will.
Thus do I love to serve,
With fingers that are masters of the tool.

Anon

About This Book

The first section of this book will guide you through some essential and helpful information about equipment, fibers, yarns, selvedges, calculations, and color. With this knowledge at your fingertips, you will be ready to move on to the main part of the book, the pattern directory. Here you'll find a vast array of weaving drafts and samples, suitable for all skill levels. Whether you want to dip in and find a pattern that takes your fancy, concentrate on a particular technique, or work through from start to finish, you'll find everything you need to weave some new and wonderful designs. Once you've woven your piece, you'll need to know how to finish it off to best effect. The end section of this book will advise you on how to do just that, with reference to hemming, smocking, fringes, whipping, and laundry care.

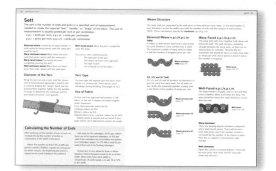

p6–25 Introduction

The beginning of this book provides a background to the fundamental aspects of weaving, such as the equipment you'll need, how to thread a selvedge, and how to calculate warp length. There is plenty of interesting information on fibers and yarns, and a useful color wheel to help you choose the right colors for your projects.

p26–241 Pattern Directory

The main bulk of the book, the directory, is divided into four main sections: Basic Threadings, Block Drafts, Lace Weaves, and Special Threadings. Each type of weave within that category is introduced with written detail on the technical aspects, before progressing to the drafts and samples.

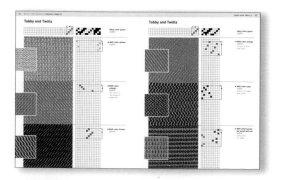

The Weaving Drafts

A typical page will start with the warp-thread weave draft shown at the top, with written instruction to the right. Full-color photographs of woven samples follow below, each accompanied with written technical instructions—regarding the weft thread and other details—to the far right, with the draft in between. See "Understanding the Weaving Drafts" opposite for full details.

Understanding the Weaving Drafts

1. Warp threading draft
The grid at the top of the page is the warp threading draft. The lines of horizontal rules represent the four shafts (top rule = shaft 4; bottom rule = shaft 1). The draft is read from right to left. Each blocked-in square is in the color of the thread used in the samples.

2. Threading pattern repeats
Red vertical rules indicate where a single repeat of the threading pattern draft starts and finishes. The circular black arrow indicates where the threading pattern is repeated. The red arrow shows the direction in which the pattern is threaded.

7. Sample A full-color sample of the weave is pictured from the front.

8. Reverse A smaller full-color sample of most of the weaves is pictured from the reverse.

9. Close-up Many of the weaves have a close-up image to show even more detail.

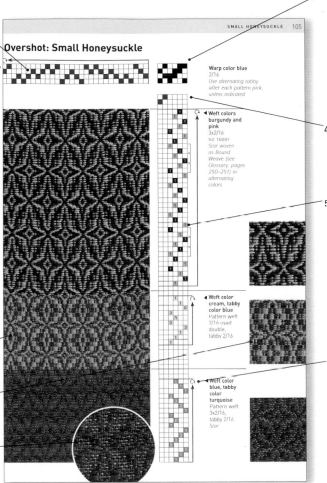

SMALL HONEYSUCKLE 105

Overshot: Small Honeysuckle

Warp color blue
2/16
Use alternating tabby
after each pattern pick,
unless indicated

◄ Weft colors
burgundy and
pink
3x2/16
NO TABBY
Star woven
as Bound
Weave (see
Glossary, pages
250–251) in
alternating
colors

◄ Weft color
cream, tabby
color blue
Pattern weft
2/16 used
double,
tabby 2/16

◄ Weft color
blue, tabby
color
turquoise
Pattern weft
3x2/16,
tabby 2/16
Star

3. Shaft combination (tie-up grid)
Blocked-in squares in the boxed grid show the shafts that are to be lifted together. NOTE: If you have a foot-controlled loom that depresses the shafts, then read the combinations to be treadled as the empty squares.

4. Using plain weave
If plain weave (tabby) is to be used, it is indicated at the top of the weaving draft.

5. Weaving draft
A blocked-in square indicates that the combination of shafts indicated in the boxed grid directly above that column is to be used for the row (pick). Colors used correspond to the color of the thread used in the sample. A number inside a blocked-in square indicates that the pick is to be repeated that number of times.

6. Weaving pattern repeats
The red arrow marks a single repeat and shows the direction in which the draft should be read— from the bottom upward (the same direction as the weaving grows on the loom). The circular black arrow indicates where the weaving pattern should be repeated.

Gamps

Some samples are featured across two pages as blocks of three adjacent but different threading drafts within one piece. Three different weaving drafts are woven across the whole piece, resulting in a "gamp" (sample combination) of nine different woven patterns.

NOTE

The warp threading drafts for the samples adhere to the rules as outlined in the technical details relating to the threading sequences in the introduction to each section, but may be worked in a different direction, or indeed start on a different shaft.

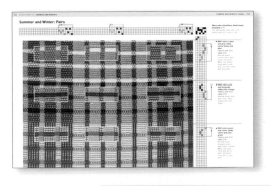

Flap

Don't forget to make use of the handy pull-out flap at the back of this book, which is a quick-reference guide to understanding the weaving drafts. You can pull this out and leave it open alongside the page you're working from, so you can keep those fingers busy weaving instead of turning backwards and forwards!

Basic Equipment

Items of equipment range from the essential to the useful, with variations of type for many. Some items can be homemade rather than bought.

Loom

If possible, try several before buying. It must be sturdy. Tapestry and floor rugs can be woven on special equipment or on a four-shaft loom. "Multishaft" refers to looms with more than four shafts, but, as this book shows, there are so many possibilities that can be woven using a four-shaft loom that it may be all you need.

Floor loom

The shafts can be raised, lowered, or both, simultaneously using treadles. Because the feet power the loom, the hands are free to throw the shuttle and beat the weft into place.

Loom bench

For use with a floor loom (see above), this should preferably be adjustable in height, so that the weaver's waist is above the weaving.

Table loom

The shafts are usually raised to create the sheds by means of hand-operated levers or pulleys. Some have a folding castle for ease of storage; some can be converted to floor models.

Recommended

Raddle
Useful as a "comb" to both separate the warp ends evenly across the width and to check for any slackness in the warp during warping.

Shed sticks
Form a firm base for the initial heading.

Pick-up stick
Used to pick up warp thread. You can use a stick shuttle but a pointed pick-up stick is easier.

Rug beater or fork
For weft-face weaves.

Useful

Cone holder
Used to hold multiple cones while warping. Tip: Make a cone holder by hammering in long nails right through a flat piece of board.

Spool holder
Holds a single spool in place while winding warp or shuttle.

Spool rack
A method of holding several spools, especially when winding fine warps.

Shuttles

The choice of shuttle you use will come down to your own preference—but it's best to try new types whenever possible.
Stick: straight, netting, ski, rug.
Boat: roller or flat; single or double; center-feed or end-feed.

To be kept on hand while working:

- Weaver's snips or scissors—a small size is best.
- Tape measure.
- Fine, smooth yarn—for marking woven warp-length measurements. Only a short length is needed. After winding on, insert into the next pick somewhere in the center of the weaving by placing under two raised ends, over about 1 inch (2.5 cm), and then under two raised ends. Leave this in the weaving until it is necessary to wind on again and measure the length of woven cloth before pulling out the fine yarn and reinserting. Make sure you record the new length (or total length). Sticking a length of masking tape onto your loom ensures you always have the record visible and on hand.
- A few pins for mending broken ends.
- Notebook and pencil for recording progress details and comments.

Bobbin winder

For boat shuttles.
Tip: Make bobbins out of circles of paper.

Heddles

Wire, string, or polyester.
Tip: Make your own heddles using a template of four nails.

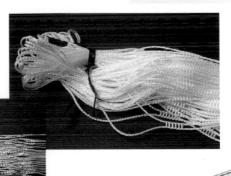

Threading hook

For threading the warp ends through the heddles.

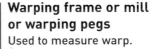

Reed hook or fish

You can use the threading hook, but the fish is easier to draw several strands together through the dents.

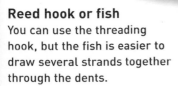

Warping frame or mill or warping pegs

Used to measure warp.

Warping sticks or

lengths of strong paper for winding on, so that the warp ends don't become embedded within each other. Can be used together or alone.

Fibers

Fibers come from several sources, falling into three main groups: animal, vegetable, and synthetic. They are usually thin and hairlike. Alone they are weak, but when twisted together fibers create a strong thread. The length of an individual fiber is called the staple, and this affects the strength and appearance of the yarn spun from the fiber.

Animal (Protein) Fibers

Wool

There are many breeds of sheep, producing wool fibers of very different staple lengths, counts, and qualities. Wool can shed water, and when worn can absorb excessive moisture, so wool garments do not make you cold and clammy. Wool insulates and is also fire resistant.

Some sheep produce long fibers, others short; some fibers are fine, others coarse; some fibers are almost straight, others curly and "crimped." The length of the staple can vary from 1 to 15 inches (2.5 to 40 cm). Generally, the shorter staples produce usually finer, warmer fibers with a high degree of crimp. They will felt easily. The longer staples produce thicker and stronger fibers, but will have less softness and crimp. Some longer staples have a good luster.

Yarns spun from wool fibers

Hair

From the coats of several animals. It is often more expensive than wool.

Mohair From the Angora goat. A strong fiber, as long as 10 inches (25 cm). Springy and lustrous. Does not felt easily.

Cashmere From the undercoat of the Cashmere/Tibetan goat. Soft, short, warm, and downy fiber with a slight luster. Staple is 1½ to 3½ inches (4 to 9 cm) long.

Alpaca From the coat of the Peruvian camelid (which has coarse outer hair). Highly lustrous with little crimp. Softer than mohair but not as soft as camel or cashmere.

Camel Fibers from the outer coat are tough and coarse. The undercoat is most often used: fibers are soft, short, and fine.

Goat From the outer coat of any breed of goat. Coarse and hard-wearing. Can be blended with wool for a tweedy-effect yarn.

Angora Not from the goat but from the Angora breed of rabbit. Fine, soft, and fluffy fibers.

Silk Extruded by the silk moth when forming its cocoon, silk is the only natural filament (continuous fiber). Filaments can be as long as 1 mile (1.6 km), and are fine, strong, and lustrous with good elasticity. Silk is warm, soft, and delicate, naturally crease resistant and drapes well. The two common silks are: Bombyx mori—the whitest, most lustrous, and finest filament; and tussah—less lustrous filaments, ivory or deeper in color, and coarser.

Dyed alpaca

Angora

Vegetable (Cellulose) Fibers

Cotton From the seedpod—or boll—of the cotton plant. Warm and soft. A short, fine staple. The average staple length is 1 inch (2.5 cm), with Sea Island cotton having the longest, finest, and most lustrous staples; Indian cotton the shortest and coarsest.

Kapok Similar to cotton, but much shorter and silkier. It is not easy to spin, so is often used for stuffing.

Bast fibers

Inner fibers from plant stems. Lack elasticity.

Linen and Hemp From the woody stems of the flax or hemp plant. Strong, lustrous, and smooth. Absorbs moisture, dries quickly.

Nettle Fine and lustrous.

Bamboo Highly absorbent. The plant is ground and wrung to create short fibers.

Jute Coarse and not very strong. Jute, especially, deteriorates with moisture.

Ramie Strong, lustrous, and reasonably fine.

Leaf fibers

New Zealand flax From the phormium plant. Several types, producing different lengths and luster. Traditionally not truly spun but the fibers are twisted together to form yarn as long as 3 yards (2.7 m).

Pinna Fibers from pineapple leaves. Filmy and shiny.

Raffia From palm leaves.

Regenerated fibers

Rayon and Tencel Regenerated from cellulose reduced to a viscous pulp.

Soya Regenerated from the bean pulp after oil has been extracted.

Synthetic Fibers

Polyester Usually described as such. Similar to cotton. Looks and feels better than nylon. Fairly crease resistant.

Olefin Most common types: polypropylene and polyethylene. These are unlike any natural fibers—they have their own unique properties.

Polyacrylic Most common type: acrylic. Not as strong as nylon and polyester. Widely used in knitting yarn because it resembles wool.

Polyamide Most common type: nylon. Made from petro-chemicals and dissimilar from any natural fibers. First created in New York and London, hence its name. Very strong, with good elasticity.

Spinning

The nature of a yarn reflects the fiber from which it is spun. While filament (continuous) fibers are grouped and lightly twisted together, shorter fibers need to be spun to create a yarn. The twist increases the strength of the fibers.

The individual fibers are drawn out to produce overlapping lengths that are then twisted or spun to become a continuous length of yarn. The twist of the spinning can be tight or loose. This initial single twisting or spinning produces a single yarn. It can be used for weaving, but sometimes has a tendency to snarl or whiz back on itself.

There are two main spinning techniques, used for all types of fibers:

Fibers can be twisted in either direction: S or Z. S-spun yarns have the angle of twist running from top left to bottom right; Z-spun yarns have their angle of twist from top right to bottom left. It is easy to remember the direction because it is the angle of the center of the letter.

Woolen Spun

The fibers are carded before spinning to make them lie in different directions. This produces a yarn that contains a great deal of air within it. It is warm and soft with good elasticity, maintaining the shrinkage and any felting properties of the fiber used.

Worsted Spun

The fibers are combed before spinning to make them lie straight and parallel. Produces a smoother and harder yarn than woolen spun. The natural luster of the fibers used shows up well. Usually plied, it is hard-wearing and crease resistant, with good insulation properties.

Different types of fiber may be combined—blended—to produce yarn. An expensive fiber can be blended with a less expensive one. If there is less than 10 percent of a fiber in the blend, there is little effect upon the nature of the other fiber.

Yarns

The properties of a yarn depend on the type(s) of fiber used to create it.

Plied Yarns

Plied yarns are stronger and more stable than single yarns. For these, two or more singles are twisted together. The direction of twist for the ply is usually the opposite to that of the singles that are used. By twisting in the opposite direction the emphasis of the twist is neutralized.

Two singles yarns plied together produce two-ply. Three singles form three-ply, and so on. Three-ply or greater produces a rounder, more even yarn than two-ply, which is simply a series of rotating flat planes.

The thickness of the singles, and thus of the plied yarns, can vary. Knitting yarns were originally designated as two-ply, three-ply, etc., according to the number of standardized singles used. Double Knitting was twice the thickness of four-ply and Chunky was twice the thickness of Double Knitting. Now knitting yarns are no longer categorized by just these names.

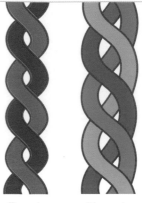

Two-ply   Three-ply

Silks

Reeled silk The combination of five or six cocoon filaments reeled together to produce a single yarn. Its shrinkage is nil.
Spun silk Short lengths of the filament, often from broken cocoons or the ends of reeled silk, spun to create a yarn. Spun in a worsted manner, it is usually plied (see above). It is not as lustrous as reeled silk because of its shorter fibers. It is lovely to use. The shrinkage is about 10 percent.
Nubbed and noil silk yarns Even the rejects and the tangled noils from the spun silk can be used to make textured yarns.

Linen

Linen soils less easily than cotton. It is cool and fairly hard-wearing. It absorbs water very easily. Unfortunately it also creases easily. Although linen has little or no elasticity when dry, a degree can be added during weaving by laying a wet cloth on the warp threads behind the heddles. Leave for a very short while for the moisture to be absorbed by the linen, remove the cloth and weave, repeating each time you wind on. This is less messy than spraying.

Mercerized Cotton

The yarn is finished in a bath of caustic soda— which makes it contract—and then it is stretched to its original length, which makes the yarn silky and lustrous. Finally the yarn is neutralized and laundered. This is not easy to do at home! Mercerized cotton is easy to work with, being strong, crisp, and durable.

Fancy Yarns

Use with discretion. Fancy yarns need careful planning if they are to be used as one of the main weaving yarns, even if used as a main weft thread. They can be used as highlights, and are easiest to use in the weft because there can be problems getting them through the heddle eye.

Choosing Warp and Weft Yarns

Different yarn types can be combined safely in a single piece of weaving, one as warp and another as weft. Before placing both together in either the warp or weft, however, check to see that take-up and shrinkage is the same.

Weft Yarns

Weft yarns can be anything! Even the most fragile and unstable yarns can be used.

Warp Yarns

These need to be strong, firm, and compact, with some elasticity to accommodate the lowering and raising of the shafts when making the shed. They need to be compact to cope with the beating of the reed and rubbing of the dents, and firm to withstand the pressure of the heddles.

Hold a length of yarn with your hands about 18 inches (45 cm) apart. Gently pull to see if the yarn remains stable. If it doesn't, then it's unsuitable as a warp yarn.

Mixing Yarns

Using yarns spun from different fibers. Sometimes a yarn itself is created from more than one type of fiber. If this is the case, it is a good idea to launder the fabric according to the requirements of the most delicate of the fibers.

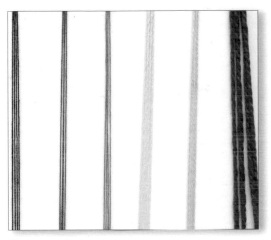

Warp or weft yarns.

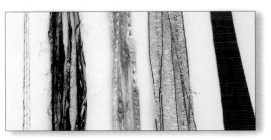

Fancy yarns using mixed fibers.

THE SAMPLES IN THIS BOOK

The yarns used for the samples in this book are all cotton, in two sizes. The finer yarn is 2/16: two sixteenth singles plied together, twisted S. The thicker yarn is composed of three of the 2/16 yarns loosely twisted together (3×2/16), twisted Z.

Threading the Selvedges

The selvedge—which literally means "self edge"—is the closed woven edge formed on either side of the cloth. The selvedges can be additions to the warp or incorporated within the pattern. There is a simple formula for threading the selvedges, which will help to maintain the correct number of picks per inch (p.p.i.) or picks per centimeter (p.p.c.m.).

Separate selvedge, balanced weave

A separately warped selvedge on a straight-entry threading draft.

Use 12 ends for each selvedge. Thread the 4 extreme outer threads in single order, then thread the next 8 threads as doubles.

Thread these 12 selvedge ends through the reed at double the sett of the main fabric—if the main sett is 2 ends per dent (i.e., 2 ends between two teeth in the reed), then all of the selvedge will be at 4 ends per dent, using 3 dents overall.

There are more intersections with the weft in the singles section at the extreme edge than there are for the double entries just inside these.

main pattern

			1				2	
		1				2		
	1				2			
1				2				

			2				1
		2				1	
	2				1		
2				1			

The ends that have been threaded through at double the sett, compressing into a tighter space, will help to maintain the correct weft sett across the main fabric as the picks cannot be beaten too closely. The formula works for twill, too (below right).

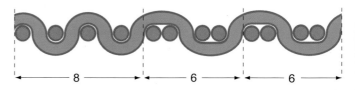

Selvedge interlacement 4 ends per dent, tabby

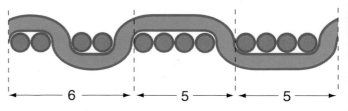

Selvedge interlacement 4 ends per dent, 2/2 twill

Patterns worked to the edge If you want the pattern to go right to the edge of the fabric, then double the ends that are 4 inside the edge and thread the 12 outer ends through the reed as above.

Warp-face As the ends are already set closely together there is no need for a separately calculated or threaded selvedge.

Weft-face Double the 2 or 3 outer threads at each side.

Warp-dominant Double outer 4 only.

Weft-dominant Treat as a balanced weave.

Selvedges on tabby

Floating selvedge This is an extra end at the extreme outer edge that is not threaded through any heddle and so does not move when the shed is opened. It is therefore simple to insert the shuttle either above or below the floating selvedge, and equally easy for the shuttle to exit from the shed either above or below. Several weave structures, for example a point-shedded twill, will have the same ends raised or lowered for consecutive picks. By taking the weft around the floating selvedge it will be woven right to the edges of the work.

The easiest way to use a floating selvedge is to always enter the shuttle into the shed either above or below, and to exit in the opposite way. Which way you do this is up to you; there is no right or wrong way—so either enter above and leave below or enter below and leave above. Do the same for every pick, no matter from which side—even, if using two shuttles, if consecutive picks are from the same side. They will, after all, be entering at a different level than they each exited from their previous pick.

It is often useful to use a doubled thread for the floating selvedge. Add to the rest of the warp ends and sley it separately through the reed, otherwise it may intertwine with the other warp ends in the selvedge. If the tension of the floating warp does become loose, it is easy to hang a weight on it just under the warp beam.

Beating the Weft

It is important that the weft is beaten correctly, so that the weft fits against the fell.

Table Loom

Balanced weave Insert the weft at an angle and hold the shuttle without any overt tension so that the weft just fits against the far selvedge. Beat very gently until the weft is almost in place. Change the shed and beat again into position.

Warp-face Hold the weft under tension at right angles to the warp, change the shed and beat firmly. Tug the weft slightly before entering the next pick—this will undo any buckling that may have occurred at the selvedge.

Weft-face The weft needs to be slack enough to curve under and over the warp without pulling in the edges. Insert the weft at an angle. Starting at the entry side, and using your fingers, draw the weft down into a series of curves across the warp. Beat into place, change the shed, and beat hard to confirm.

Floor Loom

Balanced weave Work as for table loom, but close the shed before beating and open the next shed as you push the beater away from the fell.

Warp-face Work as for table loom, but if you hold the weft under tension as you beat, there will be no buckling to undo.

Weft-face Insert the weft at an angle and curve as for table loom. Close the shed, beat into place, open the next shed and beat hard before inserting the next pick.

Sett

The sett is the number of ends and picks in a specified unit of measurement needed to create the required "feel," "handle," or "drape" of the fabric. The unit of measurement is usually quoted per inch or per centimeter:

e.p.i. = ends per inch; e.p.c.m. = ends per centimeter

p.p.i. = picks per inch; p.p.c.m. = picks per centimeter

Balanced weave Created by an equal number of ends and picks being woven, with the same yarn used for each.
Warp-dominant weave When there are more ends than picks, woven with the same yarn.
Warp-faced weave Formed by the ends completely covering the weft.
Weft-dominant weave When there are more picks than ends, woven with the same yarn.

Weft-faced weave When the picks completely cover the warp.

The correct sett is determined by:
1   The diameter of the yarn
2   The weave structure (see opposite)
3   The type of yarn
4   The eventual use of the fabric.

Diameter of the Yarn

Wrap the yarn around a ruler until the chosen unit of measurement (generally 1 inch/2.5 cm) is covered, making the "wraps" touch, but not pushing them together tightly. Use the number of wraps to determine the maximum sett for your weave structure—see opposite.

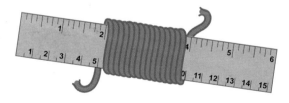

Yarn Type

The yarn type will depend upon the fibers from which it is constructed. There will be some shrinkage during finishing. (See pages 12–15.)

Use of Fabric

A close sett (see opposite) will produce a stiff fabric, so the sett is always calculated slightly under maximum:
Firm, hard-wearing: reduce by 5%
Clothing: reduce by 10%
Woolen: reduce by 15%
Draping fabrics (e.g., scarves): reduce by 20–25%
    Always weave a sample and wet finish it (see page 247) to see if adjustments need to be made.

Calculating the Number of Ends

After working out the number of e.p.i. or e.p.c.m., multiply this by the number of inches or centimeters in the width of the piece.

Adjust the number so that it fits in with any pattern repeats. (Pattern repeats do not have to be whole repeats; the beginning and end of a repeat can be used to balance the pattern.)

Add ends for the selvedges: 24 (12 per side) if there are to be separate selvedges, or 8 (4 per side) if the selvedges are to be within the pattern (see Selvedges, pages 16–17). Add 4 ends (2 per side) if there are to be floating selvedges.

Remember to also allow for draw-in when weaving. Unless the piece needs to be a certain width, allow even more extra width to compensate. A useful guide is to add 10 to 12% to the width.

Weave Structure

The warp ends are separated by the weft yarns as they intersect each other, so the total number of yarn diameters across the width uses both the number of ends and the number of intersections. NOTE: These calculations specify the **maximum** e.p.i./e.p.c.m.

Balanced Weave e.p.i./e.p.c.m.

Tabby

In tabby, or plain weave, each end is intersected by a pick (shown in cross-section over 4 ends). The maximum number of warp ends for tabby is half the number of wrapped yarns per unit.

Weave structure tabby (page 27)

2/2, 1/3, and 3/1 Twill

2/2, 1/3, and 3/1 twill all produce six diameters of yarn for every four warp ends. For all twills on four shafts the maximum number of warp ends is two thirds of the number of wraps per unit.

Weave structure 2/2 (page 27)

Weave structure 1/3 (page 27)

Weave structure 3/1 (page 27)

Warp-Faced e.p.i./e.p.c.m.

The warp ends will close together both above and below the weft. The weft remains completely straight between the warp ends, so there are no intersections to consider. Theoretically the maximum sett would be twice as many warp ends as wraps per unit, but in practice about 1½ times the number is required.

Warp-faced (pages 230-231)

Weft-Faced e.p.i./e.p.c.m.

The warp remains straight, and it is the weft that closes together above and below the warp. The warp should be about the same thickness or less than the weft.

Weft-faced (pages 236–237)

Warp-dominant

There are varying degrees between a balanced and a warp-faced weave. There will be more ends than picks, but if the number of ends is increased by the number of decreases of picks, then this is a guide to achieving the right number.

Weft-dominant

Again this can be to varying degrees. There will be more picks than ends and the warp will show and intersect.

Calculating the Warp Length

Once you've worked out the sett of fabric required, you need to consider a number of other factors when calculating the warp length.

Again allowances need to be made—this time for the take-up during weaving. (The exception is for weft-faced weaves, where the warp will remain absolutely straight between the curving weft threads.) A useful guide is to add about 10 to 12 percent to the total required finished length.

You will also need to add on "loom waste." This is the length of warp needed for tying the warp on the loom, and also for the length of warp needed at the end of the piece, stretching from the final edge, through the heddles, and to the apron rod. If the apron rod, holding the end of the warp, comes too close behind the shafts, the sheds can't be opened properly. Add about 27 inches (70 cm) for a table loom, or 1 yard (90 cm) for a floor loom.

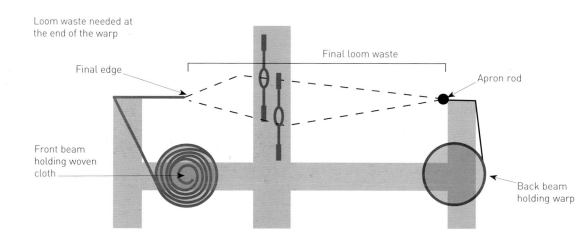

Loom waste needed at the end of the warp

Final loom waste

Final edge

Apron rod

Front beam holding woven cloth

Back beam holding warp

Other additions include a length for fringes between pieces; allowance for headings; extra lengths for any turned hems; and a length for an initial test piece. It is better to overestimate— rather than underestimate—these additions.

Fringes For fringes between pieces, add an extra allowance of about 50 percent to the required fringe lengths if they are to be twisted or braided. The loom waste can be used for fringes at the very beginning and end.
Headings Headings are short (see Finishings, pages 244–246), but you do need to include them at both the beginning and end of each piece.
Hems Also fairly short, but if you don't include them in your calculations, you could end up with too short a warp length.

Test pieces Add about 6 inches (15 cm) to produce a short test piece at the start of weaving. This is to check the threading and tension of the warp and to achieve the correct p.p.i./p.p.c.m. It can be satisfying to add a further 20 inches (50 cm) for experimenting with other weft colors and patterns after the main piece has been woven.

NOTE: If the floating selvedges are to be threaded and weighted separately, the length of each must be longer than the warp because you need to be able to hang it over the back of the loom, even when the apron rod has moved up to the weaving level.

Warp Length Calculations

The calculations you'll need are set out below.

Total required finished length		-----
Headings and hems	+	-----
Short test piece	+	6" (15 cm)
add together		total A

Take up: add 10–12% to total A	+	10–12%
add to total A		total B

Total fringe lengths	+	-----
add to total B		total C

Add shrinkage	I	
add to total C		total D

Experiments (optional)	+	20" (50 cm)
Loom waste: 27" [70 cm] table		
or 1 yard [90 cm] floor	+	-----
add to total D for total warp length		total E

REMEMBER: Always round up rather than down!

Color Theory

Understanding color is key to producing attractive woven items—colors are closely intertwined, so it's important to work with the right combination from the outset.

The Color Wheel

A color wheel is an invaluable tool for anyone designing textiles.

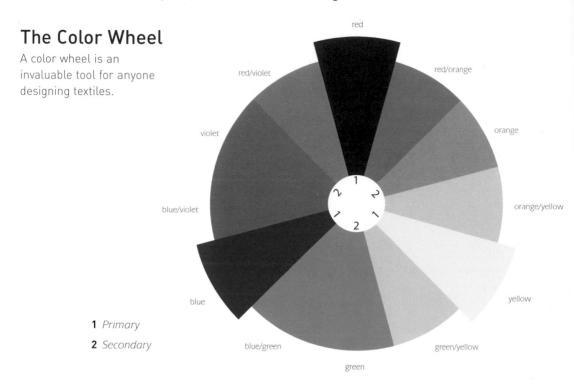

1 *Primary*

2 *Secondary*

Complementary colors on the opposite side of the wheel produce the greatest contrast when placed together, for example, red and green. Combining a pair of complementary colors produces black (or near-black).

Tertiary colors are made by mixing secondary colors.

Split complementary is one color plus one or two of the tertiary colors on either side of the complementary.

Harmonious colors sit within any quarter of the wheel. Cut a circle to the same size as the color wheel, and cut out one quarter. Placing this on top of the wheel, and turning it around, shows the harmonious sections clearly.

Triad colors are an equilateral triangle of colors from the wheel, such as all three primaries, or all three secondaries.

Tetrad colors are the four colors at the corners of a square or rectangle placed on the wheel.

Achromatic colors are white, black, and gray (a combination of black and white). The intensity of the base color can be decreased by adding achromatic colors.

Monochromatic colors are tints, shades, and tones of a single hue. Small accents of a hue can be added to highlight.

Value of a color refers to whether it is naturally light or dark. Not all pure colors have the same value. Yellow is light, purple dark. Adding achromatic colors also alters the value of pure hues: adding black gives a shade; gray gives a tone; white gives a tint.

Temperature Warm colors—reds and oranges—are dominant; cool colors—blues and violets—tend to be recessive. If two colors of equal temperature are placed together they vibrate. The temperature is altered by any background color. If the background is warm, then the color appears cooler; and if cool, it appears warmer.

True Colors

Textiles never have a completely flat surface. Fibers and yarns are three-dimensional, and weaving with yarns creates an even more textured surface. Between the woven yarns are spaces, which receive less light and are therefore in shadow, and which themselves receive a weakened reflection of color from the yarn. Different colored yarns will not only reflect onto the shadows but also onto the yarns next to them, altering the perceived color.

Type of spin Shiny and smooth yarns reflect the light and are therefore lighter and brighter; hairy, soft, and textured yarns absorb the light and appear duller and darker.

Weight of yarn If the yarn is very fine, the weaving surface is smoother and therefore lighter and brighter. If it is thick, the weaving surface is textured, with more shadows. Fine yarns also allow the colors to blend more.

Weave structure Loose weaves create shadows. A lacy weave in black will not show the structure as well as the same pattern in a pale color.

Closeness of the fabric to the eye When held close to the eye, the colors are defined more easily. If the fabric is farther away, they tend to blend more.

Lighting This can be a minefield. Hues react to different colors of light, and many artificial lights do not give out the same color. Where will your fabric be seen—indoors, outdoors, or both? The position of the light source can also make a difference—will it be at the side, in front, or behind?

To gauge the finished effect, try positioning samples in various light conditions; against different backgrounds; and in combination with other colors or patterns.

Dominant Color

Lighter, purer, and warmer colors will be dominant, as will those covering a larger area. Your chosen color must dominate in at least one of these categories to have the desired effect. (The covering area refers to the total within the piece, which may be one large block or a combination of several small ones.)

Remember that on a dark background, light colors stand out, whereas on a light background the dark colors are dominant. (Colors on a contrasting background need less area to dominate, while colors on a similar background will need more area to do so.) Although, generally, warm colors advance and cool colors recede, the lightness or darkness of the colors can alter the dominance: light blue (cool) dominates dark red (warm), for example.

When choosing the dominant color for a design, there are a number of factors you may want to consider:

Practicality Are you making something to tone with work clothes, room furnishings, or is it an item for a special occasion?

Individual preference and taste This is sometimes influenced by cultural upbringing. Nowadays "fashion" also has an influence.

Psychological responses Colors can affect your mood, feelings, and concentration—and this can vary according to the degree of purity. A pure hue will evoke the most extreme response. (See Color Scheming, page 25, for further details.)

Symbolism Historically great symbolism was placed on certain colors found throughout nature, such as red (meaning danger in Western culture). Only the elite could wear the "royal" purple, and plague-ridden ships had to fly the yellow "duster" to forewarn other vessels. Color symbolism is not as emotive nowadays, due to the merging of cultures.

Making a Sample

There are two main methods of sampling color combinations: wrapping and twisting.

Wrapping

Use a small, narrow piece of card and wrap colored yarn around it. Place colors adjacent to each color in the selection. One color can dramatically change the appearance of another when placed next to it. Use varying numbers of wraps to replicate the proportions of the colors in the piece. You may need to make several wraps to choose a preferred combination and order.

Twisting

When yarns are woven they are not seen side by side, so sometimes twisting colors together gives the effect of the interlacements. Take lengths of yarns in the proportion to be used and twist together. This readily shows if an accent yarn has too great a proportion or dominance. To keep the twists, either tape each end onto a piece of card, or overtwist and allow to "ply" back on itself. Put the wraps and/or twists where you can see them clearly, leave for a while, then look at them again with fresh eyes.

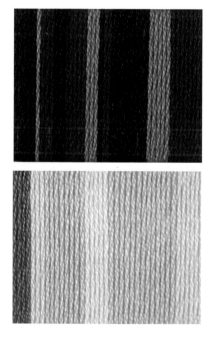

Wrapping

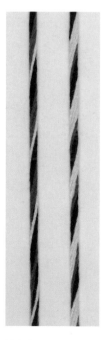

Twisting

Color Scheming

The following list shows you some effective ways to use a chosen color.

Red

Bright, warm, cheerful, inviting

- Combine with orange, terracotta, pink, purple, moss green.
- Combine with pairs of colors: terracotta and cream, lemon and brick, black and lemon, gray and pink, yellow and ocher.
- Add accents of blue, gray, green, black.
- Use to accent pink and white, black and aqua, white and blue, gray and dark gray, black and yellow.

Orange

Bright, cheerful, lively

- Combine with yellow, ocher, tan, brown, red shades.
- Combine with pairs of colors: yellow and red, cream and red tints, brown and cream, brown and moss green, brown and red.
- Add accents of blue, black, green, white, moss green, brown.
- Use to accent white and blue, brown and white, black and lemon, dark green and brown, black and white.

Yellow

Bright and sunny

- Combine with cream, orange, light bright green, moss green, terracotta.
- Combine with pairs of colors: light green and white, brick and cream, brown and fawn, dark or bright green and moss green.
- Add accents of dark turquoise, black, red, blue.
- Use to accent black and pale blue, aqua and orange, white and mid-blue, gray and black, orange and aqua.

Green

Refreshing, natural, restful

- Combine with blue, gray, aqua, lime, mid-blue, dark green.
- Combine with pairs of colors: mid- and pale or bright green, green tint and violet, any pale tone and green shade, dark green and moss.
- Add accents of yellow, navy, white, terracotta, black.
- Use to accent white and any pale tint, blue and white, black and yellow, white and red, orange and black.

Blue

Cool, bracing, refreshing

- Combine with blue-gray, mid- or dark aqua, mid-blue, navy.
- Combine with pairs of colors: pale tone and tint of purple, aqua and aqua tint, gray and cream, pale tone and tint of gray, black and mid-blue.
- Add accents of orange, leaf green, pale lemon, yellow, black.
- Use to accent black and cream, pale blue and pink, white and deep aqua, red and white, black and orange.

Violet

Luxurious, elegant

- Combine with other single colors: red, lavender, moss green, black, orange, pink.
- Combine with pairs of colors: gray and navy, mid-blue and black, powder blue and ocher, moss green and red, fawn and gray.
- Add accents of pink, lemon, terracotta, lime, russet, aqua.
- Use to accent lavender and russet, mid-blue and pink shade, pale and mid-green, gray and cream.

Basic Threadings

It is the order in which the warp threads, or ends, are threaded through the heddles on the different shafts and how they are tied up and treadled that determines which weave structures can be woven.

Scarf in broken twill, with braided fringe, merino.

There are only four possible choices at any one time when threading a four-shaft loom, but because the warp threads can be raised or lowered either singly or in groups, a total of fourteen different sheds (separation of the warp threads to make an opening for the weft) can be produced:

4 singles: 1; 2; 3; 4
6 pairs: (1, 2); (1, 3); (1, 4); (2,3); (2, 4); (3, 4)
4 triples: (1, 2, 3); (1, 2, 4); (1, 3, 4); (2, 3, 4)

This means that each warp thread, usually referred to as an "end," can be used in conjunction with the other ends in several different ways.

The ends need to be threaded for each particular pattern or design. Some of these can be simple, such as tabby or plain weave; others are more complicated, and the entire pattern repeat can spread over many ends.

Straight draft (straight entry; or straight threaded) This is the simplest draft and, threading from the **right**, can move from 4 to 1 (Z threading) or 1 to 4 (S threading). The direction of the threading is in the same direction as the center portion of the letters S and Z.

Point draft (point entry; return; or reverse entry) This uses both S and Z directions. The point refers to the reversal of direction, which can be regular or irregular, frequent or long, repeating or random.

Block drafts These are composed of threading units using two, three or four shafts, which can be repeated and/or positioned against others to create pattern blocks.

Lace It is not possible to weave true lace, but lacy effects can be produced. Several of these are also block weaves, but their special nature places them in their own section.

Special Really all threadings are special in that they are especially made to create a desired pattern or effect. While several threading drafts can be woven "As If" they were a different weave, some are only suitable for weaving in a limited manner.

Tabby

Plain weave, or tabby, is the interlacing of the warp and weft 1:1. Alternate warp threads move over one weft thread (or pick), and then under one pick. This results in alternate picks also curving over and then under alternate ends.

Tabby can be woven on a two-shaft or rigid-heddle loom, but weaving on four shafts means that the heddles are less crowded on the shafts.

On a four-shaft loom the tabby shed is usually created by raising shafts one and three and then shafts two and four. Sometimes the threading is such that different combinations are used, for example, for Ms and Os, and Summer and Winter, and indeed sometimes tabby is not possible at all, as with herringbone.

It may seem plain, but use of color in warp and weft produces extremely interesting designs. Variation can also be made by different thicknesses and types of thread used in conjunction with each other.

Tabby is the most stable of all the weaves and forms the background, or stabilizer, to many other weave structures. If just tabby is to be woven, it does not need a floating selvedge.

Twill

Sometimes called "tweel" in old manuals, twill is the interlacing of warp threads over or under two or more picks; each successive pick moving one end sideways, thus producing a diagonal structure.

Twill can be woven on three, four, or more shafts. A balanced twill on four shafts has two shafts up and two shafts down for each pick, and is written 2/2. Two other twills are possible on a four-shaft loom—3/1, where the warp end passes over three picks then goes under one; and 1/3, where the warp end goes over one pick then under three. The symbols 2/2, 3/1, and 1/3 are representations of the pathway that the warp is taking, over and under the picks.

Hopsack, or basket weave, uses twill sheds, and so is placed after twill in the samples. The result is similar to tabby, but shows clearer color and weave effects. The picks are "on opposites" either pairs: (1, 2) and (3, 4); or (1, 4) and (2, 3); or singles with the opposite triples (1) and (2, 3, 4); (2) and (1, 3, 4); (3) and (1, 2, 4); (4) and (1, 2, 3).

Many threading drafts can be woven "As If" they were for a different technique. A complicated draft can often be woven as tabby, but can sometimes be woven "As If" it were a different draft.

TAW is the abbreviation for "trompe as writ" or "woven as drawn in." It means that the weaving sequence is the same as the threading sequence.

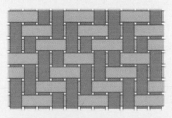

The diagonal direction can be changed by use of a point weaving sequence. At the reversal point on a 2/2 twill the warp will float over and under one and three picks.

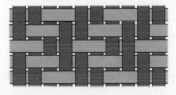

In a 1/3 or 3/1 point twill the warp will float over or under 1, 3, and 5 ends.

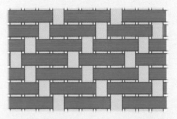

A Herringbone sequence skips one shaft or pick at the reversal, resulting in a broken point with no extra-long floats.

Straight Drafts
(also known as straight entry draft, straight threaded draft)

A straight draft is threaded in a continuous diagonal sequence, using the next adjacent shaft, in one direction only. Although it can be threaded S or Z direction, all the straight drafts in this book are threaded in the Z direction. S and Z refer to the direction of the threading in relation to the center bar of the letter.

All the 14 sheds can be made. Tabby is woven using (1, 3) and then (2, 4). Changing the direction of the lift sequence in a twill results in a vertical point or zigzag. This can be close or far apart, even or uneven, regular or irregular. There are various names for the types of point weaving sequences, and these are given alongside the samples.

Different types of twills can be combined with each other and with tabby. When using both tabby and twill in the same structure the sett needs to be as that for twill, otherwise the twill picks will beat down too closely resulting in a "weft-dominant" or even a "weft-faced" structure—one in which the weft dominates. If there are deep bands of tabby, in between twill bands, these will tend to push the edges of the weaving outward—a point to consider when designing.

NOTES

Selvedges: These follow the direction of the threading draft. See pages 16–17.

Sett: See pages 18–19.

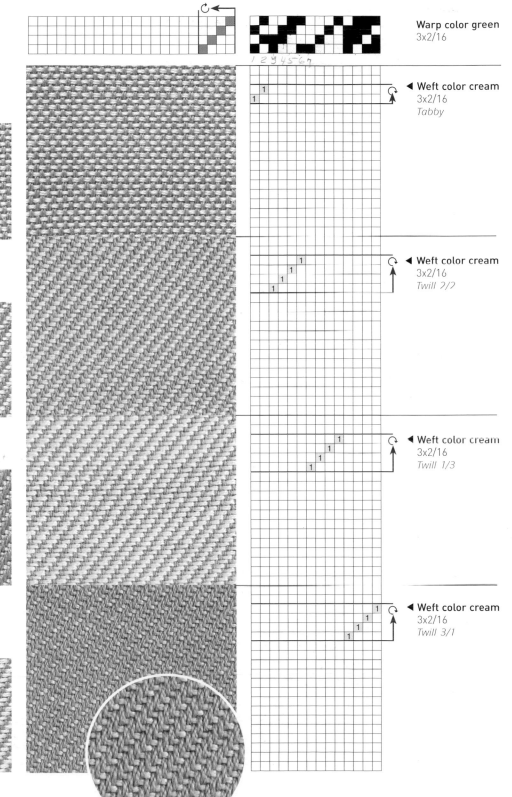

Warp color green
3x2/16

◀ **Weft color cream**
3x2/16
Tabby

◀ **Weft color cream**
3x2/16
Twill 2/2

◀ **Weft color cream**
3x2/16
Twill 1/3

◀ **Weft color cream**
3x2/16
Twill 3/1

Tabby

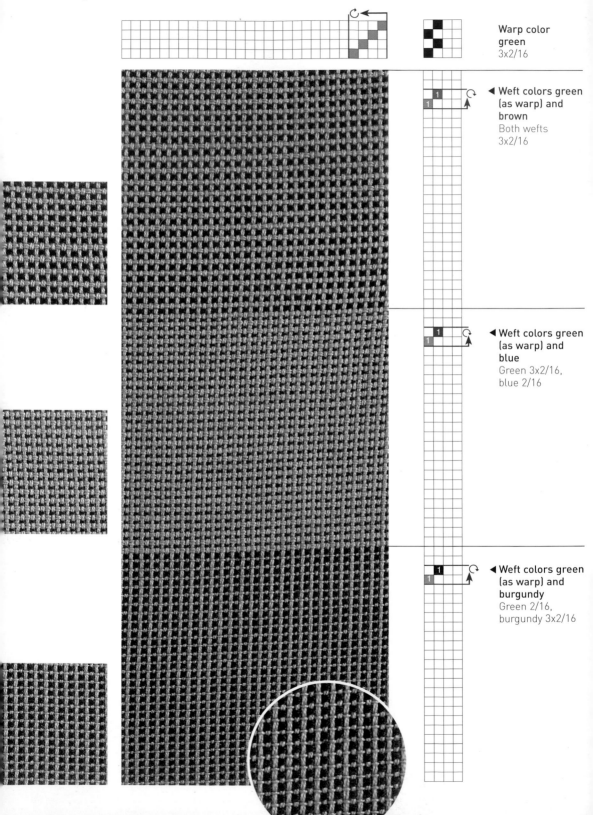

Warp color
green
3x2/16

◀ Weft colors green
(as warp) and
brown
Both wefts
3x2/16

◀ Weft colors green
(as warp) and
blue
Green 3x2/16,
blue 2/16

◀ Weft colors green
(as warp) and
burgundy
Green 2/16,
burgundy 3x2/16

Tabby

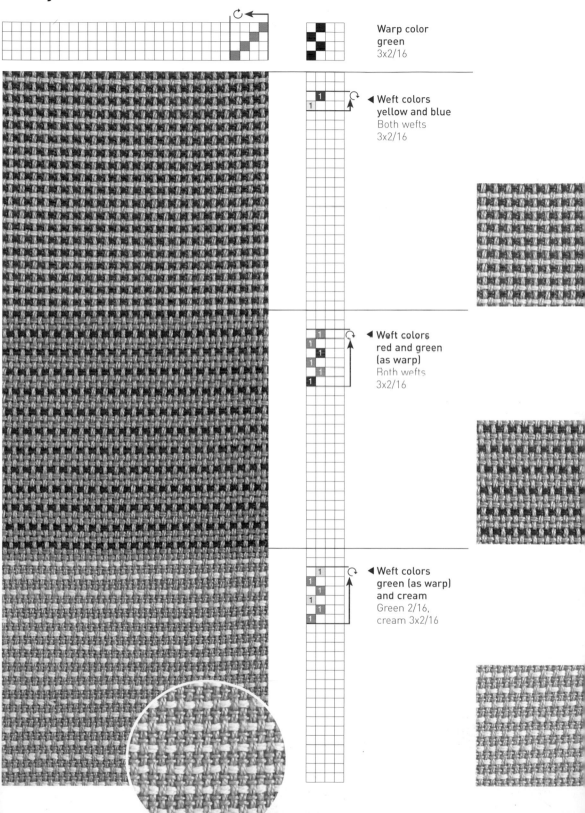

Warp color
green
3x2/16

◀ Weft colors
yellow and blue
Both wefts
3x2/16

◀ Weft colors
red and green
(as warp)
Both wefts
3x2/16

◀ Weft colors
green (as warp)
and cream
Green 2/16,
cream 3x2/16

2/2 Twill

Warp color green
3x2/16

◀ **Weft color orange**
3x2/16
S diagonal

◀ **Weft color yellow**
3x2/16
Vertical zigzag over 6 picks

◀ **Weft color burgundy**
3x2/16
Uneven vertical zigzag

2/2 Twill

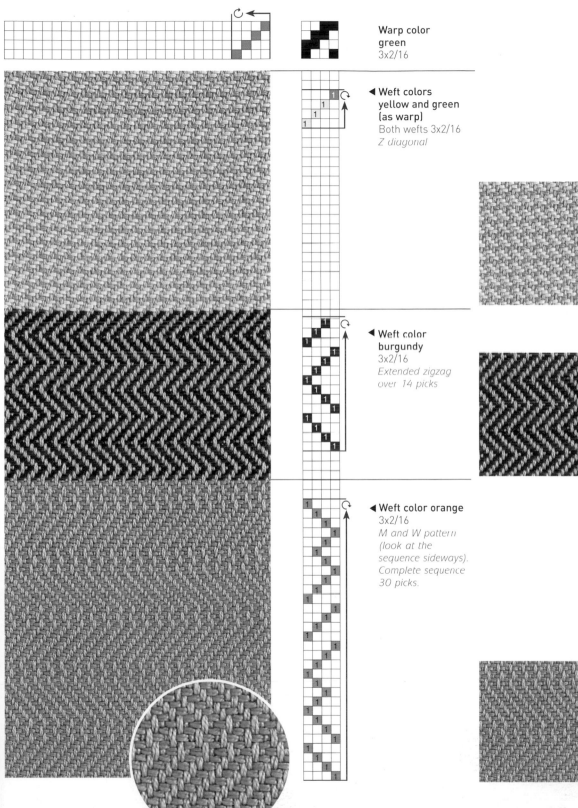

Warp color green
3x2/16

◄ **Weft colors yellow and green (as warp)**
Both wefts 3x2/16
Z diagonal

◄ **Weft color burgundy**
3x2/16
Extended zigzag over 14 picks

◄ **Weft color orange**
3x2/16
M and W pattern (look at the sequence sideways). Complete sequence 30 picks.

2/2 Twill

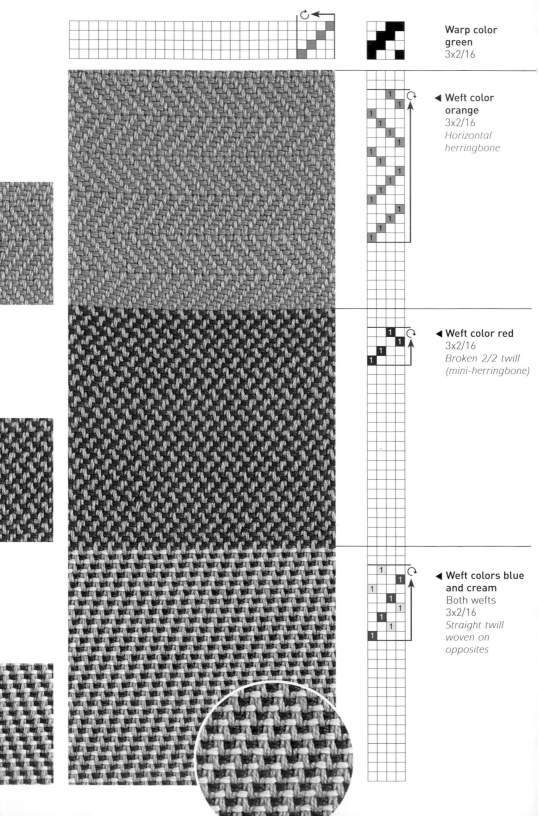

Warp color
green
3x2/16

◄ Weft color
orange
3x2/16
*Horizontal
herringbone*

◄ Weft color red
3x2/16
*Broken 2/2 twill
(mini-herringbone)*

◄ Weft colors blue
and cream
Both wefts
3x2/16
*Straight twill
woven on
opposites*

2/2 Twill

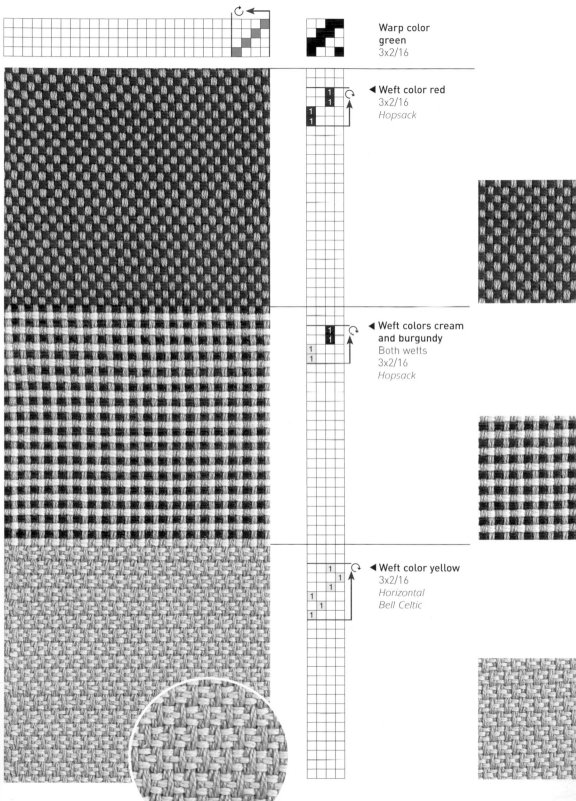

Warp color
green
3x2/16

◀ Weft color red
3x2/16
Hopsack

◀ Weft colors cream
and burgundy
Both wefts
3x2/16
Hopsack

◀ Weft color yellow
3x2/16
*Horizontal
Bell Celtic*

1/3 Twill

Warp color
green
3x2/16

◄ Weft color yellow
3x2/16
S diagonal

◄ Weft color red
3x2/16
*Vertical point over
8 picks*

◄ Weft color
orange
3x2/16
*Broken 1/3 twill,
sometimes called
Mock Sateen.
The reverse,
with longer
warp floats, is
Mock Satin.
True satin and
sateen cannot
be woven on less
than 5 shafts.*

3/1 Twill

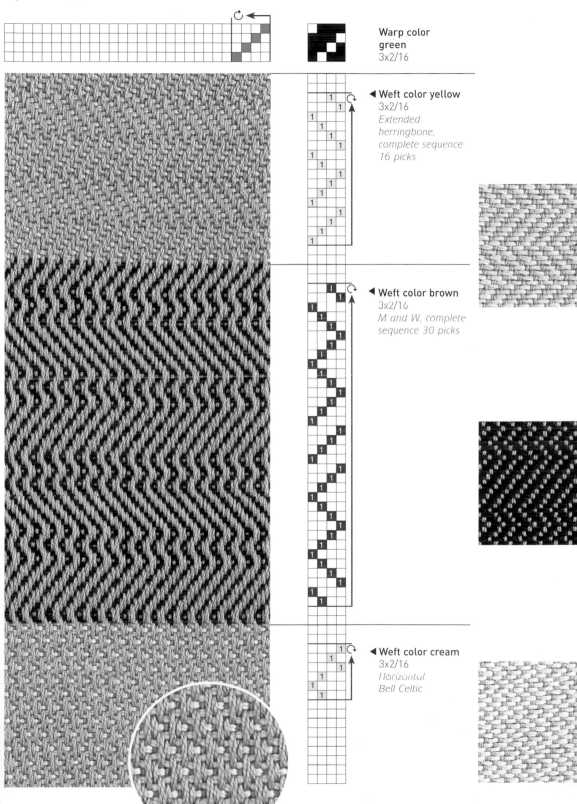

Warp color green
3x2/16

◀ **Weft color yellow**
3x2/16
Extended herringbone, complete sequence 16 picks

◀ **Weft color brown**
3x2/16
M and W, complete sequence 30 picks

◀ **Weft color cream**
3x2/16
Horizontal Bell Celtic

Mixed Twills

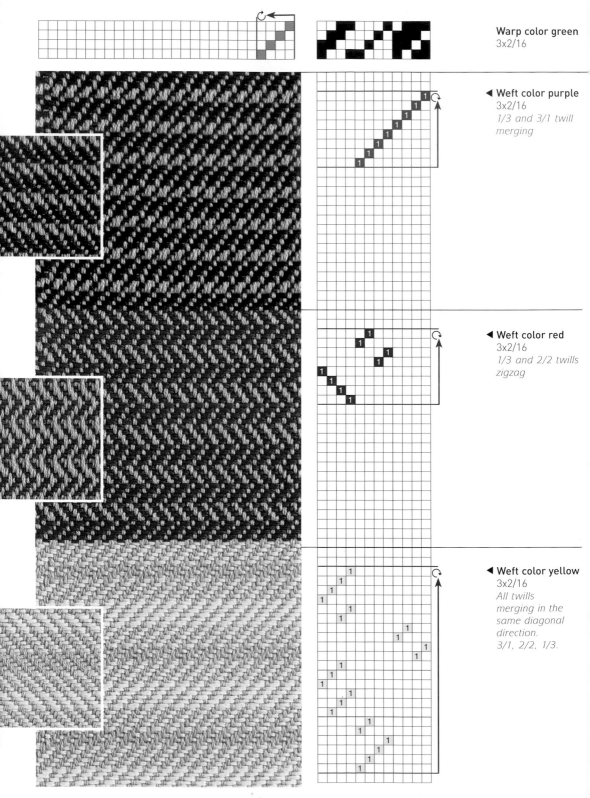

Warp color green
3x2/16

◄ **Weft color purple**
3x2/16
*1/3 and 3/1 twill
merging*

◄ **Weft color red**
3x2/16
*1/3 and 2/2 twills
zigzag*

◄ **Weft color yellow**
3x2/16
*All twills
merging in the
same diagonal
direction.
3/1, 2/2, 1/3.*

Selected Mixed Twills

Warp color green
3x2/16

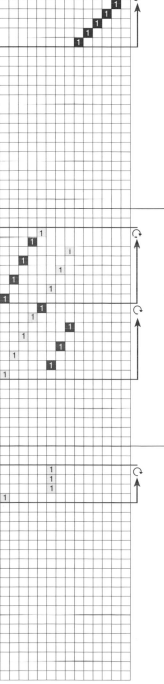

◀ **Weft color red**
3x2/16
*Beat gently to
preserve balance
and the pattern*

◀ **Weft colors cream
and purple**
Both wefts 3x2/16
*1/3 and 3/1 twill
lifts on opposites.
(Note how the
3/1 pick almost
disappears under
the 1/3 pick.)
Creates reversal of
colors on back.*

◀ **Weft color yellow**
3x2/16
*1/3 and 3/1
hopsack*

Tabby and 2/2 High Twill

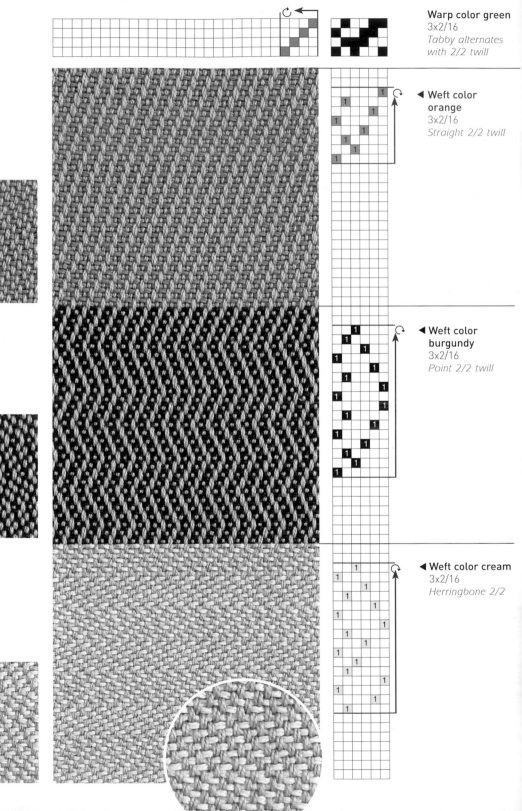

Warp color green
3x2/16
*Tabby alternates
with 2/2 twill*

◄ **Weft color
orange**
3x2/16
Straight 2/2 twill

◄ **Weft color
burgundy**
3x2/16
Point 2/2 twill

◄ **Weft color cream**
3x2/16
Herringbone 2/2

Tabby and Twills

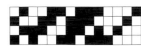

Warp color
green
3x2/16

◀ Weft colors cream
and green (as
warp)
Both wefts 3x2/16

◀ Weft color yellow
3x2/16

◀ Weft color purple
3x2/16

Tabby and Twills

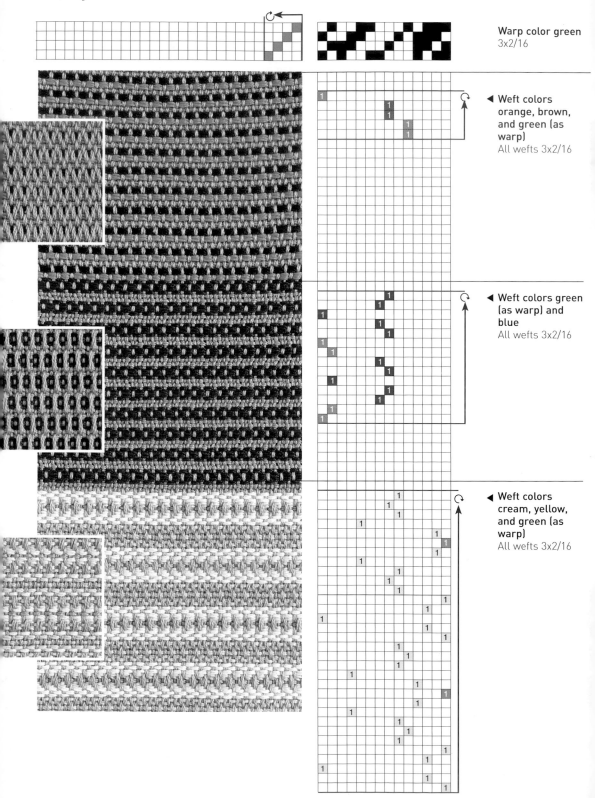

Warp color green
3x2/16

◄ Weft colors
orange, brown,
and green (as
warp)
All wefts 3x2/16

◄ Weft colors green
(as warp) and
blue
All wefts 3x2/16

◄ Weft colors
cream, yellow,
and green (as
warp)
All wefts 3x2/16

Tabby and Twills

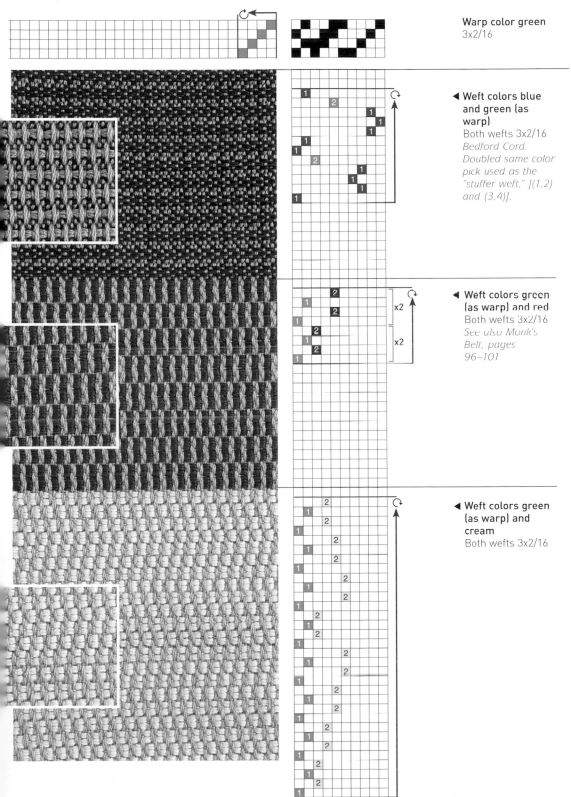

Warp color green
3x2/16

◄ **Weft colors blue and green (as warp)**
Both wefts 3x2/16 Bedford Cord. Doubled same color pick used as the "stuffer weft," [(1.2) and (3.4)].

◄ **Weft colors green (as warp) and red**
Both wefts 3x2/16 See also Monk's Belt, pages 96–101

◄ **Weft colors green (as warp) and cream**
Both wefts 3x2/16

Tabby and Twills

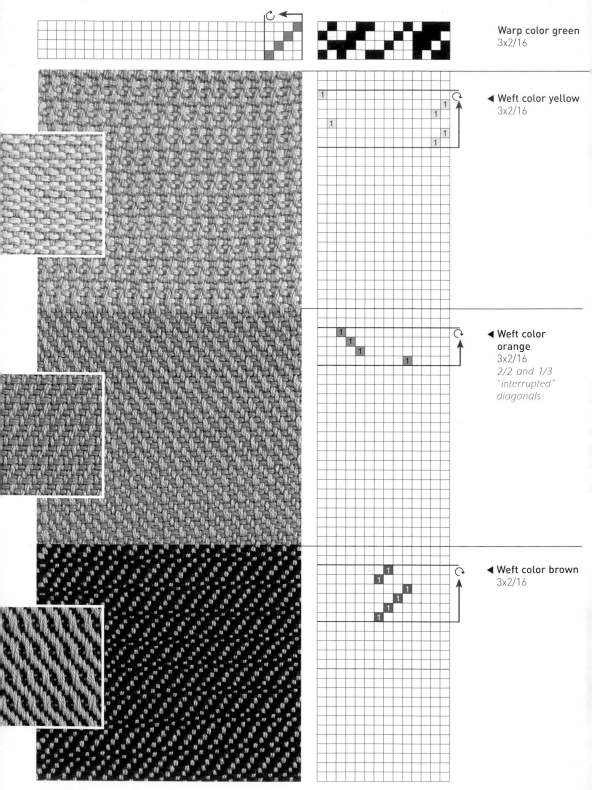

Warp color green
3x2/16

◀ **Weft color yellow**
3x2/16

◀ **Weft color orange**
3x2/16
*2/2 and 1/3
"interrupted"
diagonals*

◀ **Weft color brown**
3x2/16

Tabby and Twills

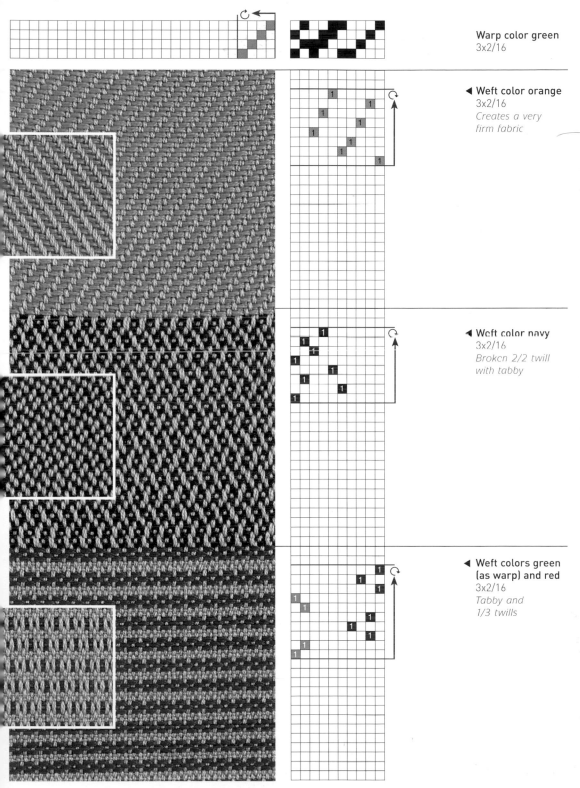

Warp color green
3x2/16

◀ Weft color orange
3x2/16
*Creates a very
firm fabric*

◀ Weft color navy
3x2/16
*Broken 2/2 twill
with tabby*

**◀ Weft colors green
(as warp) and red**
3x2/16
*Tabby and
1/3 twills*

Hopsack

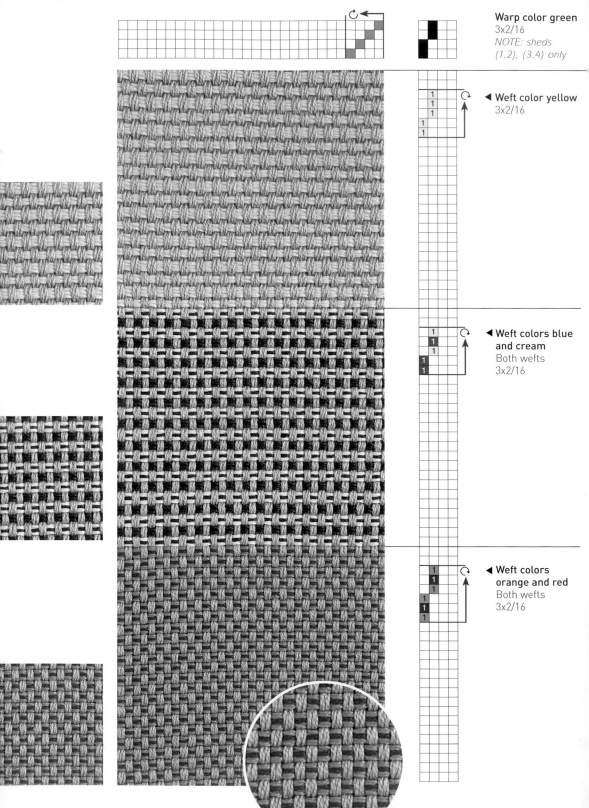

Warp color green
3x2/16
*NOTE: sheds
(1,2), (3,4) only*

◀ **Weft color yellow**
3x2/16

◀ **Weft colors blue
and cream**
Both wefts
3x2/16

◀ **Weft colors
orange and red**
Both wefts
3x2/16

Hopsack

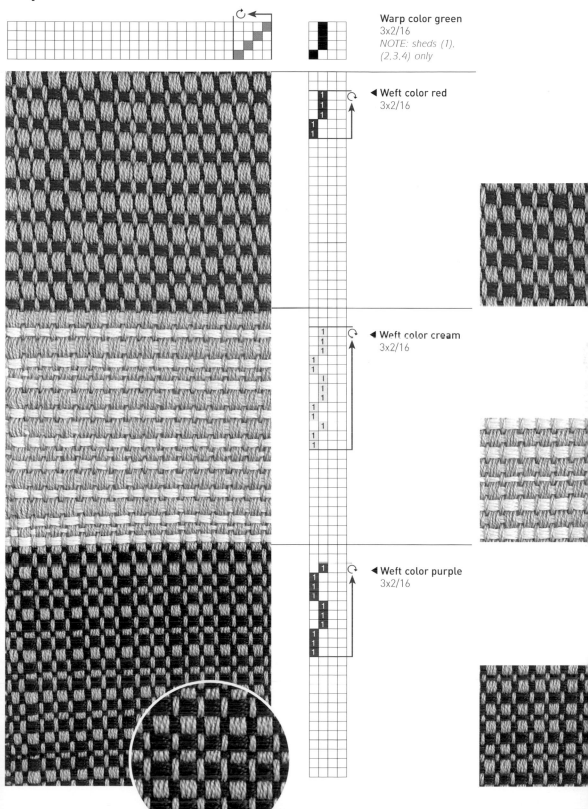

Warp color green
3x2/16
*NOTE: sheds (1),
(2,3,4) only*

◀ **Weft color red**
3x2/16

◀ **Weft color cream**
3x2/16

◀ **Weft color purple**
3x2/16

Tabby: Two-color Warp

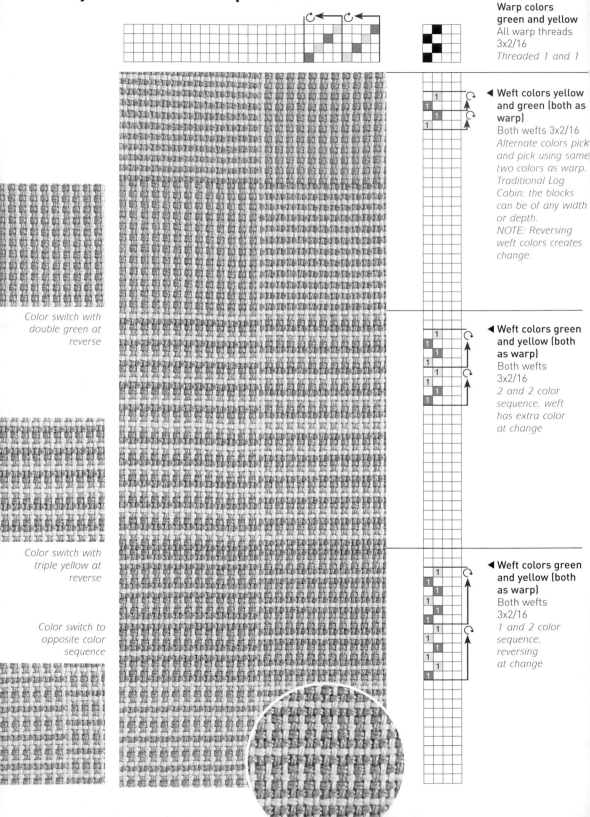

Warp colors green and yellow
All warp threads
3x2/16
Threaded 1 and 1

◄ **Weft colors yellow and green (both as warp)**
Both wefts 3x2/16
Alternate colors pick and pick using same two colors as warp.
Traditional Log Cabin: the blocks can be of any width or depth.
NOTE: Reversing weft colors creates change.

◄ **Weft colors green and yellow (both as warp)**
Both wefts 3x2/16
2 and 2 color sequence, weft has extra color at change

◄ **Weft colors green and yellow (both as warp)**
Both wefts 3x2/16
1 and 2 color sequence, reversing at change

Color switch with double green at reverse

Color switch with triple yellow at reverse

Color switch to opposite color sequence

Tabby: Two-color Warp

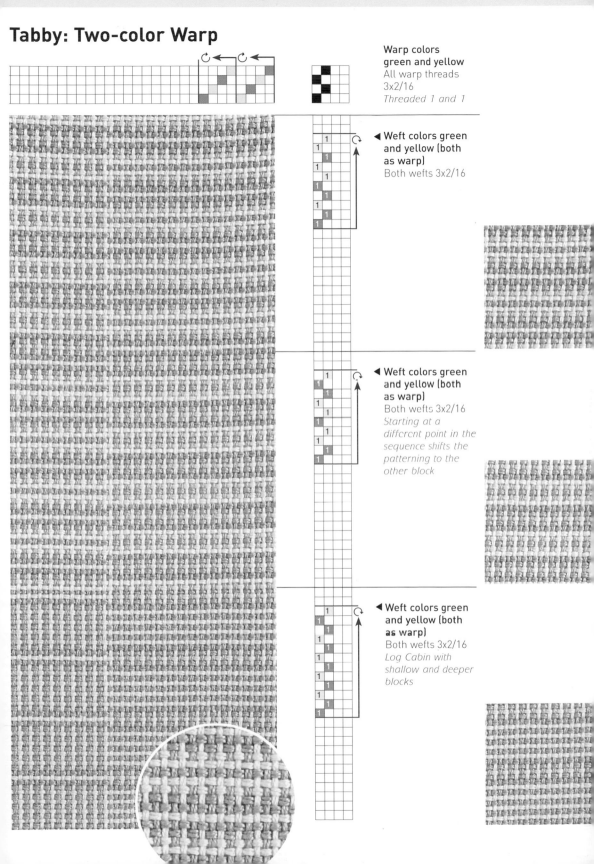

**Warp colors
green and yellow**
All warp threads
3x2/16
Threaded 1 and 1

◀ **Weft colors green
and yellow (both
as warp)**
Both wefts 3x2/16

◀ **Weft colors green
and yellow (both
as warp)**
Both wefts 3x2/16
*Starting at a
different point in the
sequence shifts the
patterning to the
other block*

◀ **Weft colors green
and yellow (both
as warp)**
Both wefts 3x2/16
*Log Cabin with
shallow and deeper
blocks*

Tabby: Two-color Warp

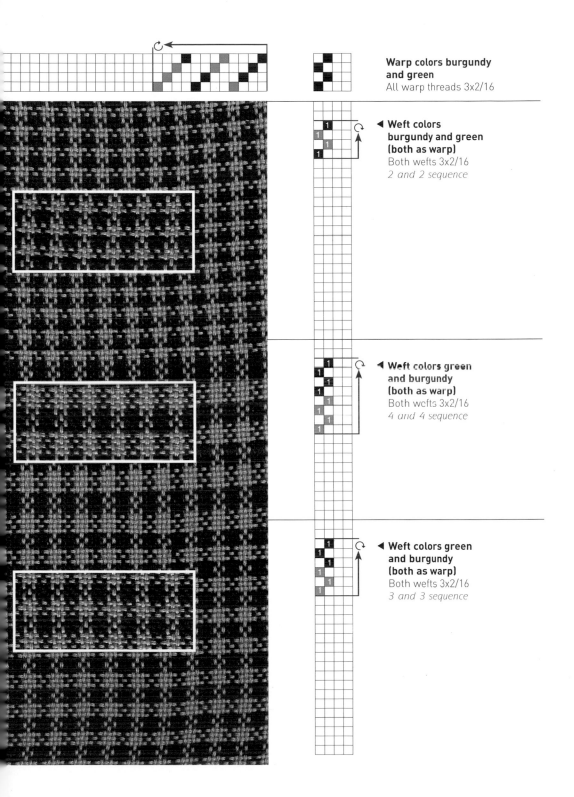

**Warp colors burgundy
and green**
All warp threads 3x2/16

◀ **Weft colors
burgundy and green
(both as warp)**
Both wefts 3x2/16
2 and 2 sequence

◀ **Weft colors green
and burgundy
(both as warp)**
Both wefts 3x2/16
4 and 4 sequence

◀ **Weft colors green
and burgundy
(both as warp)**
Both wefts 3x2/16
3 and 3 sequence

2/2 Twill: Two-color Warp

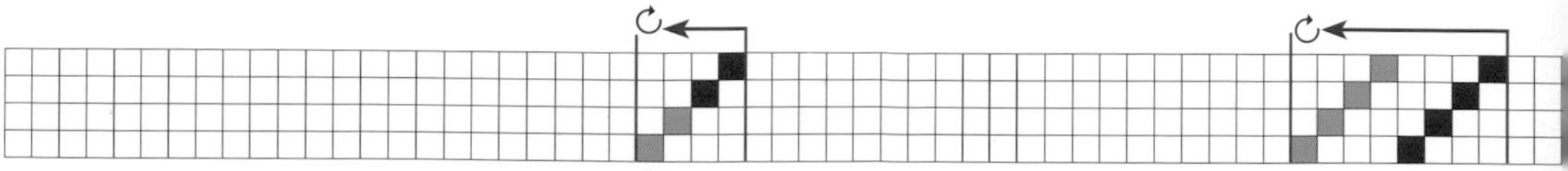

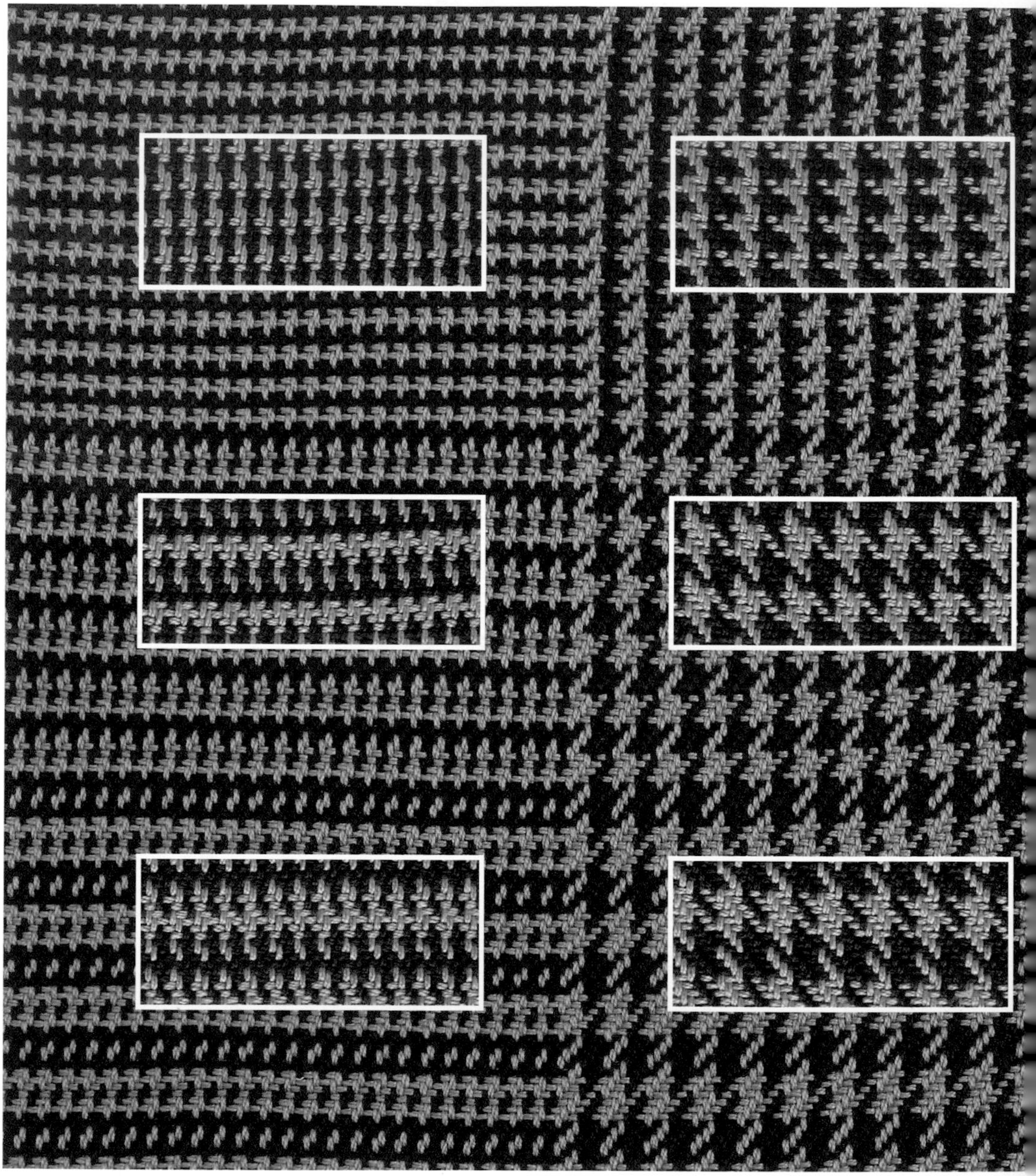

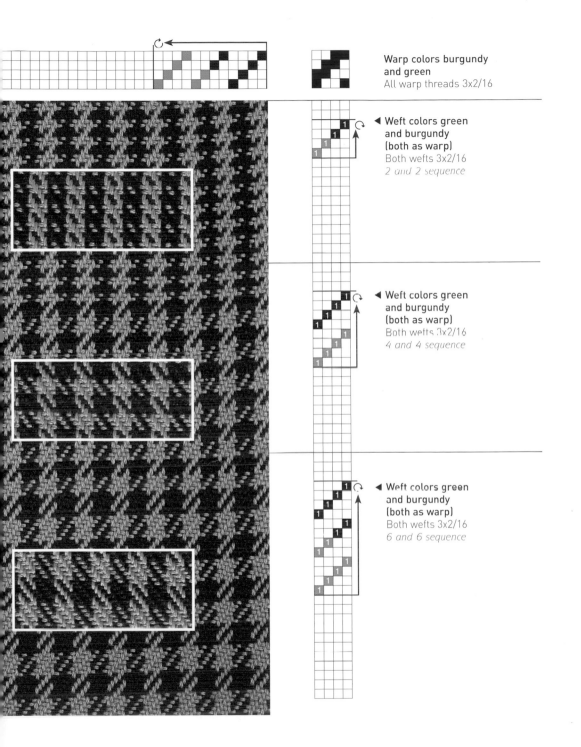

Warp colors burgundy and green
All warp threads 3x2/16

◄ **Weft colors green and burgundy (both as warp)**
Both wefts 3x2/16
2 and 2 sequence

◄ **Weft colors green and burgundy (both as warp)**
Both wefts 3x2/16
4 and 4 sequence

◄ **Weft colors green and burgundy (both as warp)**
Both wefts 3x2/16
6 and 6 sequence

1/3 and 3/1 Twill: Two-color Warp

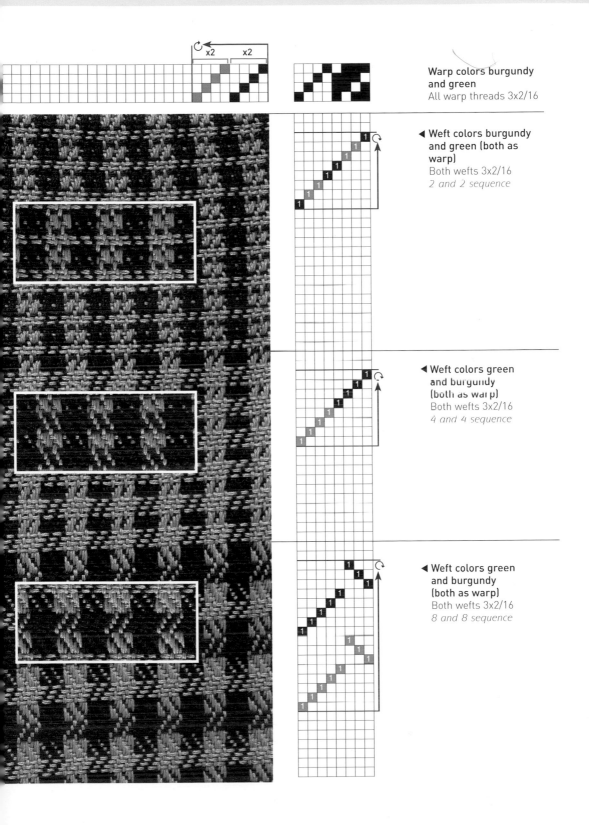

Warp colors burgundy and green
All warp threads 3x2/16

◄ **Weft colors burgundy and green (both as warp)**
Both wefts 3x2/16
2 and 2 sequence

◄ **Weft colors green and burgundy (both as warp)**
Both wefts 3x2/16
4 and 4 sequence

◄ **Weft colors green and burgundy (both as warp)**
Both wefts 3x2/16
8 and 8 sequence

2/2 Twill and Tabby: Two-color Warp

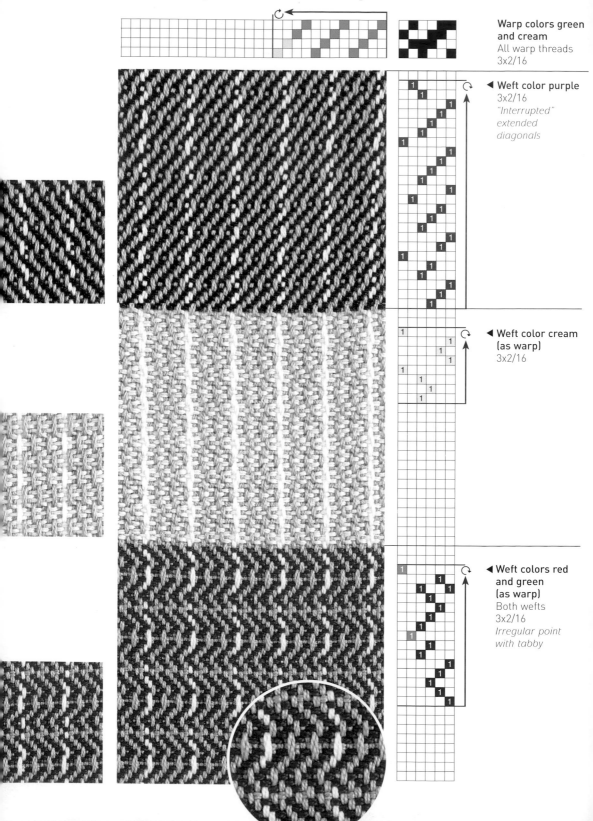

Warp colors green and cream
All warp threads
3x2/16

◀ **Weft color purple**
3x2/16
"Interrupted" extended diagonals

◀ **Weft color cream (as warp)**
3x2/16

◀ **Weft colors red and green (as warp)**
Both wefts
3x2/16
Irregular point with tabby

2/2 Twill and Tabby: Two-color Warp

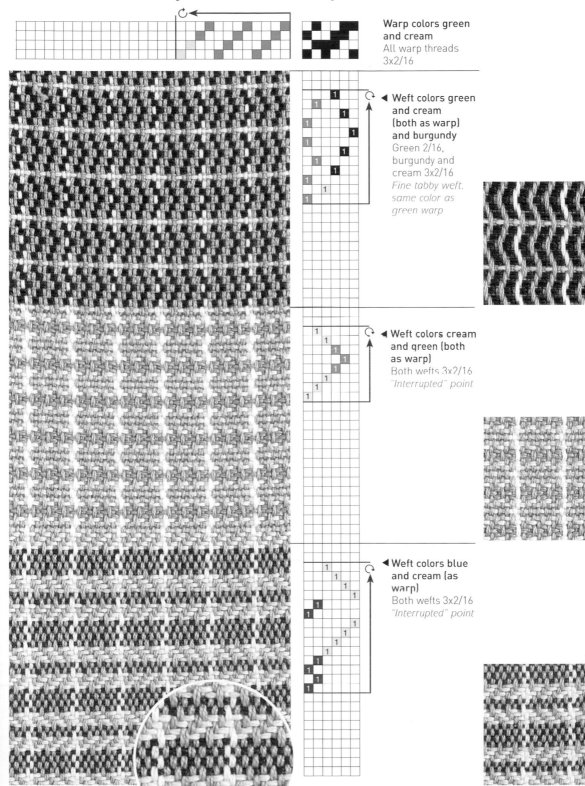

Warp colors green and cream
All warp threads 3x2/16

◀ **Weft colors green and cream (both as warp) and burgundy**
Green 2/16, burgundy and cream 3x2/16
Fine tabby weft, same color as green warp

◀ **Weft colors cream and green (both as warp)**
Both wefts 3x2/16
"Interrupted" point

◀ **Weft colors blue and cream (as warp)**
Both wefts 3x2/16
"Interrupted" point

1/3 and 3/1 Twill with Tabby: Two-color Warp

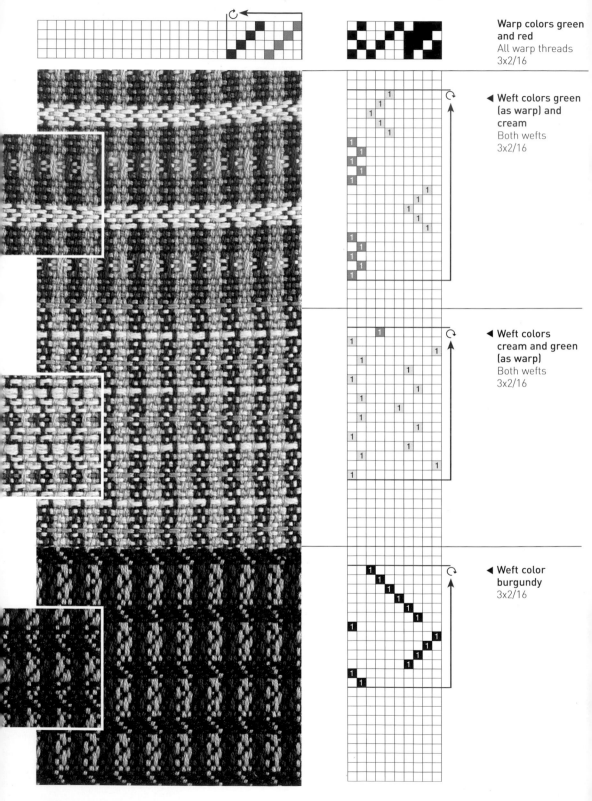

Warp colors green and red
All warp threads
3x2/16

◀ **Weft colors green (as warp) and cream**
Both wefts
3x2/16

◀ **Weft colors cream and green (as warp)**
Both wefts
3x2/16

◀ **Weft color burgundy**
3x2/16

1/3 and 3/1 Twill with Tabby: Two-color Warp

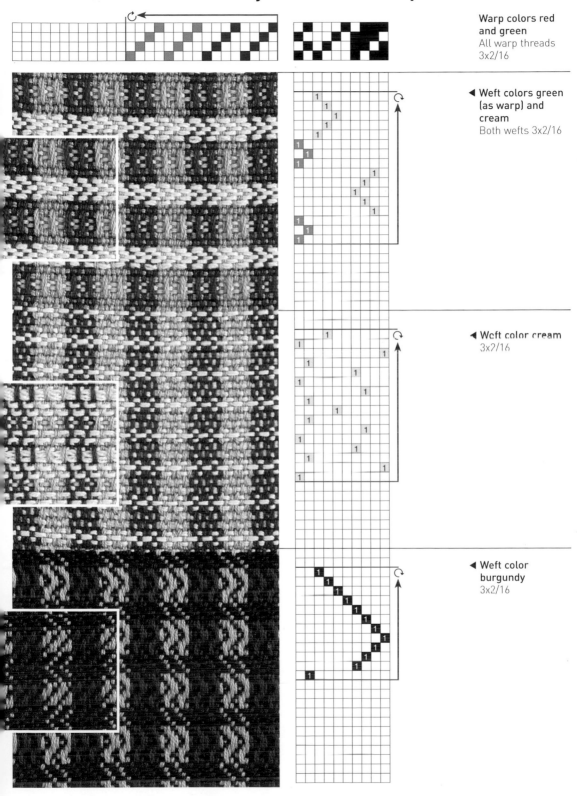

Warp colors red and green
All warp threads
3x2/16

◀ **Weft colors green (as warp) and cream**
Both wefts 3x2/16

◀ **Weft color cream**
3x2/16

◀ **Weft color burgundy**
3x2/16

Hopsack: Two-color Warp

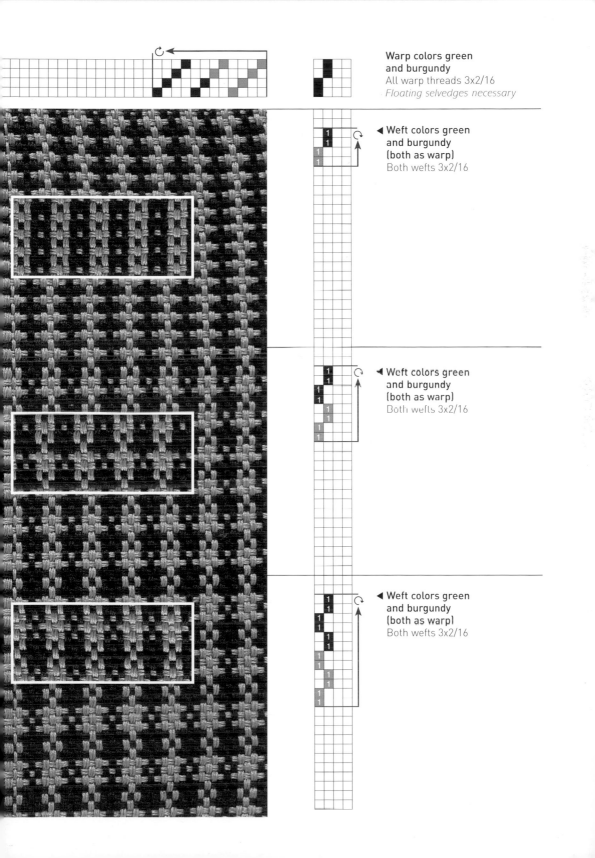

**Warp colors green
and burgundy**
All warp threads 3x2/16
Floating selvedges necessary

◀ **Weft colors green
and burgundy
(both as warp)**
Both wefts 3x2/16

◀ **Weft colors green
and burgundy
(both as warp)**
Both wefts 3x2/16

◀ **Weft colors green
and burgundy
(both as warp)**
Both wefts 3x2/16

Double Cloth

Double cloth is the term used when two layers of cloth are woven simultaneously. On a four-shaft loom only two layers of tabby can be woven. The easiest way to thread the loom is for one layer to be on shafts 1 and 3, and the other layer to be on shafts 2 and 4, in a straight entry draft.

The layers can be woven as separate layers or joined together at one or both sides. To weave separate layers, one shaft is raised for the top layer, then both the top layer ends plus one from the lower layer are raised for the next pick. Further details for weaving with a single weft for joined sides or tubes are given alongside that sample. It is important that the direction of the weft is observed— arrows at the side of each pick in the first four drafts indicate this. When weaving with two shuttles the direction of weaving is not important. The sides can also be joined by twining two separate weft threads at the sides—always do these in the same way for neatness.

An opening can be at the right, left, or center of the top layer. When the weaving is finished the cloth can be unfolded to a single layer. Drawing in at the sides means that the warp ends become more crowded there, with a packed block running along the length of the fabric. Sleying the edges farther apart can help, or a feature can be made of the packing by using a colored stripe.

A highly tensioned thicker thread can be placed alongside the side turnings. This is not a floating selvedge, as it is never caught in the weaving but remains inside the side turnings. The side thread, as long as the warp, should be fastened at the front, sleyed through the reed at least one dent beyond the rest of the ends before hanging over the back of the loom with a heavy weight. Its purpose is to keep the edges from drawing in too much. The weft always passes over it when entering or emerging from an upper layer pick, and below it when entering or emerging from a lower layer. The side thread will be removed when weaving is finished.

To weave the two layers as one, use hopsack (1, 2) and (3, 4). This can be useful when weaving a tube to make a bag or cushion. A cushion can be stuffed on the loom before closing with more hopsack.

When weaving a long piece, handsew with long stitches every 4 inches (10 cm) through both woven layers together across the width. This keeps the woven cloths together when winding on, otherwise the lower layer can creep farther on than the upper.

Although it is usual to weave the upper layer 1 with 3, and the lower 2 with 4, not only can these layers be exchanged, but the other pairs of shaft combinations can be used: (1, 2) with (3, 4), and (1, 4) with (2, 3). Horizontal tubes can be woven, either open at the edges or linked. Multicolored warps can create many variations. In the sample on page 65 the colors are very contrasted for clarity. In practice, closer colors work better.

NOTES

The **sett** is that for normal tabby, but doubled up because of the two layers. Obviously there will need to be enough extra heddles on the shafts. Especially on a rising shed loom, lifting can be easier if these extra heddles are polyester with little extra weight.

Floating selvedges are not needed for tabby. The ends on a side that is to be continuously open can be doubled for 4 ends at the selvedge.

Selvedges: See pages 16–17.

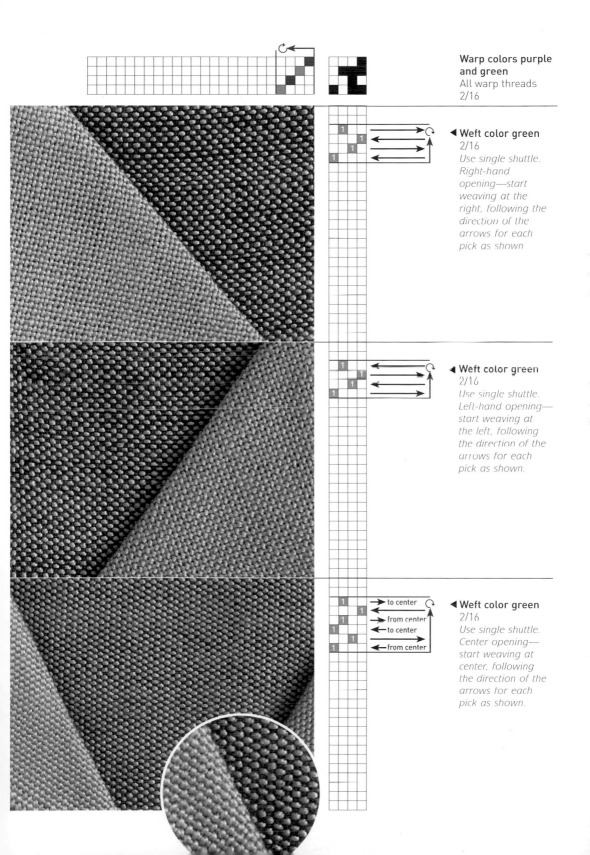

Warp colors purple and green
All warp threads 2/16

◀ **Weft color green**
2/16
Use single shuttle. Right-hand opening—start weaving at the right, following the direction of the arrows for each pick as shown

◀ **Weft color green**
2/16
Use single shuttle. Left-hand opening—start weaving at the left, following the direction of the arrows for each pick as shown.

◀ **Weft color green**
2/16
Use single shuttle. Center opening—start weaving at center, following the direction of the arrows for each pick as shown.

to center
from center
to center
from center

Separate and Tubes

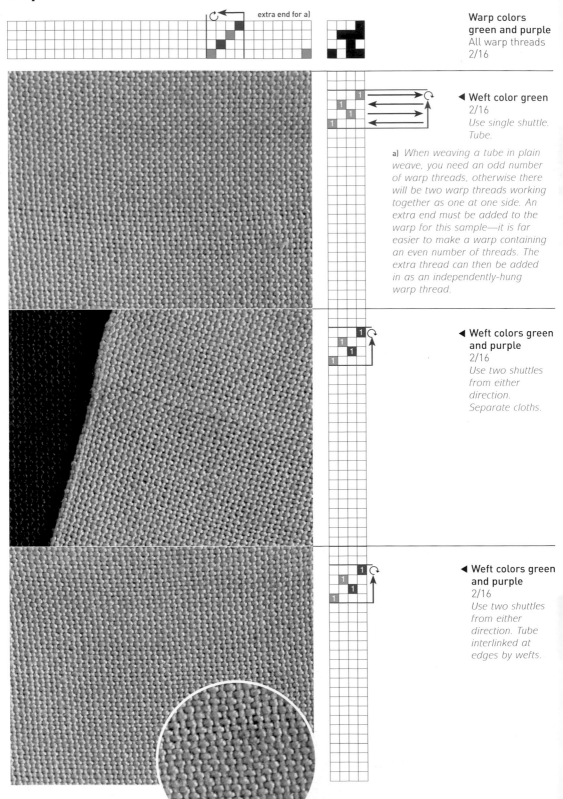

extra end for a)

Warp colors green and purple
All warp threads
2/16

◀ **Weft color green**
2/16
Use single shuttle.
Tube.

a) *When weaving a tube in plain weave, you need an odd number of warp threads, otherwise there will be two warp threads working together as one at one side. An extra end must be added to the warp for this sample—it is far easier to make a warp containing an even number of threads. The extra thread can then be added in as an independently-hung warp thread.*

◀ **Weft colors green and purple**
2/16
Use two shuttles from either direction.
Separate cloths.

◀ **Weft colors green and purple**
2/16
Use two shuttles from either direction. Tube interlinked at edges by wefts.

Four Colors in Warp

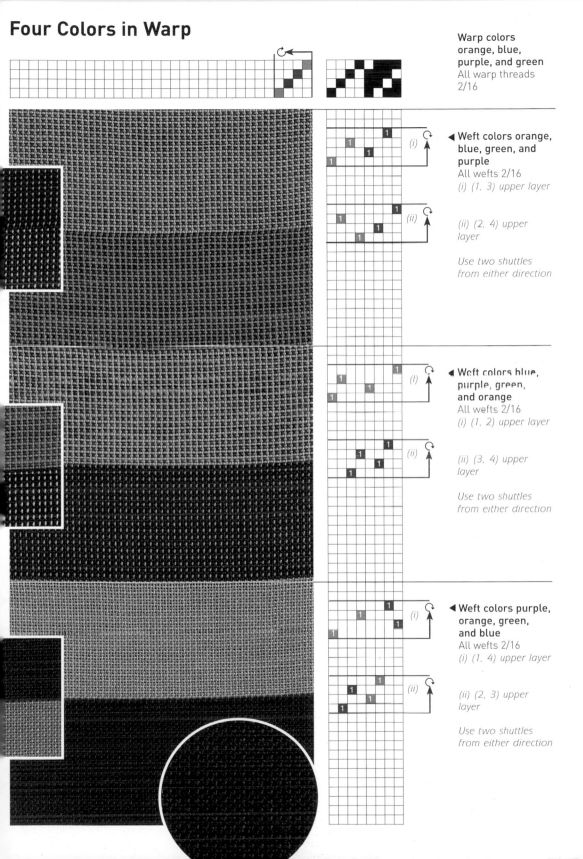

**Warp colors
orange, blue,
purple, and green**
All warp threads
2/16

◀ **Weft colors orange,
blue, green, and
purple**
All wefts 2/16
(i) (1, 3) upper layer

*(ii) (2, 4) upper
layer*

*Use two shuttles
from either direction*

◀ **Weft colors blue,
purple, green,
and orange**
All wefts 2/16
(i) (1, 2) upper layer

*(ii) (3, 4) upper
layer*

*Use two shuttles
from either direction*

◀ **Weft colors purple,
orange, green,
and blue**
All wefts 2/16
(i) (1, 4) upper layer

*(ii) (2, 3) upper
layer*

*Use two shuttles
from either direction*

Double Cloth: Vertical Selection

Not only can the two layers be separate, but they can also interact with each other across the width.

Directions for when to pick up the lower layer are given for each sample. A thin "pick-up" stick should be used—just a little longer than the width of the weaving. It should be at least 1 inch (2 cm) wide so that it can be turned "on edge" when needed to increase the height of the picked-up threads. The best results use pairs of threads to create designs that can be vertical sections of motifs.

The two layers do not have to be both woven. One layer can be left unwoven with warp floats above, below, or both above and below, the ground cloth. The warp floats can be used for insertions or left as decorative features. The warp floats can interweave with the ground either as tabby, hopsack, or 2/2 twill.

To Pick Up Groups of Warp Floats

Raise all shafts for floats. Pick up those in areas required. Close. Push stick to reed. Weave, as directed, remove stick and beat.

To Wrap Groups of Floats

Insert the next weft to halfway under the first block of floats; bring to the surface; take under the rest of the floats in that block (same direction as pick); cross back over the entire float block; go under the floats and on to where the weft emerged; insert weft into normal pick and move to the center of the next block. Pull the weft to draw in the previous float block and use the pick-up stick to push into place. (Don't remove the pick-up stick until all sections have been wrapped!) Right-handed people will find this easier to work from the right, and left-handed people from the left.

The warp ends can be of different thicknesses as well as different colors. Fine floats can be used for insertions of ribbon, fancy yarns, or other materials.

The third sample on page 69 uses a 2/2 twill for the cloth, with tabby sections for the pockets. If a very fine thread, such as "invisible" sewing thread, is used alternately in both warp and weft, then these pockets will fully display any insertions. The fine tabby upper pocket weaves evenly because it is held in place by the 2/2 twill weave.

TO WORK THE PICK-UP DESIGNS (VERTICAL SELECTION)

Lift (2, 4): Pick up all ends in areas to be raised to upper layer. Close.
Lift (1): Move pick-up stick to reed. Weave with top color, remove stick, and beat.
Lift (1, 3): Pick up all ends in areas to remain in upper layer. Close.
Lift (2): Move stick to fell and turn on edge. Weave with lower color, remove stick, and beat.
Lift (2, 4): Pick up all ends in areas to be raised to upper layer. Close.
Lift (3): Move pick-up stick to reed. Weave with top color, remove stick, and beat.
Lift (1, 3): Pick up all ends in areas to remain in upper layer. Close.
Lift (4): Move stick to fell and turn on edge. Weave with lower color, remove stick, and beat.

Netting shuttles or very thin stick shuttles are ideal for this.

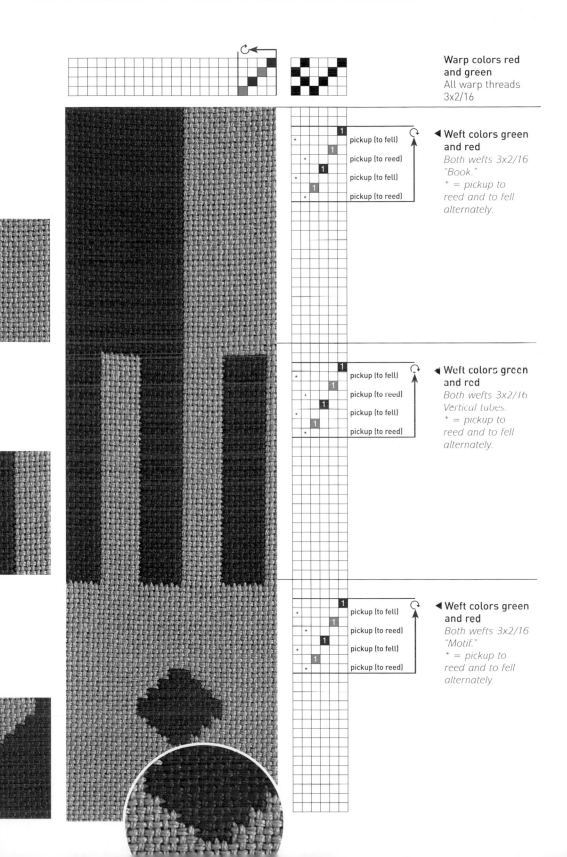

Warp colors red and green
All warp threads 3x2/16

pickup (to fell)
pickup (to reed)
pickup (to fell)
pickup (to reed)

◀ **Weft colors green and red**
Both wefts 3x2/16 "Book."
* = pickup to reed and to fell alternately.

pickup (to fell)
pickup (to reed)
pickup (to fell)
pickup (to reed)

◀ **Weft colors green and red**
Both wefts 3x2/16 Vertical tubes.
* = pickup to reed and to fell alternately.

pickup (to fell)
pickup (to reed)
pickup (to fell)
pickup (to reed)

◀ **Weft colors green and red**
Both wefts 3x2/16 "Motif."
* = pickup to reed and to fell alternately.

Thick and Thin Warp, Tabby

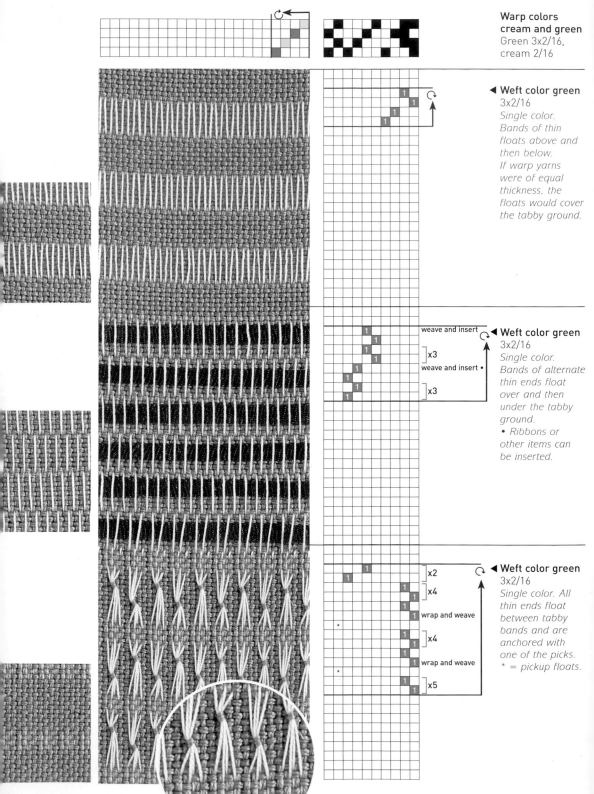

Warp colors cream and green
Green 3x2/16, cream 2/16

◀ **Weft color green**
3x2/16
Single color.
Bands of thin floats above and then below.
If warp yarns were of equal thickness, the floats would cover the tabby ground.

weave and insert

]x3

weave and insert •

]x3

◀ **Weft color green**
3x2/16
Single color.
Bands of alternate thin ends float over and then under the tabby ground.
• Ribbons or other items can be inserted.

]x2

]x4

wrap and weave

]x4

wrap and weave

]x5

◀ **Weft color green**
3x2/16
Single color. All thin ends float between tabby bands and are anchored with one of the picks.
* = pickup floats.

Thick and Thin Warp, Twill

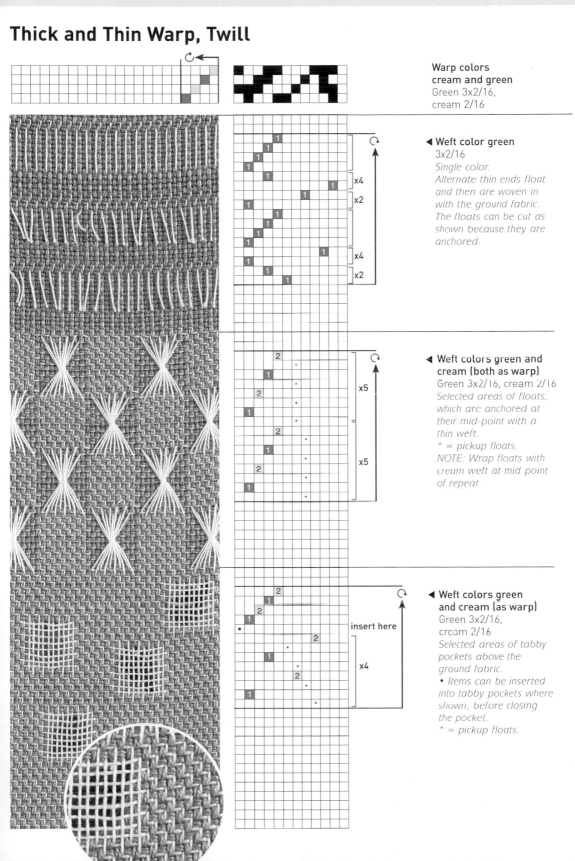

**Warp colors
cream and green**
Green 3x2/16,
cream 2/16

◄ **Weft color green**
3x2/16
*Single color.
Alternate thin ends float
and then are woven in
with the ground fabric.
The floats can be cut as
shown because they are
anchored.*

◄ **Weft colors green and
cream (both as warp)**
Green 3x2/16, cream 2/16
*Selected areas of floats,
which are anchored at
their mid-point with a
thin weft.
* = pickup floats.
NOTE: Wrap floats with
cream weft at mid point
of repeat.*

◄ **Weft colors green
and cream (as warp)**
Green 3x2/16,
cream 2/16
*Selected areas of tabby
pockets above the
ground fabric.
• Items can be inserted
into tabby pockets where
shown, before closing
the pocket.
* = pickup floats.*

Point Drafts

A point draft or twill is one that reverses the direction of threading at certain points. There are several possibilities:

Evenly
The draft reverses after a fixed number of ends in each direction, the whole sequence repeating after an even number of end entries. Tabby can be woven.

    Bird's Eye, repeat over 6 ends: 1, 2, 3, 4, 3, 2

    Rosepath, repeat over 8 ends: 1, 2, 3, 4, 1, 4, 3, 2

The sequences can be started on any shaft, working in any direction.

Irregular
This can be a repeating sequence or random. An irregular sequence can be reversed to mirror itself at regular intervals. A favorite among handweavers is "M and W," so named because the layout resembles first an M and then a W. Tabby can be woven.

Reversal
The reversal can be a direct reverse or skip one position as in Herringbone, sometimes called a Broken Twill. Tabby is not possible with a herringbone threading—if woven as tabby there will be a doubled end at the reversing points. This can be treated as a design feature.

Direction
When woven as a diagonal twill in one direction, horizontal zigzags are produced.

    The twill lifts used can be 2/2; 3/1; 1/3 or a combination of any of these.

NOTES

THERE WILL BE A LONGER FLOAT AT THE REVERSAL POINTS.

Patterns When woven with a point lifting sequence, diamond-type patterns will occur.

Selvedges are usually entered as a straight threading continuing in the same direction as the start and finish of the threading sequence. If it is important that the threading sequence is carried right up to the edges of the fabric then follow the directions on pages 16–17.

A floating selvedge will need to be used because of the reversals.

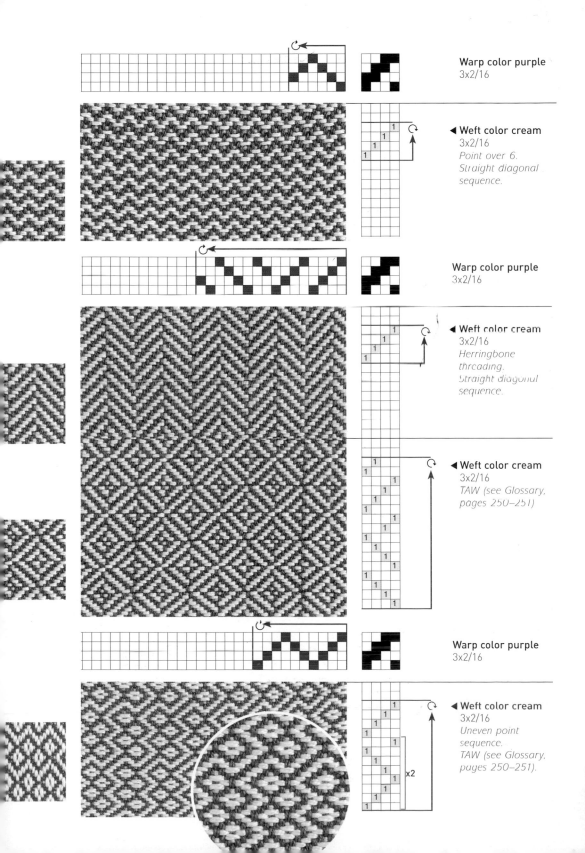

Warp color purple
3x2/16

◀ **Weft color cream**
3x2/16
*Point over 6.
Straight diagonal
sequence.*

Warp color purple
3x2/16

◀ **Weft color cream**
3x2/16
*Herringbone
threading.
Straight diagonal
sequence.*

◀ **Weft color cream**
3x2/16
*TAW (see Glossary,
pages 250–251)*

Warp color purple
3x2/16

◀ **Weft color cream**
3x2/16
*Uneven point
sequence.
TAW (see Glossary,
pages 250–251).*

Point Threading Over 6: Bird's Eye; 2/2 Twill

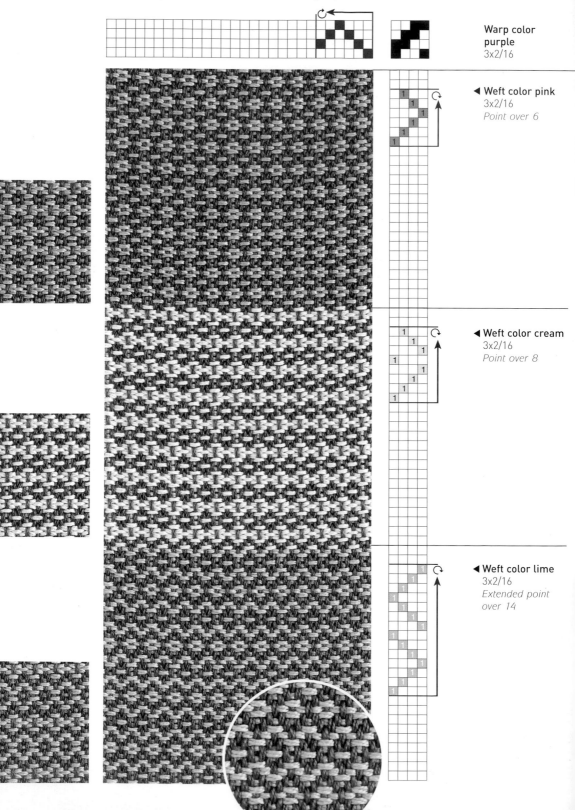

Warp color
purple
3x2/16

◀ Weft color pink
3x2/16
Point over 6

◀ Weft color cream
3x2/16
Point over 8

◀ Weft color lime
3x2/16
*Extended point
over 14*

Point Threading Over 6: Bird's Eye; 1/3 Twill

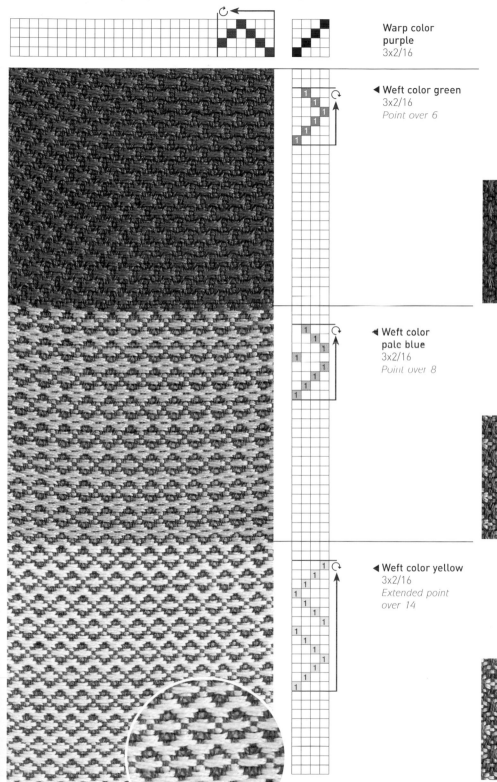

Warp color
purple
3x2/16

◀ Weft color green
3x2/16
Point over 6

◀ Weft color
pale blue
3x2/16
Point over 8

◀ Weft color yellow
3x2/16
*Extended point
over 14*

Point Threading Over 8: Rosepath; 2/2, 3/1, & 1/3 Twills

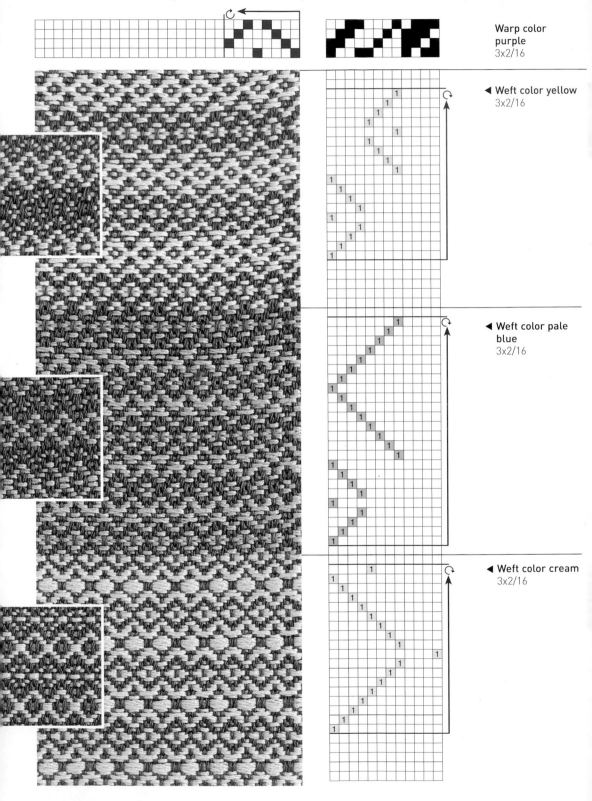

Warp color
purple
3x2/16

◀ Weft color yellow
3x2/16

◀ Weft color pale
blue
3x2/16

◀ Weft color cream
3x2/16

Point Threading Over 8: Rosepath; Mixed Twills; Borders

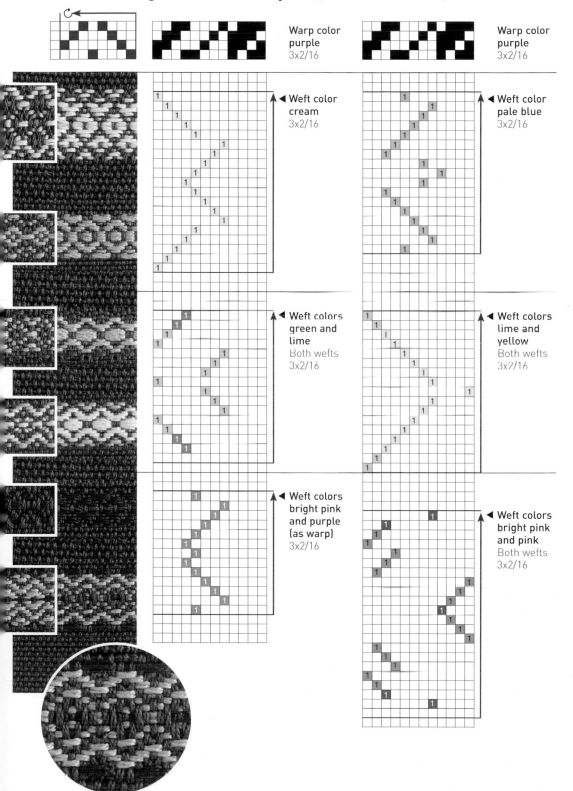

Warp color
purple
3x2/16

Warp color
purple
3x2/16

◀ Weft color
cream
3x2/16

◀ Weft color
pale blue
3x2/16

◀ Weft colors
green and
lime
Both wefts
3x2/16

◀ Weft colors
lime and
yellow
Both wefts
3x2/16

◀ Weft colors
bright pink
and purple
(as warp)
3x2/16

◀ Weft colors
bright pink
and pink
Both wefts
3x2/16

M and W Threading Over 22: 2/2 Twill

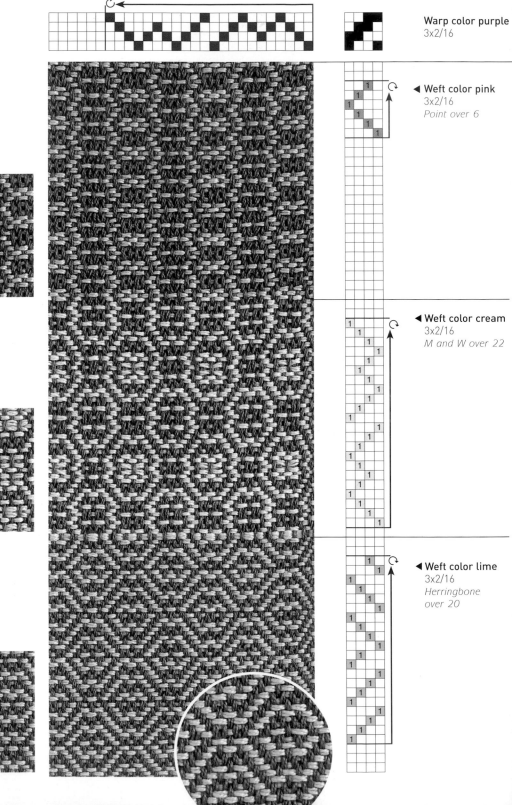

Warp color purple
3x2/16

◀ **Weft color pink**
3x2/16
Point over 6

◀ **Weft color cream**
3x2/16
M and W over 22

◀ **Weft color lime**
3x2/16
Herringbone over 20

M and W Threading Over 22: 1/3 Twill

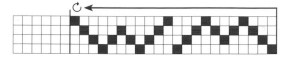

Warp color purple
3x2/16

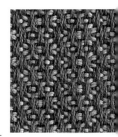

◄ **Weft color pale blue**
3x2/16
Point over 6

◄ **Weft color cream**
3x2/16
M and W over 22

◄ **Weft color yellow**
3x2/16
Herringbone over 20

Point Threading Over 6: Bird's Eye; 2/2 Twill

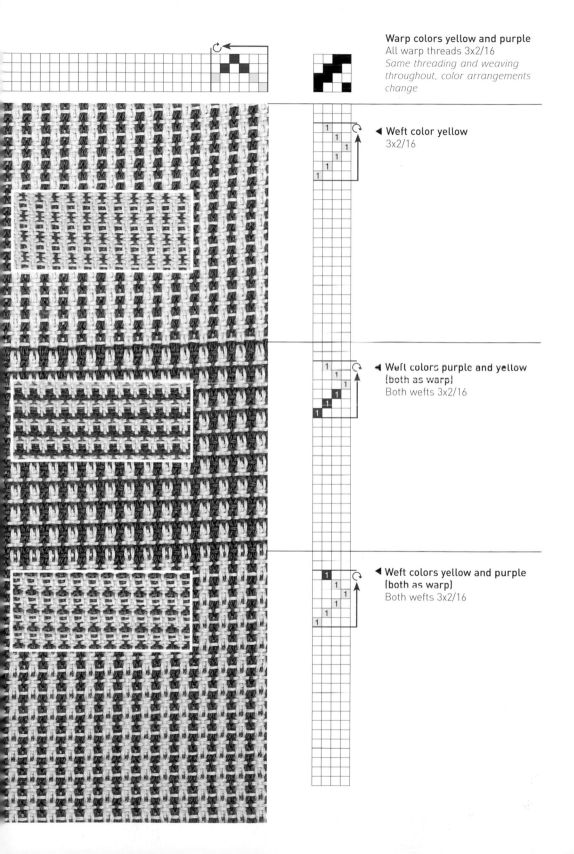

Warp colors yellow and purple
All warp threads 3x2/16
Same threading and weaving throughout, color arrangements change

◀ **Weft color yellow**
3x2/16

◀ **Weft colors purple and yellow (both as warp)**
Both wefts 3x2/16

◀ **Weft colors yellow and purple (both as warp)**
Both wefts 3x2/16

Point Threading Over 8, 10, and 12; 2/2 Twill

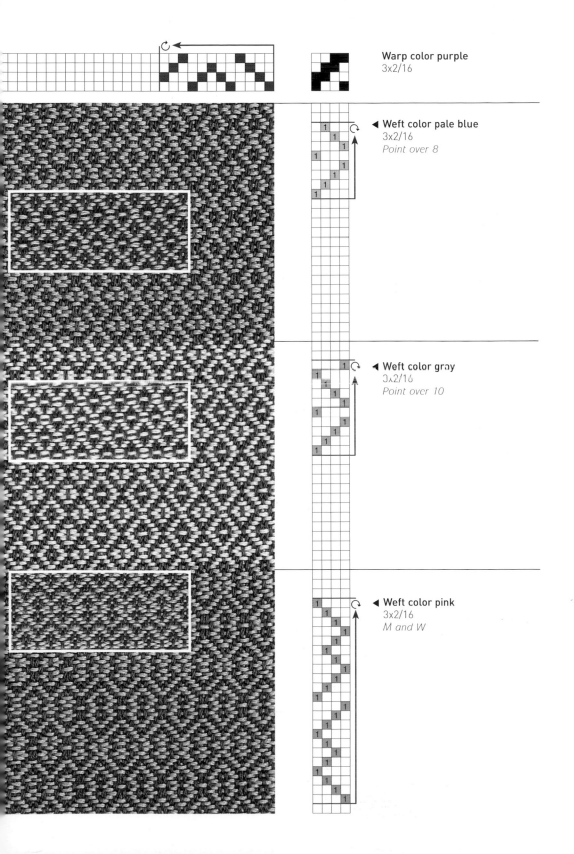

Warp color purple
3x2/16

◀ Weft color pale blue
3x2/16
Point over 8

◀ Weft color gray
3x2/16
Point over 10

◀ Weft color pink
3x2/16
M and W

Point Threading Over 8: Rosepath; 2/2 Twill

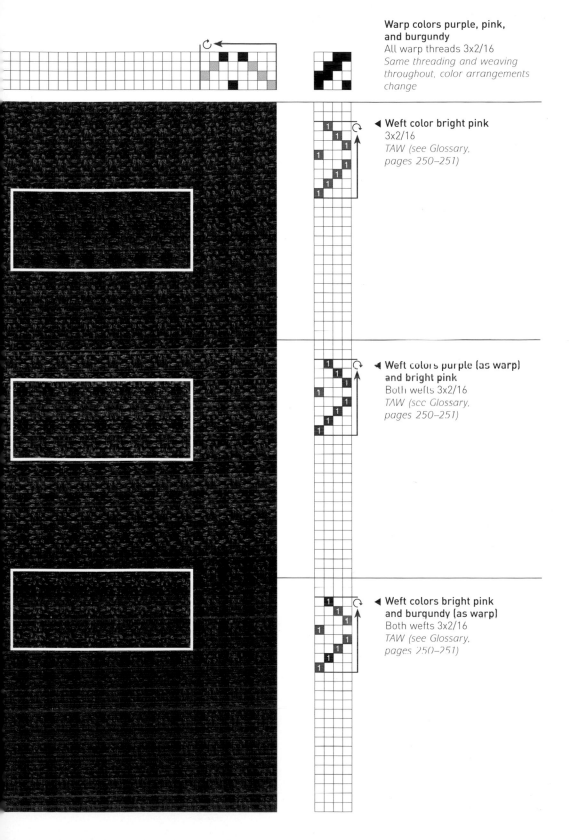

Warp colors purple, pink, and burgundy
All warp threads 3x2/16
Same threading and weaving throughout, color arrangements change

◀ **Weft color bright pink**
3x2/16
TAW (see Glossary, pages 250–251)

◀ **Weft colors purple (as warp) and bright pink**
Both wefts 3x2/16
TAW (see Glossary, pages 250–251)

◀ **Weft colors bright pink and burgundy (as warp)**
Both wefts 3x2/16
TAW (see Glossary, pages 250–251)

Point Threading Over 12

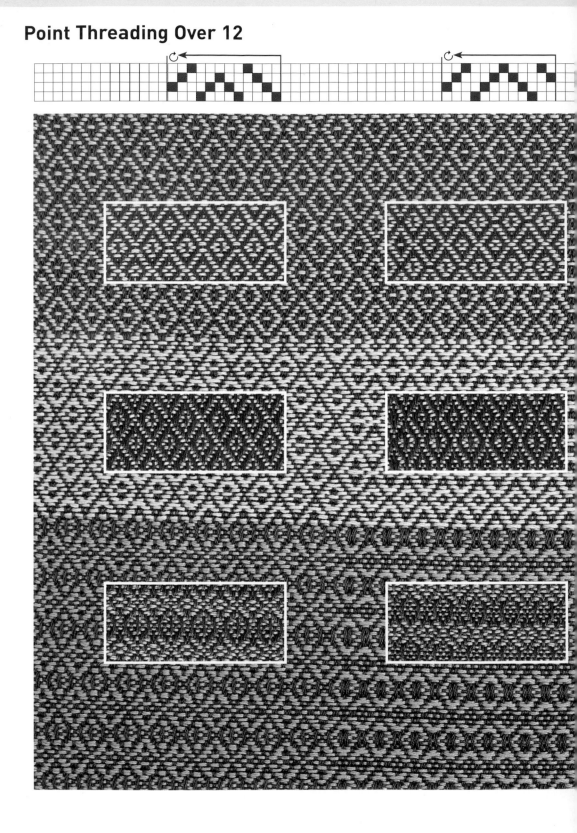

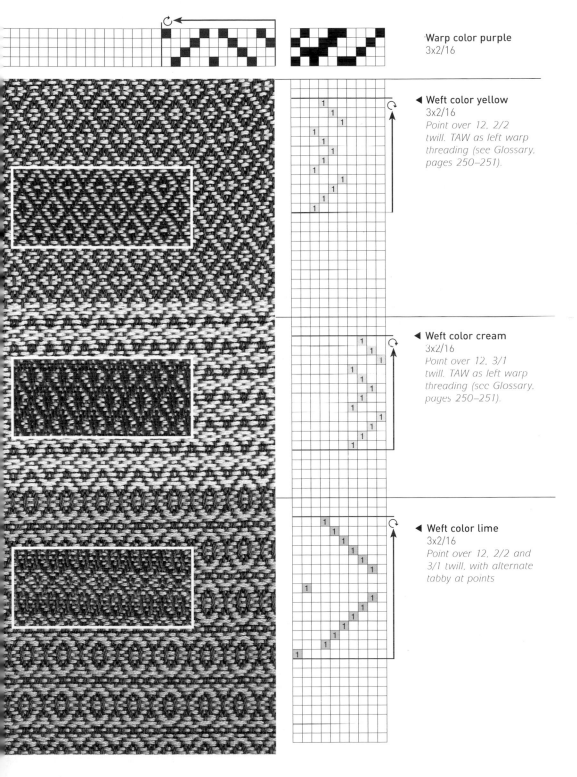

Warp color purple
3x2/16

◀ Weft color yellow
3x2/16
*Point over 12, 2/2
twill. TAW as left warp
threading (see Glossary,
pages 250–251).*

◀ Weft color cream
3x2/16
*Point over 12, 3/1
twill. TAW as left warp
threading (see Glossary,
pages 250–251).*

◀ Weft color lime
3x2/16
*Point over 12, 2/2 and
3/1 twill, with alternate
tabby at points*

Broken Point Threading: 2/2 Twill

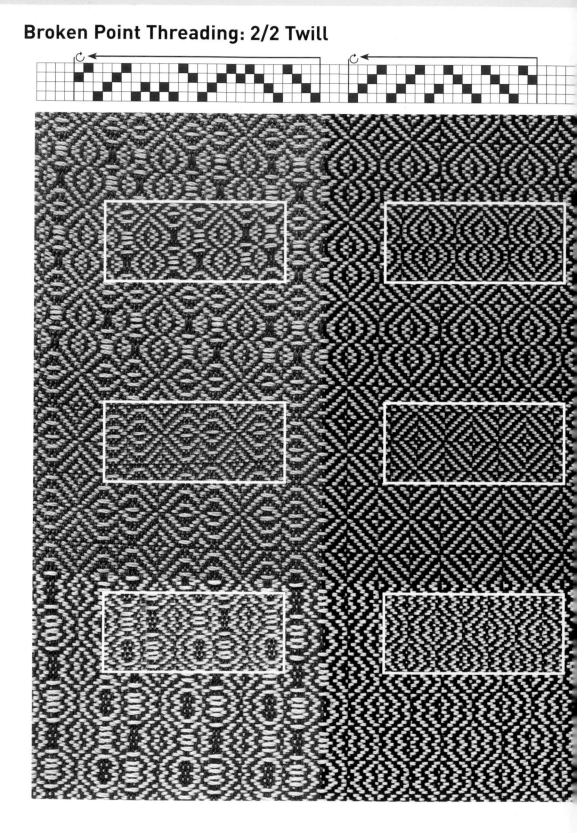

Warp color purple
3x2/16

◀ **Weft color lime**
3x2/16
*Irregular point and broken
point sequence. TAW as
left warp threading (see
Glossary, pages 250–251).*

◀ **Weft color pale blue**
3x2/16
*Classic Herringbone. TAW as
center warp threading (see
Glossary, pages 250–251).*

◀ **Weft color cream**
3x2/16
*M and W. TAW as right
warp threading (see
Glossary, pages 250–251).*

M and W Threading: 2/2 Twill

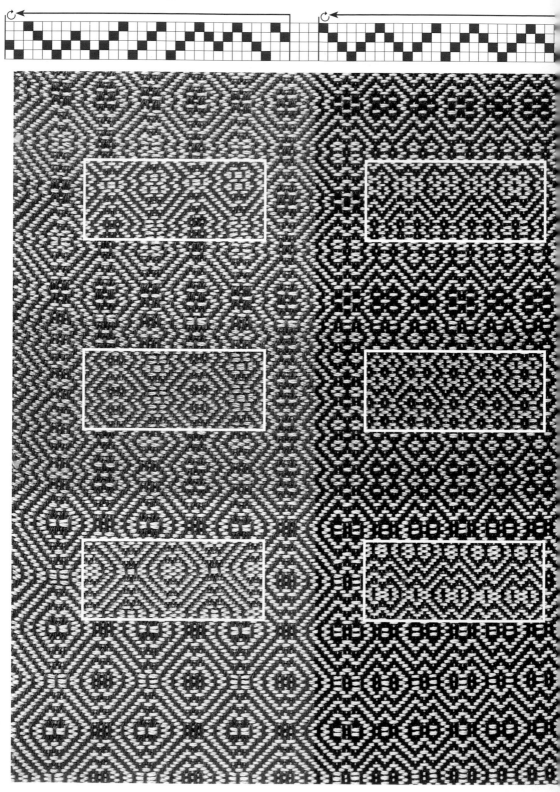

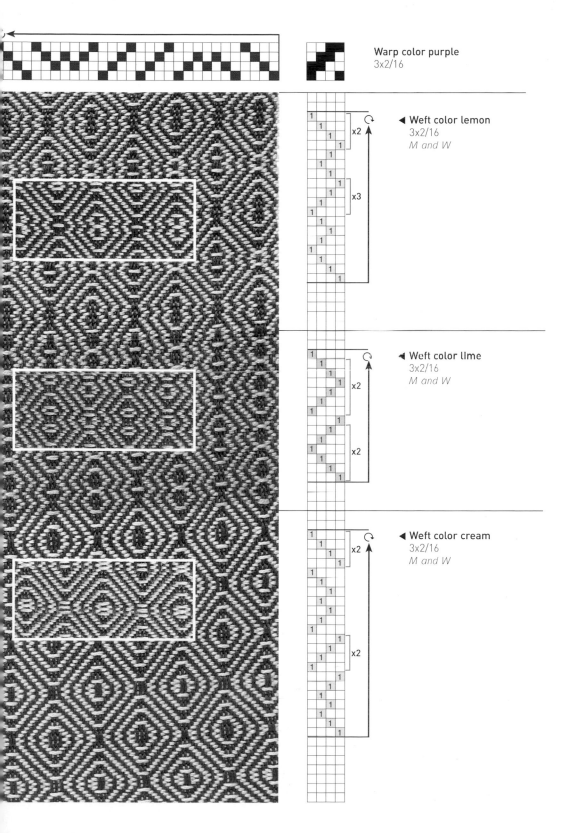

Warp color purple
3x2/16

◄ Weft color lemon
3x2/16
M and W

◄ Weft color lime
3x2/16
M and W

◄ Weft color cream
3x2/16
M and W

M and W Variations Threading: 2/2 Twill

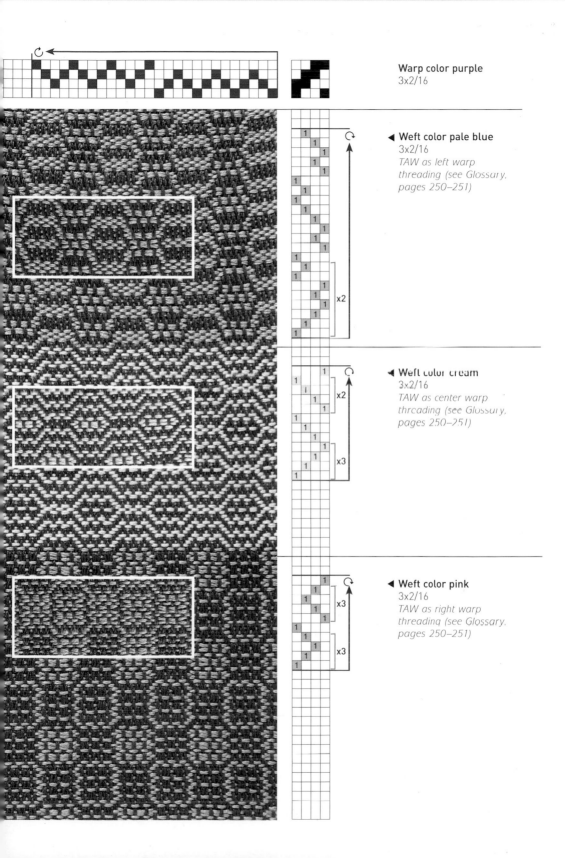

Warp color purple
3x2/16

◀ **Weft color pale blue**
3x2/16
*TAW as left warp
threading (see Glossary,
pages 250–251)*

x2

◀ **Weft color cream**
3x2/16
*TAW as center warp
threading (see Glossary,
pages 250–251)*

x2

x3

◀ **Weft color pink**
3x2/16
*TAW as right warp
threading (see Glossary,
pages 250–251)*

x3

x3

Point Threading Over 6: Bird's Eye; 2/2 Twill

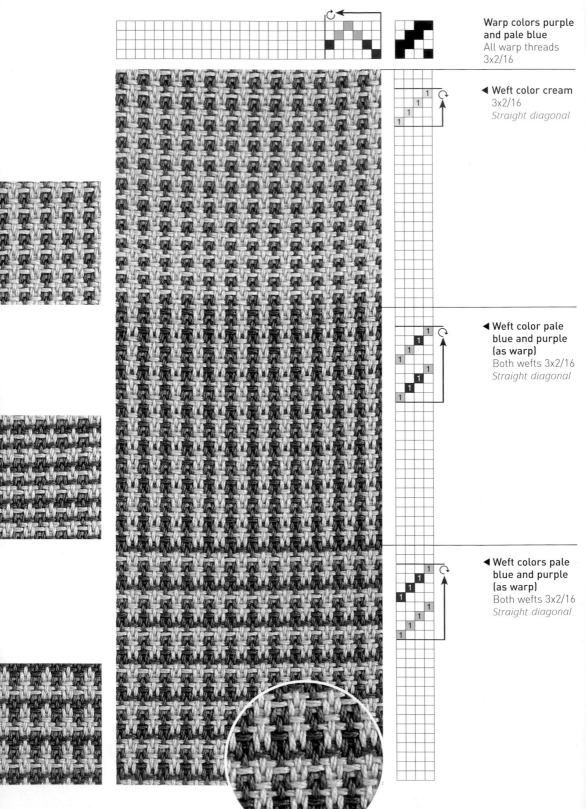

Warp colors purple and pale blue
All warp threads
3x2/16

◀ **Weft color cream**
3x2/16
Straight diagonal

◀ **Weft color pale blue and purple (as warp)**
Both wefts 3x2/16
Straight diagonal

◀ **Weft colors pale blue and purple (as warp)**
Both wefts 3x2/16
Straight diagonal

Point Threading Over 6: Bird's Eye; 2/2 Twill

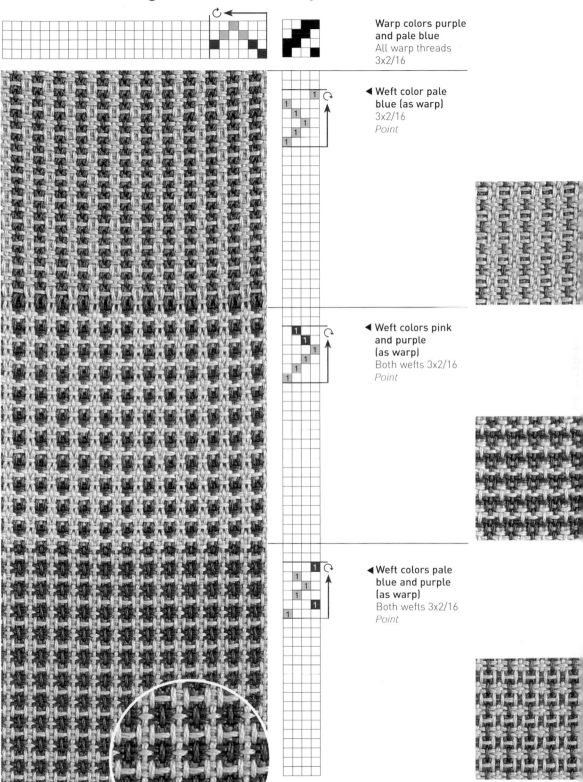

Warp colors purple and pale blue
All warp threads
3x2/16

◀ **Weft color pale blue (as warp)**
3x2/16
Point

◀ **Weft colors pink and purple (as warp)**
Both wefts 3x2/16
Point

◀ **Weft colors pale blue and purple (as warp)**
Both wefts 3x2/16
Point

Block Drafts

In this section are those patterns created from blocks composed of small repeated groups of threading. There can be multiples of groups, or even just a single group, forming the area.

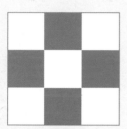

Even blocks

Uneven blocks

Blocks as a border

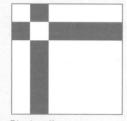

Blocks off-center

All blocks different sizes

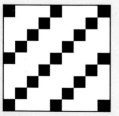

Straight diagonal order

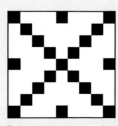

Point order

Each block is a set of warp threads written as a group on the threading draft and woven as a group in the fabric. On four shafts, the blocks can be threaded on two, three, or four shafts.

Blocks threaded on two shafts are used for Monk's Belt; Overshot; Honeycomb.

Blocks threaded on three shafts are used for Summer and Winter; Crackle.

Blocks threaded on four shafts are used in Ms and Os.

Some can only create two, but clearly different, blocks on four shafts: Monk's Belt; Honeycomb; Ms and Os; Summer and Winter. The areas of blocks, in both warp and weft, can be of different sizes, enabling the weaver to create designs with different proportions of squares and oblongs. Graph paper is useful for design work.

Four blocks are created in Overshot and Crackle, and thus have more design potential. They can be threaded in straight or point configurations.

Each technique has its own traditional or conventional method of weaving. Some have a larger variety of methods; others are more limited in range. All the techniques can also be woven in non-traditional, "As If," or other unconventional ways, with several different possibilities using the same threading. Experiment!

Use Tabby Several block drafts require the use of tabby weave to stabilize the structure. If "use tabby" is stipulated for any pattern, it means alternate each pattern pick with a tabby pick. Alternate the tabby picks: tabby **A**, pattern, tabby **B**, pattern, etc.

Silk waistcoat for page boy at a wedding, using two overshot patterns on the same threading draft. Ground threads 30/2 cream silk, doubled pattern threads space-dyed.

Threads The tabby weft is usually the same thickness and type as the warp. It is often the same color but can be different.

The pattern weft is either thicker than the warp, or the same thickness used double so that the pattern weft covers the background tabby. It is usually a contrast to the warp but can be the same color.

Any variations to the above will be noted in the sample notes.

Beating It is better to throw the doubled pattern weft twice in the same shed, rather than winding a doubled weft on the shuttle, as it both looks neater and has a better covering power. When using a doubled pattern thread, beat the first pick gently to place it against the fell before inserting the second pick, and then beat the entire pick in the usual way.

More details about the specifics of the individual block designs are at the beginning of each subsection, together with advice about the basics of designing with those blocks.

NOTE: Several of the lace weaves are also block weaves but are in their own section.

Monk's Belt

This is an extremely old design. It probably pre-dates the Christian era, but whether the pattern was actually used for monks' belts or acquired that name much later is debatable.

Monk's Belt is a two-block weave threaded in groups using ends on two adjacent shafts and woven "with tabby." On a four-shaft loom only two blocks are possible. Each group can be as small as two threads or covering 4, 6, or more.

The threading blocks first use two adjacent shafts and then the opposite two shafts (either [1, 2] and [3, 4]; or [2, 3] and [4, 1]). A two-thread block on two shafts can follow repeated blocks using six or eight threads on the other pair of shafts, before returning to a larger repeat on the first pair. If this sequence is repeated, it will create a visually larger area of blocks on the first pair of shafts, without the need for overlong floats. The threading must be odd, even, odd, even, so that tabby can be woven.

The weft pattern thread floats repeatedly over the block (and at the same time under the opposite block), creating clear areas of pattern. The vertical pattern areas can be as long as you wish, as the warp is stabilized by the use of tabby, which is used alternately between each pattern pick. Repeated horizontal blocks do not have tie-downs, so it is best not to repeat the number of warp blocks too often, as this can produce overlong weft floats.

NOTES

Threads: See page 95.

Reading the weaving draft: A number within the color block for the weft pick shows how many times that shed has to be lifted, with tabby in between.

The intersections of tabby create a plain-weave fabric with the pattern imposed into this. Theoretically it would be possible to cut away the pattern threads and be left with a plain-weave fabric.

The Monk's Belt threading can be woven "As Overshot" by using links of the other pairs of adjacent shafts.

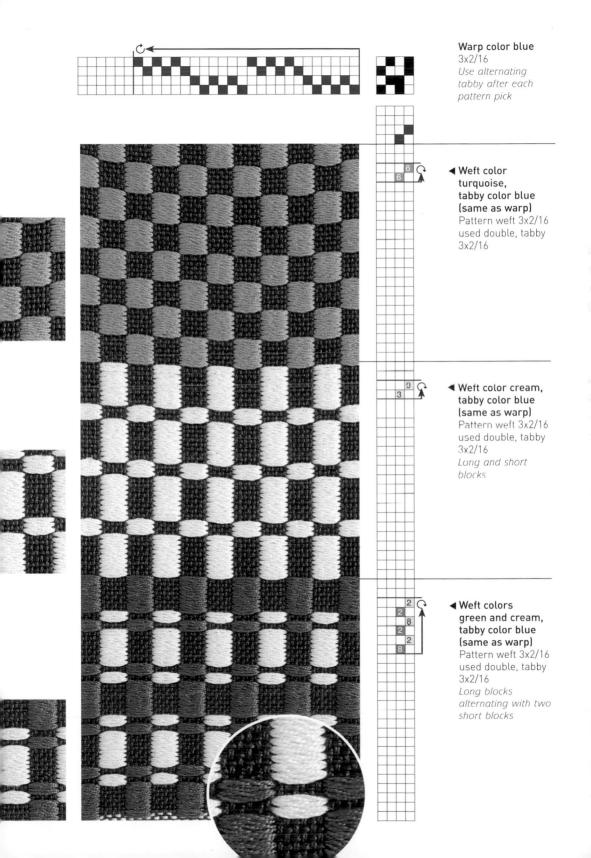

Warp color blue
3x2/16
*Use alternating
tabby after each
pattern pick*

◄ **Weft color
turquoise,
tabby color blue
(same as warp)**
Pattern weft 3x2/16
used double, tabby
3x2/16

◄ **Weft color cream,
tabby color blue
(same as warp)**
Pattern weft 3x2/16
used double, tabby
3x2/16
*Long and short
blocks*

◄ **Weft colors
green and cream,
tabby color blue
(same as warp)**
Pattern weft 3x2/16
used double, tabby
3x2/16
*Long blocks
alternating with two
short blocks*

Monk's Belt

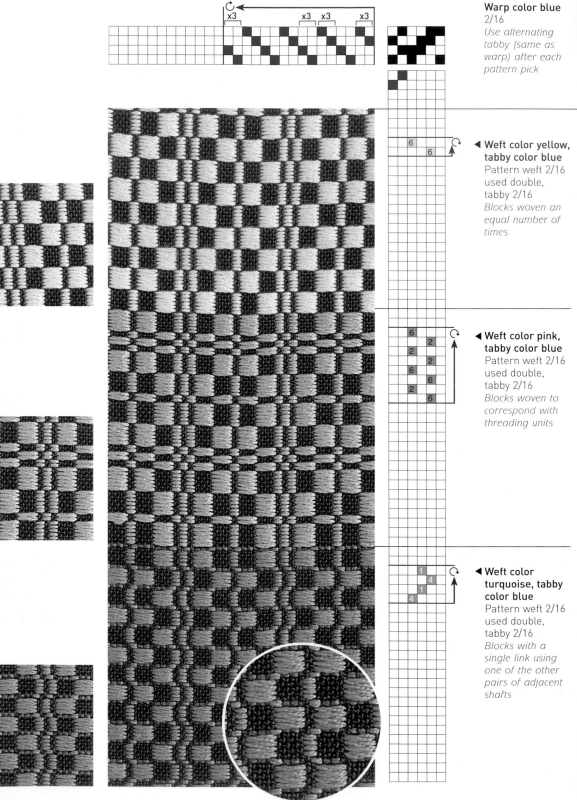

Warp color blue
2/16
Use alternating tabby (same as warp) after each pattern pick

◄ **Weft color yellow, tabby color blue**
Pattern weft 2/16 used double, tabby 2/16
Blocks woven an equal number of times

◄ **Weft color pink, tabby color blue**
Pattern weft 2/16 used double, tabby 2/16
Blocks woven to correspond with threading units

◄ **Weft color turquoise, tabby color blue**
Pattern weft 2/16 used double, tabby 2/16
Blocks with a single link using one of the other pairs of adjacent shafts

Monk's Belt Borders

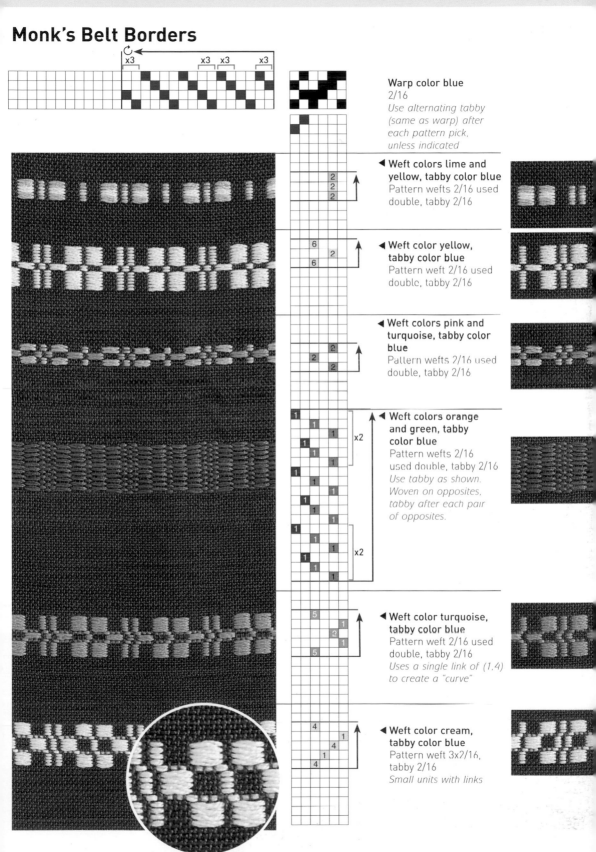

Warp color blue
2/16
*Use alternating tabby
(same as warp) after
each pattern pick,
unless indicated*

◀ Weft colors lime and
yellow, tabby color blue
Pattern wefts 2/16 used
double, tabby 2/16

◀ Weft color yellow,
tabby color blue
Pattern weft 2/16 used
double, tabby 2/16

◀ Weft colors pink and
turquoise, tabby color
blue
Pattern wefts 2/16 used
double, tabby 2/16

◀ Weft colors orange
and green, tabby
color blue
Pattern wefts 2/16
used double, tabby 2/16
*Use tabby as shown.
Woven on opposites,
tabby after each pair
of opposites.*

◀ Weft color turquoise,
tabby color blue
Pattern weft 2/16 used
double, tabby 2/16
*Uses a single link of (1,4)
to create a "curve"*

◀ Weft color cream,
tabby color blue
Pattern weft 3x2/16,
tabby 2/16
Small units with links

Monk's Belt

Warp color blue
2/16
Use alternating tabby (same as warp) after each pattern pick

◀ **Weft color cream, tabby color blue**
Pattern weft 3x2/16, tabby 2/16
Very traditional patterning, blocks woven as warp arrangement

◀ **Weft color pink, tabby color blue**
Pattern weft 3x2/16, tabby 2/16
Border, using the "link" sheds to create diagonal movement

◀ **Weft colors green and yellow, tabby color blue**
Pattern weft 3x2/16, tabby 2/16
Border

Monk's Belt

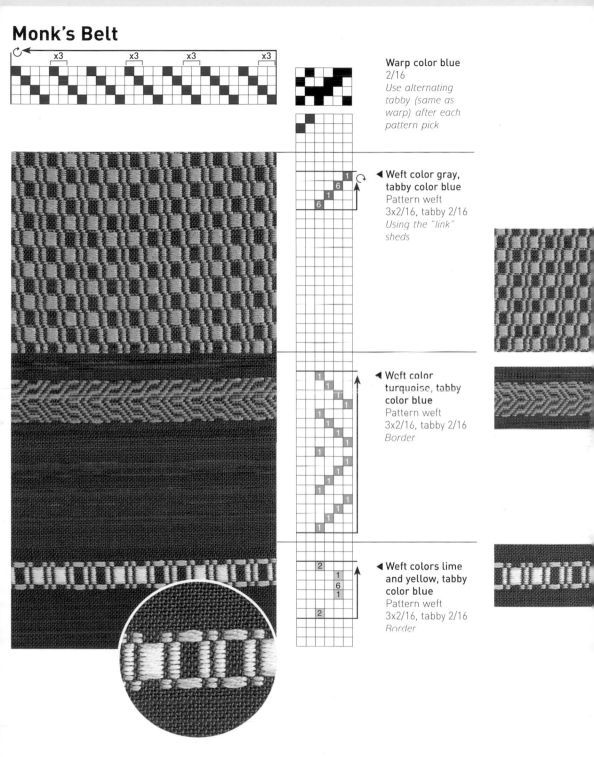

Warp color blue
2/16
*Use alternating
tabby (same as
warp) after each
pattern pick*

◀ Weft color gray,
tabby color blue
Pattern weft
3x2/16, tabby 2/16
*Using the "link"
sheds*

◀ Weft color
turquoise, tabby
color blue
Pattern weft
3x2/16, tabby 2/16
Border

◀ Weft colors lime
and yellow, tabby
color blue
Pattern weft
3x2/16, tabby 2/16
Border

Overshot

Overshot is so named because the weft "shoots" over the ground cloth according to the threaded pattern blocks. It is similar to Monk's Belt; however, all four pairs of adjacent shafts are used for the four pattern block.

Blocks are composed of threading repeats on two adjacent shafts—not too many at once or the pattern floats will be overlong. The pattern pick floats over and below the ground cloth on opposite blocks, but is woven in with the tabby ground cloth between these, showing as small specks in the pattern. The threading must be odd, even, odd, even, so that tabby can be woven. The thread at the end of each block is also part of the adjacent block.

The pattern can be woven as drawn in (TAW) in three different ways:

Star
Count the intervals between the ends in a block, and then use this pair of shafts the same number of times for the pattern.

Intervals between 1 and 2 in threading = number of picks on (1, 2)

Intervals between 2 and 3 in threading = number of picks on (2, 3)

Intervals between 3 and 4 in threading = number of picks on (3, 4)

Intervals between 4 and 1 in threading = number of picks on (4, 1)

e.g., thread 1, 2, 1, 2, 1, 2 = 5 intervals, so 5 consecutive pattern picks on (1, 2)

There will always be a straight X at the center of the pattern of either tabby background or pattern threads.

"Rose 1"
The position on the lifting draft is moved to the next pair. (1, 2) becomes (2, 3); (2, 3) becomes (3, 4) and so on. The pattern is more curved.

"Rose 2"
The changes on the lifting draft are slightly different than "Rose 1."

(1, 2) moves to (2, 3); and (2, 3) moves to (1, 2).

(3, 4) moves to (4, 1); and (4, 1) moves to (3, 4).

The pattern is again curved.

Usually adjacent pairs of shafts are used for the pattern. The 1/3 or 3/1 twill picks can also be used but the floats can be very long. This can work if the cloth is to be lined.

The pattern can be woven in many other combinations. Two adjacent blocks could be "on opposites."

With a sinking shed loom it is the pattern weft that produces the descriptive pattern on the upper surface using the above formulas. However, when using a rising or lifted shed this shows on the underside of the cloth.

NOTES

Threads: See page 95.

Selvedges and sett: Use a straight draft for the selvedges. Use a floating selvedge to catch the pattern wefts. Use a sett suitable for tabby.

Reading the weaving draft: A number within the color block for the picks shows how many times that shed has to be used, with tabby in between.

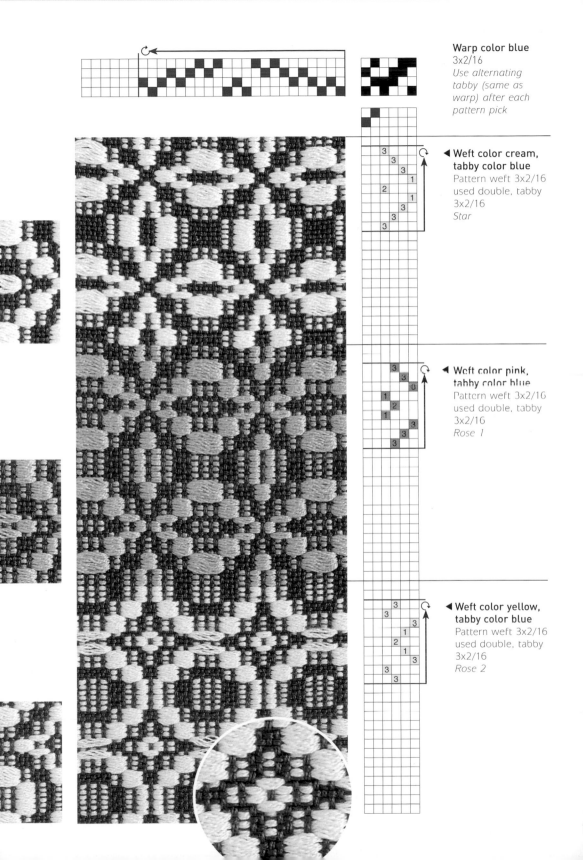

Warp color blue
3x2/16
*Use alternating
tabby (same as
warp) after each
pattern pick*

◀ **Weft color cream,
tabby color blue**
Pattern weft 3x2/16
used double, tabby
3x2/16
Star

◀ **Weft color pink,
tabby color blue**
Pattern weft 3x2/16
used double, tabby
3x2/16
Rose 1

◀ **Weft color yellow,
tabby color blue**
Pattern weft 3x2/16
used double, tabby
3x2/16
Rose 2

Overshot: Small Honeysuckle

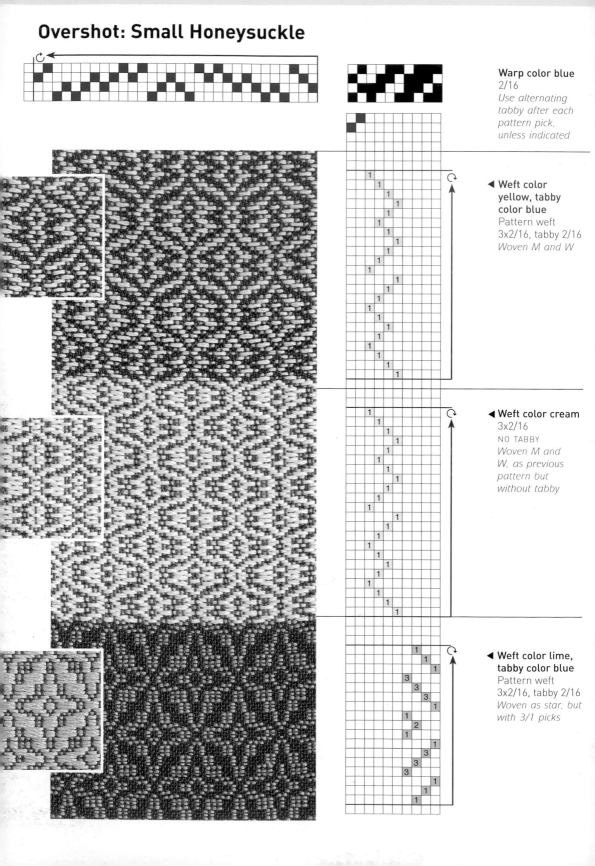

Warp color blue
2/16
Use alternating tabby after each pattern pick, unless indicated

◀ **Weft color yellow, tabby color blue**
Pattern weft 3x2/16, tabby 2/16
Woven M and W

◀ **Weft color cream**
3x2/16
NO TABBY
Woven M and W, as previous pattern but without tabby

◀ **Weft color lime, tabby color blue**
Pattern weft 3x2/16, tabby 2/16
Woven as star, but with 3/1 picks

Overshot: Small Honeysuckle

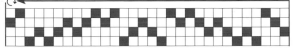

Warp color blue
2/16
*Use alternating tabby
after each pattern pick,
unless indicated*

◀ **Weft colors
burgundy and
pink**
3x2/16
NO TABBY
*Star woven
as Bound
Weave (see
Glossary, pages
250–251) in
alternating
colors*

x3
x3
x3

x3
x3
x3

◀ **Weft color
cream, tabby
color blue**
Pattern weft
2/16 used
double,
tabby 2/16

◀ **Weft color
blue, tabby
color
turquoise**
Pattern weft
3x2/16,
tabby 2/16
Star

Overshot: Small Honeysuckle

Warp color blue
2/16
Use alternating tabby after each pattern pick

◄ **Weft color turquoise, tabby color blue**
Pattern weft 3x2/16, tabby 2/16
Star

◄ **Weft color pink, tabby color blue**
Pattern weft 2/16 used double, tabby 2/16
Rose 1

◄ **Weft color cream, tabby color green**
Pattern weft 3x2/16, tabby 2/16
Rose 2

Overshot: Small Honeysuckle Borders

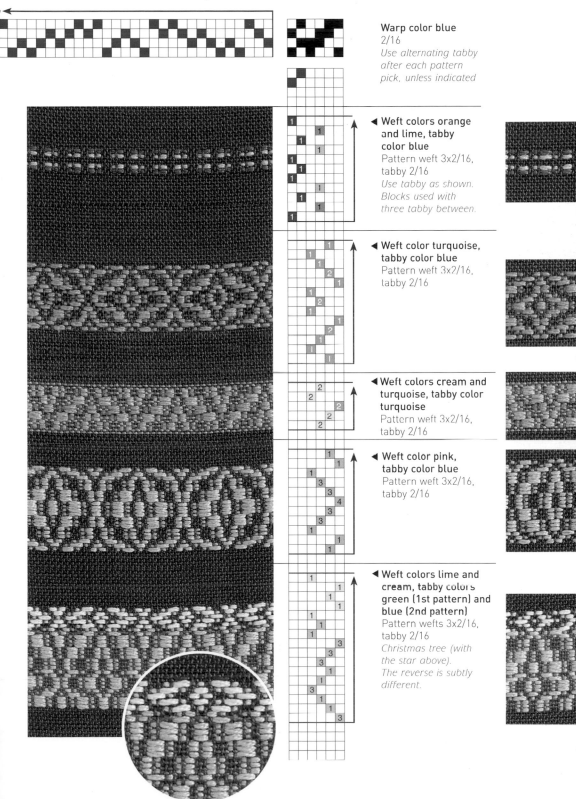

Warp color blue
2/16
*Use alternating tabby
after each pattern
pick, unless indicated*

◀ Weft colors orange
and lime, tabby
color blue
Pattern weft 3x2/16,
tabby 2/16
*Use tabby as shown.
Blocks used with
three tabby between.*

◀ Weft color turquoise,
tabby color blue
Pattern weft 3x2/16,
tabby 2/16

◀ Weft colors cream and
turquoise, tabby color
turquoise
Pattern weft 3x2/16,
tabby 2/16

◀ Weft color pink,
tabby color blue
Pattern weft 3x2/16,
tabby 2/16

◀ Weft colors lime and
cream, tabby colors
green (1st pattern) and
blue (2nd pattern)
Pattern wefts 3x2/16,
tabby 2/16
*Christmas tree (with
the star above).
The reverse is subtly
different.*

Overshot: Star and Rose

Warp color blue
2/16
Use alternating tabby after each pattern pick

◀ **Weft color yellow, tabby color blue**
Pattern weft 3x2/16, tabby 2/16
Star and Rose lifting sequence

◀ **Weft color gray, tabby color blue**
Pattern weft 3x2/16, tabby 2/16
Border

◀ **Weft color pink, tabby color blue**
Pattern weft 3x2/16, tabby 2/16
Border

Overshot: Enigma

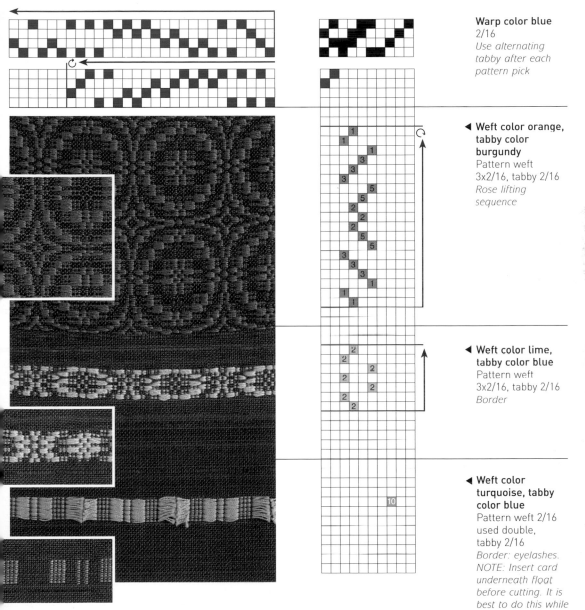

Warp color blue
2/16
*Use alternating
tabby after each
pattern pick*

◀ **Weft color orange,
tabby color
burgundy**
Pattern weft
3x2/16, tabby 2/16
*Rose lifting
sequence*

◀ **Weft color lime,
tabby color blue**
Pattern weft
3x2/16, tabby 2/16
Border

◀ **Weft color
turquoise, tabby
color blue**
Pattern weft 2/16
used double,
tabby 2/16
*Border: eyelashes.
NOTE: Insert card
underneath float
before cutting. It is
best to do this while
on the loom.*

Overshot: Charlotte

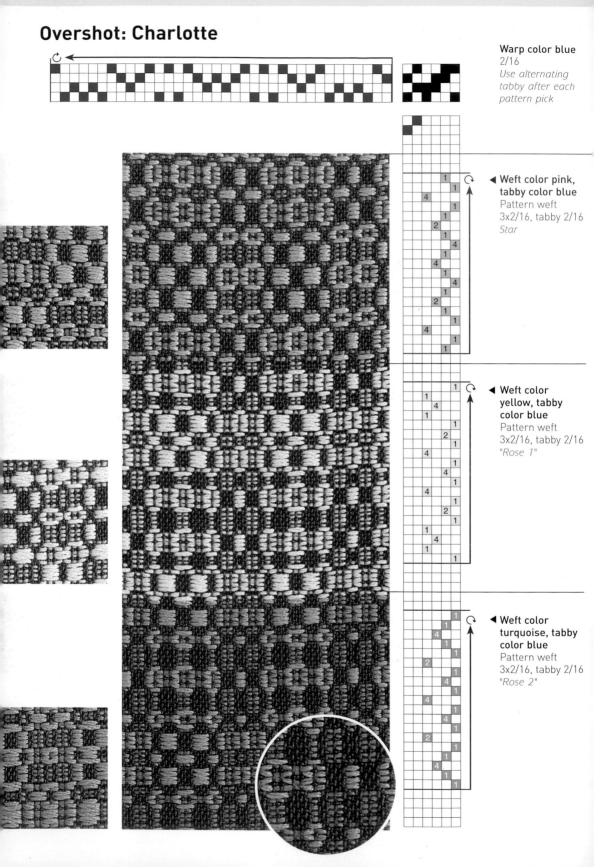

Warp color blue
2/16
Use alternating tabby after each pattern pick

◀ **Weft color pink, tabby color blue**
Pattern weft
3x2/16, tabby 2/16
Star

◀ **Weft color yellow, tabby color blue**
Pattern weft
3x2/16, tabby 2/16
"Rose 1"

◀ **Weft color turquoise, tabby color blue**
Pattern weft
3x2/16, tabby 2/16
"Rose 2"

Overshot: Charlotte

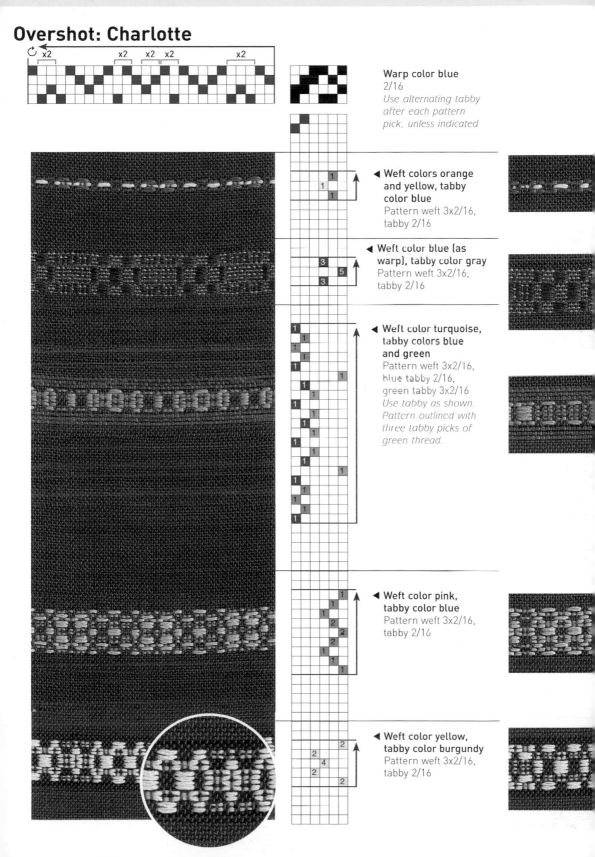

Warp color blue
2/16
*Use alternating tabby
after each pattern
pick, unless indicated*

◀ Weft colors orange
and yellow, tabby
color blue
Pattern weft 3x2/16,
tabby 2/16

◀ Weft color blue (as
warp), tabby color gray
Pattern weft 3x2/16,
tabby 2/16

◀ Weft color turquoise,
tabby colors blue
and green
Pattern weft 3x2/16,
blue tabby 2/16,
green tabby 3x2/16
*Use tabby as shown.
Pattern outlined with
three tabby picks of
green thread.*

◀ Weft color pink,
tabby color blue
Pattern weft 3x2/16,
tabby 2/16

◀ Weft color yellow,
tabby color burgundy
Pattern weft 3x2/16,
tabby 2/16

Overshot: Floral Dance

Warp color blue
2/16
Use alternating tabby after each pattern pick

◀ **Weft color lime, tabby color blue**
Pattern weft 3x2/16, tabby 2/16
Star

◀ **Weft color cream, tabby color blue**
Pattern weft 3x2/16, tabby 2/16
"Rose 1"

◀ **Weft color turquoise, tabby color blue**
Pattern weft 3x2/16, tabby 2/16
"Rose 2"

Overshot: Floral Dance

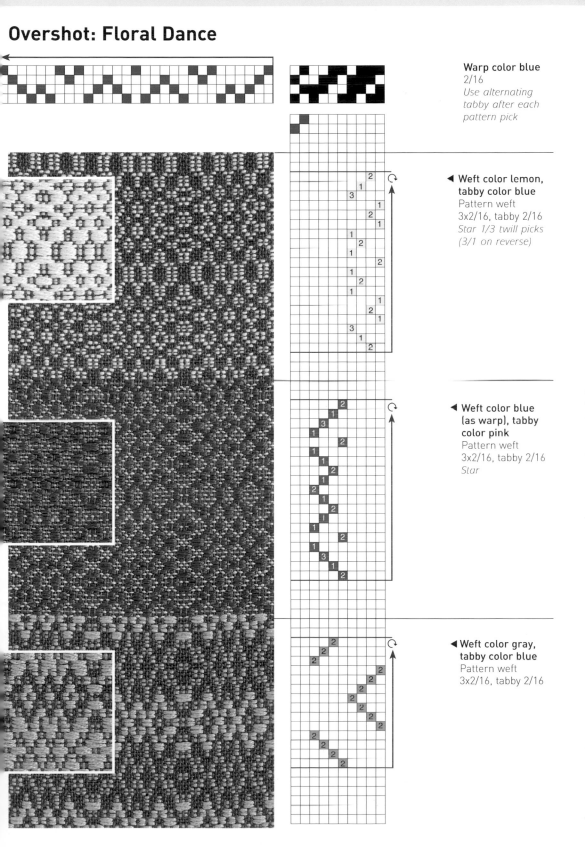

Warp color blue
2/16
Use alternating tabby after each pattern pick

◀ **Weft color lemon, tabby color blue**
Pattern weft 3x2/16, tabby 2/16
Star 1/3 twill picks (3/1 on reverse)

◀ **Weft color blue (as warp), tabby color pink**
Pattern weft 3x2/16, tabby 2/16
Star

◀ **Weft color gray, tabby color blue**
Pattern weft 3x2/16, tabby 2/16

Overshot: Annabel

Warp color blue
2/16
Use alternating tabby after each pattern pick

◄ **Weft color yellow, tabby color blue**
Pattern weft 3x2/16, tabby 2/16
Star

◄ **Weft color turquoise, tabby color turquoise**
Pattern weft 2/16 used double, tabby 2/16
"Rose 1."
Tabby and pattern weft the same color.

◄ **Weft color orange, tabby color burgundy**
Pattern weft 3x2/16, tabby 2/16
"Rose 2"

Overshot: Annabel

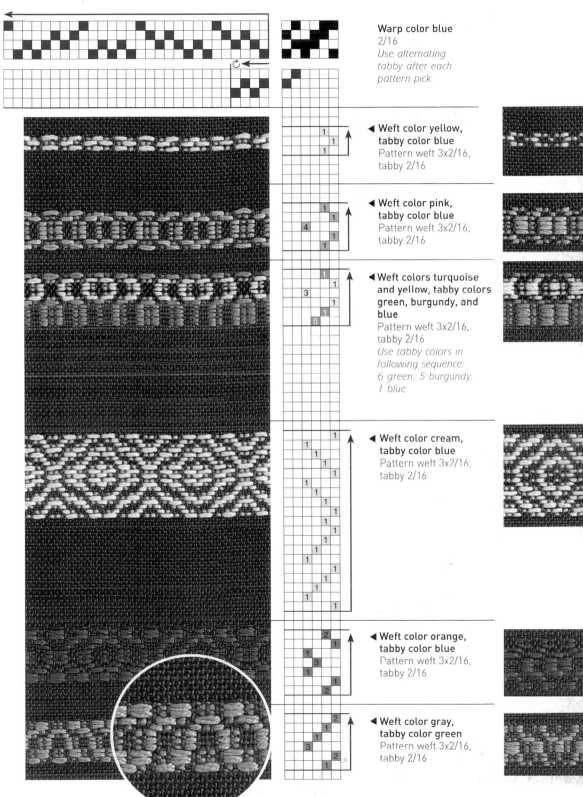

Warp color blue
2/16
Use alternating tabby after each pattern pick

◀ **Weft color yellow, tabby color blue**
Pattern weft 3x2/16, tabby 2/16

◀ **Weft color pink, tabby color blue**
Pattern weft 3x2/16, tabby 2/16

◀ **Weft colors turquoise and yellow, tabby colors green, burgundy, and blue**
Pattern weft 3x2/16, tabby 2/16
Use tabby colors in following sequence: 6 green, 5 burgundy, 1 blue

◀ **Weft color cream, tabby color blue**
Pattern weft 3x2/16, tabby 2/16

◀ **Weft color orange, tabby color blue**
Pattern weft 3x2/16, tabby 2/16

◀ **Weft color gray, tabby color green**
Pattern weft 3x2/16, tabby 2/16

Overshot: Trellis

Warp color blue
2/16
Use alternating tabby after each pattern pick, unless indicated

◀ **Weft color lime, tabby color blue**
Pattern weft 3x2/16, tabby 2/16
Star

◀ **Weft color pink, tabby color blue**
Pattern weft 3x2/16, tabby 2/16
"Rose 1"

◀ **Weft color yellow**
2/16 used double
NO TABBY
TAW (see Glossary, pages 250–251)

Overshot: Trellis

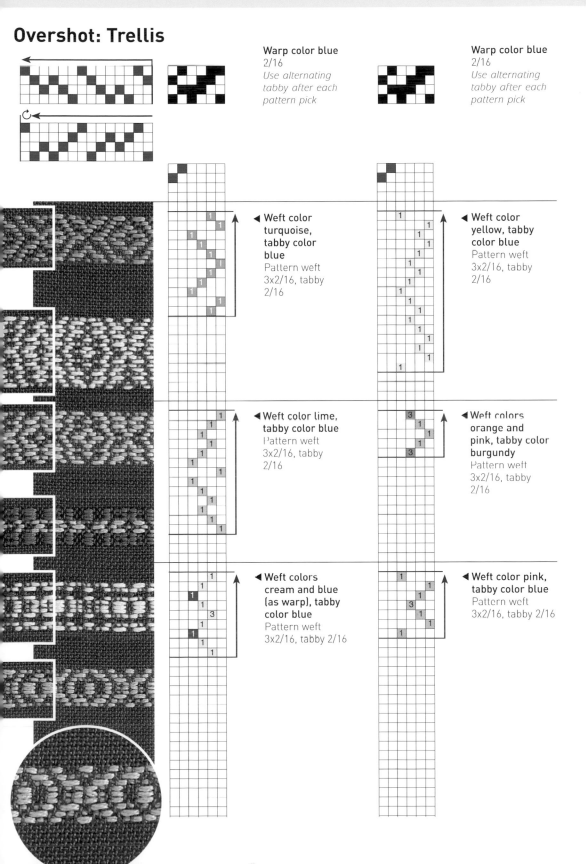

Warp color blue
2/16
*Use alternating
tabby after each
pattern pick*

Warp color blue
2/16
*Use alternating
tabby after each
pattern pick*

◄ Weft color
turquoise,
tabby color
blue
Pattern weft
3x2/16, tabby
2/16

◄ Weft color
yellow, tabby
color blue
Pattern weft
3x2/16, tabby
2/16

◄ Weft color lime,
tabby color blue
Pattern weft
3x2/16, tabby
2/16

◄ Weft colors
orange and
pink, tabby color
burgundy
Pattern weft
3x2/16, tabby
2/16

◄ Weft colors
cream and blue
(as warp), tabby
color blue
Pattern weft
3x2/16, tabby 2/16

◄ Weft color pink,
tabby color blue
Pattern weft
3x2/16, tabby 2/16

Overshot: Leaves

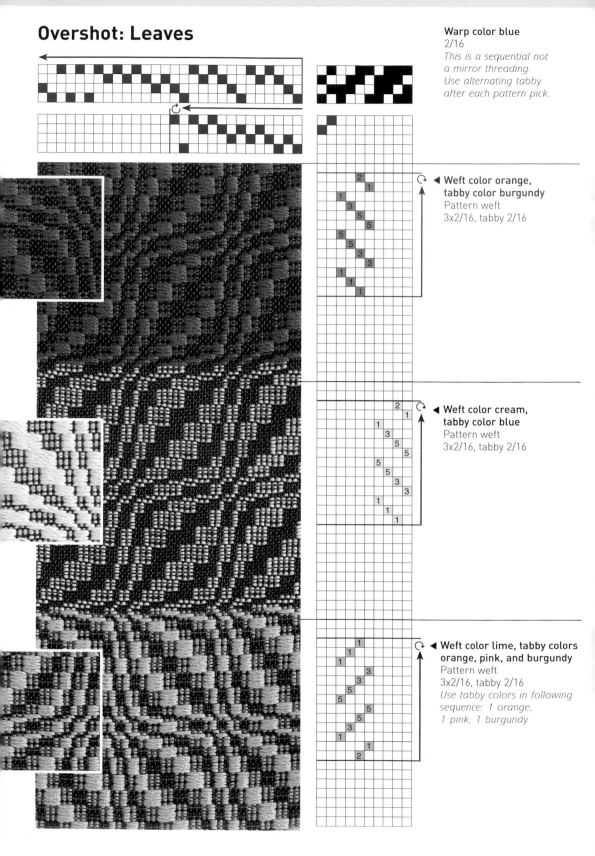

Warp color blue
2/16
*This is a sequential not
a mirror threading.
Use alternating tabby
after each pattern pick.*

◀ **Weft color orange,
tabby color burgundy**
Pattern weft
3x2/16, tabby 2/16

◀ **Weft color cream,
tabby color blue**
Pattern weft
3x2/16, tabby 2/16

◀ **Weft color lime, tabby colors
orange, pink, and burgundy**
Pattern weft
3x2/16, tabby 2/16
*Use tabby colors in following
sequence: 1 orange,
1 pink, 1 burgundy*

Overshot: Leaves

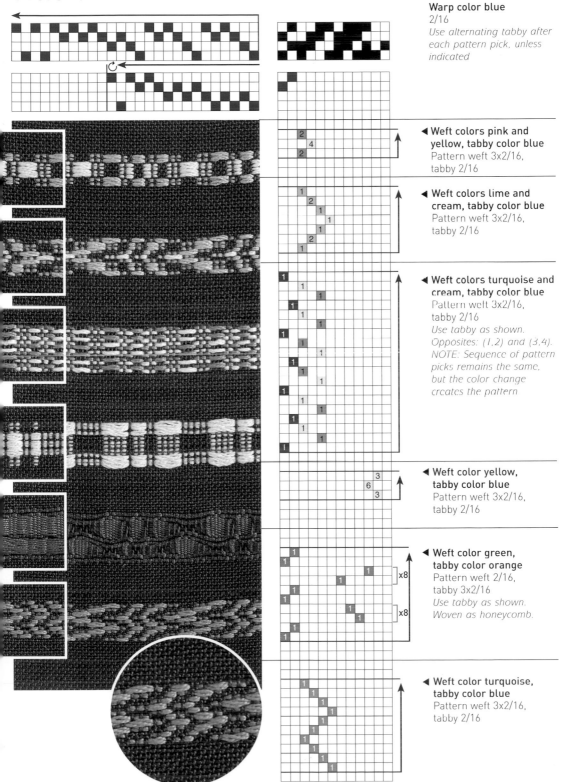

Warp color blue
2/16
Use alternating tabby after each pattern pick, unless indicated

◄ Weft colors pink and yellow, tabby color blue
Pattern weft 3x2/16, tabby 2/16

◄ Weft colors lime and cream, tabby color blue
Pattern weft 3x2/16, tabby 2/16

◄ Weft colors turquoise and cream, tabby color blue
Pattern weft 3x2/16, tabby 2/16
Use tabby as shown. Opposites: (1,2) and (3,4). NOTE: Sequence of pattern picks remains the same, but the color change creates the pattern

◄ Weft color yellow, tabby color blue
Pattern weft 3x2/16, tabby 2/16

◄ Weft color green, tabby color orange
Pattern weft 2/16, tabby 3x2/16
Use tabby as shown. Woven as honeycomb.

◄ Weft color turquoise, tabby color blue
Pattern weft 3x2/16, tabby 2/16

Overshot: Patchwork

Warp color blue
2/16
Use alternating tabby after each pattern pick

◄ **Weft color turquoise, tabby color blue**
Pattern weft 3x2/16, tabby 2/16
Star

◄ **Weft color yellow, tabby color blue**
Pattern weft 3x2/16, tabby 2/16
"Rose 2"

◄ **Weft color lime, tabby color blue**
Pattern weft 3x2/16, tabby 2/16
Chains

Overshot: Patchwork

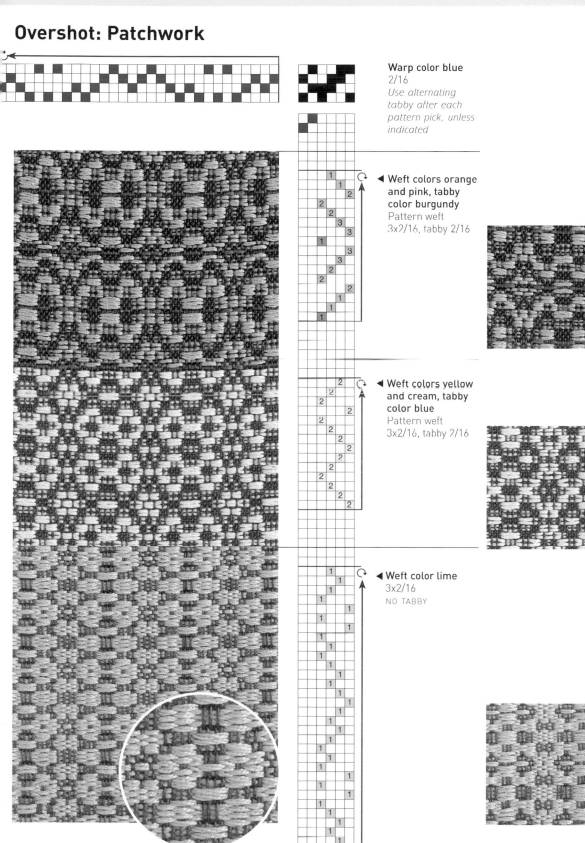

Warp color blue
2/16
Use alternating tabby after each pattern pick, unless indicated

◀ **Weft colors orange and pink, tabby color burgundy**
Pattern weft 3x2/16, tabby 2/16

◀ **Weft colors yellow and cream, tabby color blue**
Pattern weft 3x2/16, tabby 2/16

◀ **Weft color lime**
3x2/16
NO TABBY

Overshot: Same But Different

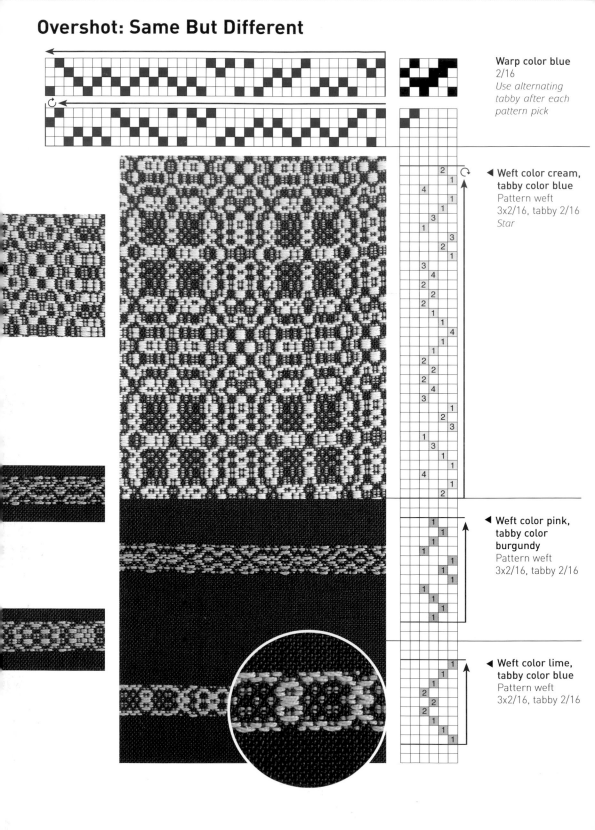

Warp color blue
2/16
Use alternating tabby after each pattern pick

◀ **Weft color cream, tabby color blue**
Pattern weft 3x2/16, tabby 2/16
Star

◀ **Weft color pink, tabby color burgundy**
Pattern weft 3x2/16, tabby 2/16

◀ **Weft color lime, tabby color blue**
Pattern weft 3x2/16, tabby 2/16

Overshot: Same But Different

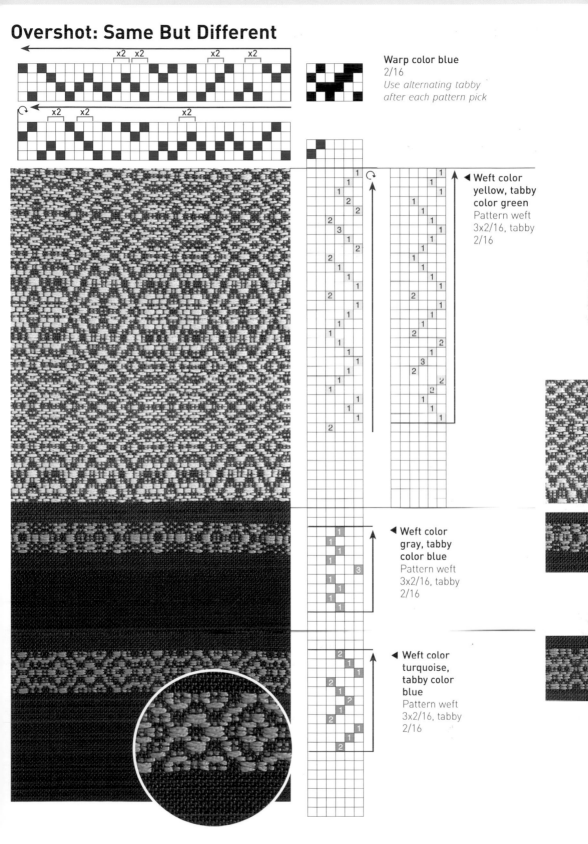

Warp color blue
2/16
*Use alternating tabby
after each pattern pick*

◀ Weft color
yellow, tabby
color green
Pattern weft
3x2/16, tabby
2/16

◀ Weft color
gray, tabby
color blue
Pattern weft
3x2/16, tabby
2/16

◀ Weft color
turquoise,
tabby color
blue
Pattern weft
3x2/16, tabby
2/16

Overshot: Three Small Patterns

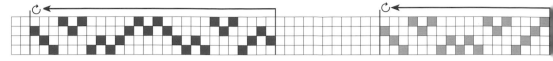

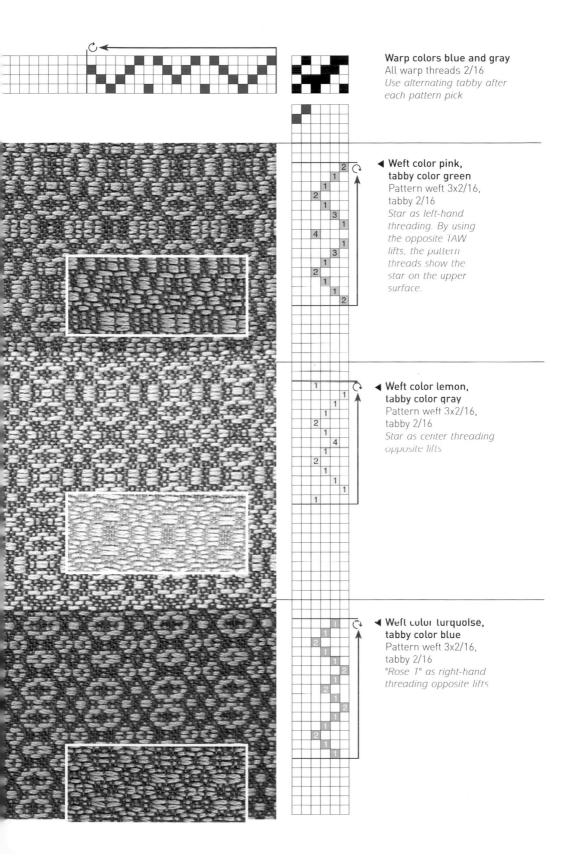

Warp colors blue and gray
All warp threads 2/16
*Use alternating tabby after
each pattern pick*

◄ **Weft color pink,
tabby color green**
Pattern weft 3x2/16,
tabby 2/16
*Star as left-hand
threading. By using
the opposite TAW
lifts, the pattern
threads show the
star on the upper
surface.*

◄ **Weft color lemon,
tabby color gray**
Pattern weft 3x2/16,
tabby 2/16
*Star as center threading
opposite lifts*

◄ **Weft color turquoise,
tabby color blue**
Pattern weft 3x2/16,
tabby 2/16
*"Rose 1" as right-hand
threading opposite lifts*

Ms and Os

Ms and Os has two blocks: tabby and texture. The texture is a loose weft rib. It is woven with a single shuttle, with a weft thread thicker than the warp. Each block is composed of eight threads using all four shafts: either 1, 2, 1, 2, 3, 4, 3, 4 or 1, 3, 1, 3, 2, 4, 2, 4. Half blocks can be used. Occasionally blocks can be of four threads: 1, 2, 3, 4 or 1, 3, 2, 4.

Blocks can be repeated to create any length block. When woven for texture, wide blocks are best woven shallow, with narrow blocks as deep as required.

As the weft rib is looser than the tabby, the edges of the blocks become curved around the tabby areas.

It is not possible to weave true tabby across the entire width. Instead, a close approximation, "Mock Tabby," is woven (1, 4), (2, 3).

NOTES FOR WEAVING Ms AND Os

Threads: The weft thread is thicker than the warp. A single thicker thread rather than two fine ones is preferable as thin threads tend to separate and slide more in the pattern areas.

The weft thread is usually a contrast to the warp but could be the same color.

Selvedges and sett: For the left-hand selvedge use [float, 4, 2, 3, 1, 44, 33, 22, 11]. For the right-hand selvedge use [44, 33, 22, 11, 4, 2, 3, 1, float].

The floating selvedge must be used.

Use a sett suitable for tabby as if using the same thread for weft as warp.

Reading the weaving draft: Note the tie-up grid.

There are great possibilities for alternative patterns using the same threading. Some samples of these are shown.

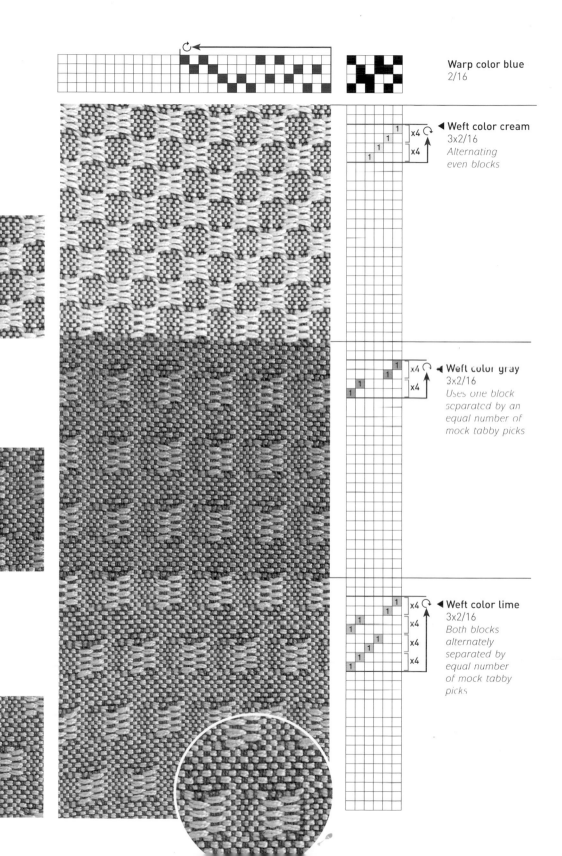

Warp color blue
2/16

◀ **Weft color cream**
3x2/16
*Alternating
even blocks*

◀ **Weft color gray**
3x2/16
*Uses one block
separated by an
equal number of
mock tabby picks*

◀ **Weft color lime**
3x2/16
*Both blocks
alternately
separated by
equal number
of mock tabby
picks*

Ms and Os

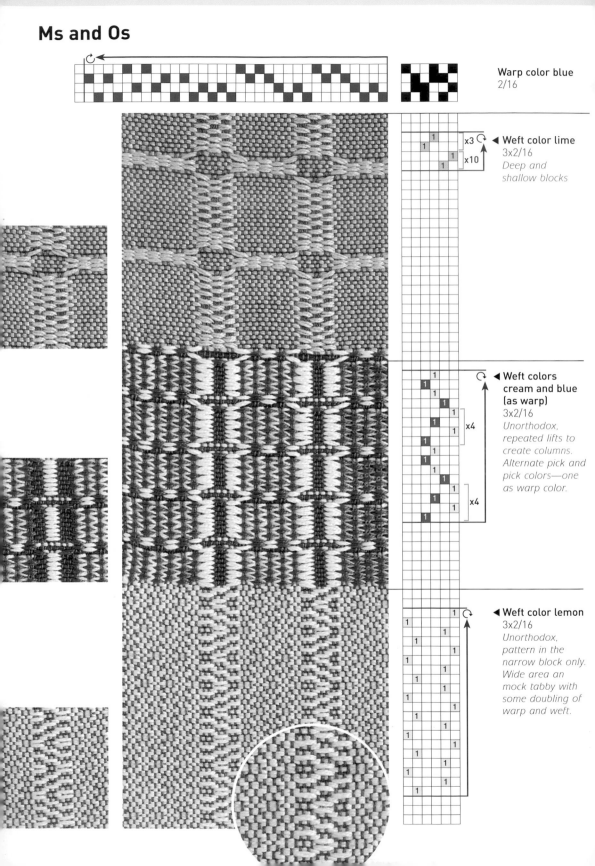

Warp color blue
2/16

◄ **Weft color lime**
3x2/16
*Deep and
shallow blocks*

x3
x10

◄ **Weft colors
cream and blue
(as warp)**
3x2/16
*Unorthodox,
repeated lifts to
create columns.
Alternate pick and
pick colors—one
as warp color.*

x4
x4

◄ **Weft color lemon**
3x2/16
*Unorthodox,
pattern in the
narrow block only.
Wide area an
mock tabby with
some doubling of
warp and weft.*

Ms and Os

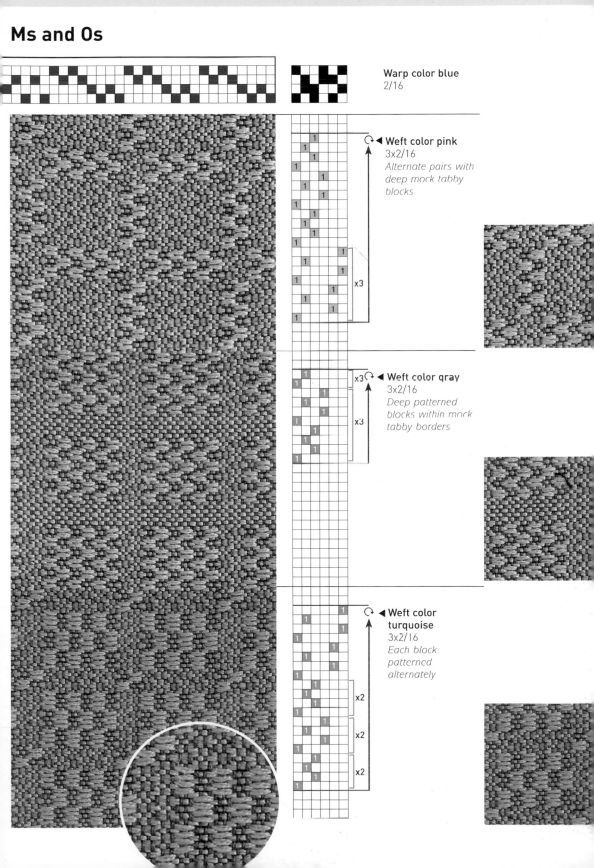

Warp color blue
2/16

◀ Weft color pink
3x2/16
*Alternate pairs with
deep mock tabby
blocks*

x3

x3 ◀ Weft color gray
3x2/16
*Deep patterned
blocks within mock
tabby borders*

x3

◀ Weft color
turquoise
3x2/16
*Each block
patterned
alternately*

x2

x2

x2

Crackle

Alternatively known as Jämtlands Væv, Jämtlandsvavar, or Jämtlandsdrall (names that reveal its Scandinavian origins), this weave suggested the crackled glazing on old pottery to Mary Meigs Atwater who first called it "Crackle."

Four different blocks are possible on four shafts, each block threaded using three shafts. Repeated blocks can be as wide as wished because there are no long floats, but as tabby must be woven the threading blocks must be alternately on odd and even shafts.

The four units are (reading each from the right):

[i] 2, 3, 2, 1
[ii] 3, 4, 3, 2
[iii] 4, 1, 4, 3
[iv] 1, 2, 1, 4

Blocks can be repeated, but, when moving to a new block, thread an extra end on the same shaft as the current block started. The extra end is only added to the draft at the completion of the repeated blocks:

(Reading each from the right, as threading order)

extra end on shaft 1 for block repeating [2, 3, 2, 1] = [**1**, 2, 3, 2, 1]
extra end on shaft 2 for block repeating [3, 4, 3, 2] = [**2**, 3, 4, 3, 2]
extra end on shaft 3 for block repeating [4, 1, 4, 3] = [**3**, 4, 1, 4, 3]
extra end on shaft 4 for block repeating [1, 2, 1, 4] = [**4**, 1, 2, 1, 4]

When moving to a block that is two away, add an extra threading end as before, and then another additional one moving in the same line:

From [i] to [iii] add 1 and 2, from [ii] to [iv] add 2 and 3, from [iii] to [i] add 3 and 2, from [iv] to [ii] add 4 and 3.

Continuous straight diagonal repeats can be inserted after any of the linking threads, providing that there are no areas of four threads on only two shafts.

Crackle can be woven as overshot, on opposites, or TAW without tabby.

Overshot patterns can be rewritten as Crackle changing the unit on (2 and 1) to a unit on (2, 3, 2, 1) and similarly for the other units.

NOTES

Threads: See page 95.

Selvedges and sett: Use a straight draft for the selvedges. Use a floating selvedge to catch the pattern wefts. Use a sett suitable for tabby.

Reading the weaving draft: A number within the color block for the picks shows how many times that shed has to be used, with tabby in between.

It is often easier to write a Crackle draft than to interpret a design!

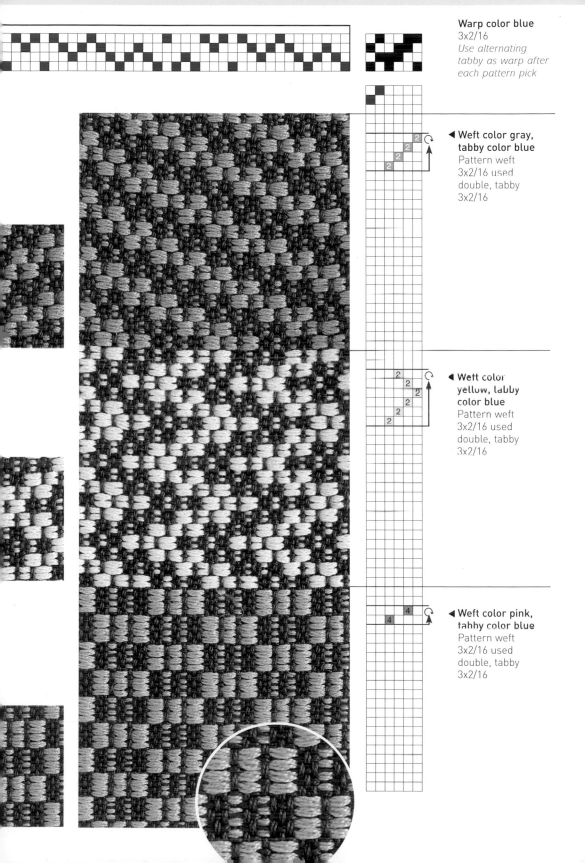

Warp color blue
3x2/16
*Use alternating
tabby as warp after
each pattern pick*

◄ **Weft color gray,
tabby color blue**
Pattern weft
3x2/16 used
double, tabby
3x2/16

◄ **Weft color
yellow, tabby
color blue**
Pattern weft
3x2/16 used
double, tabby
3x2/16

◄ **Weft color pink,
tabby color blue**
Pattern weft
3x2/16 used
double, tabby
3x2/16

Crackle: Blocks

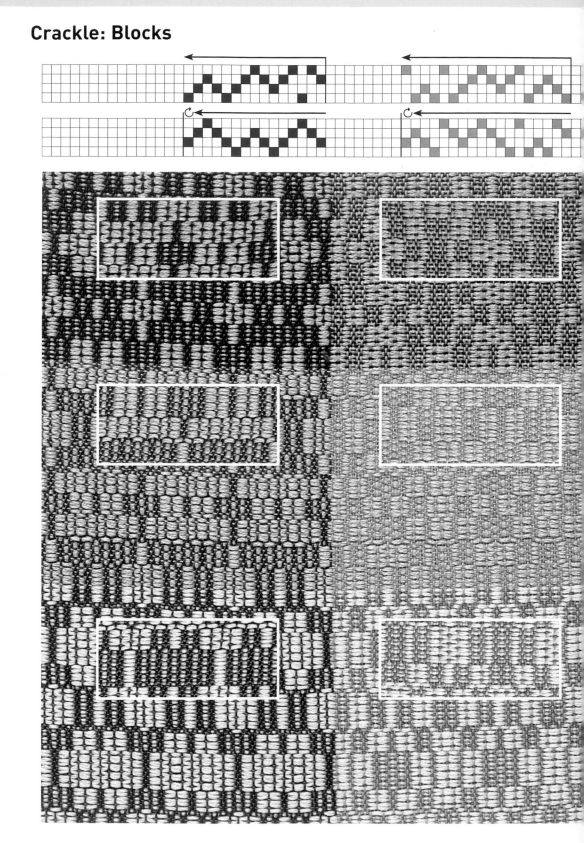

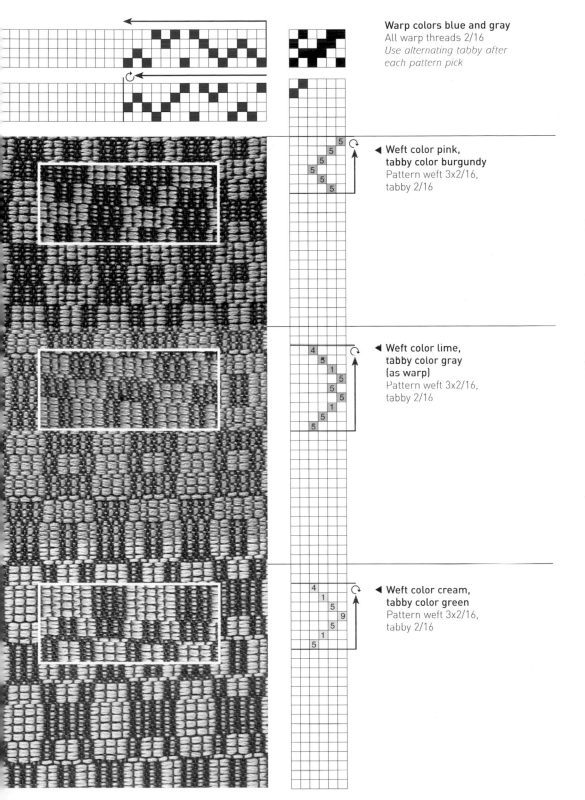

Warp colors blue and gray
All warp threads 2/16
Use alternating tabby after each pattern pick

◄ **Weft color pink,**
tabby color burgundy
Pattern weft 3x2/16,
tabby 2/16

◄ **Weft color lime,**
tabby color gray
(as warp)
Pattern weft 3x2/16,
tabby 2/16

◄ **Weft color cream,**
tabby color green
Pattern weft 3x2/16,
tabby 2/16

Crackle: Pairs

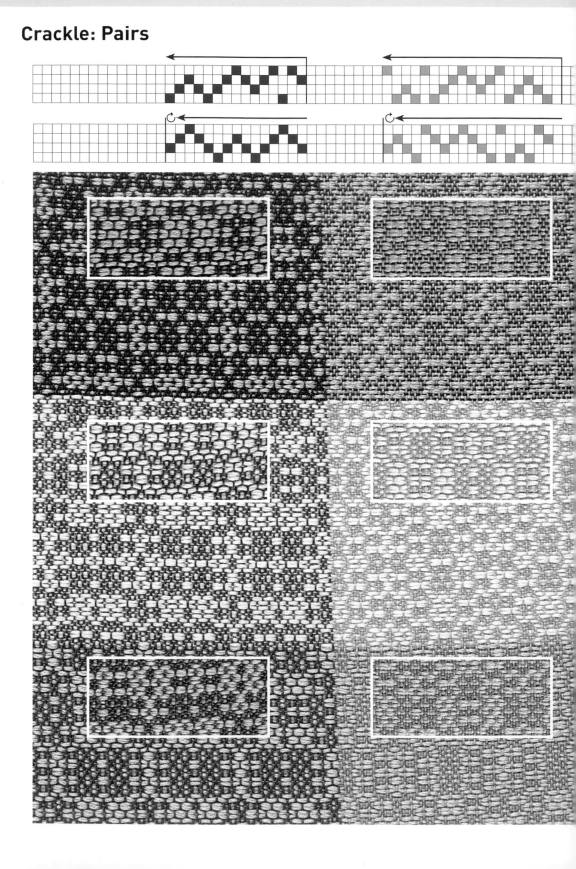

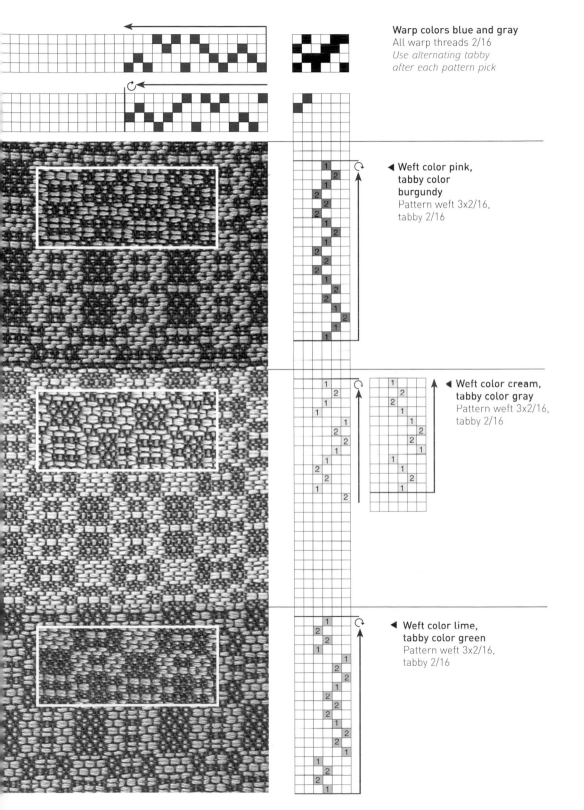

Warp colors blue and gray
All warp threads 2/16
*Use alternating tabby
after each pattern pick*

◄ **Weft color pink,
tabby color
burgundy**
Pattern weft 3x2/16,
tabby 2/16

◄ **Weft color cream,
tabby color gray**
Pattern weft 3x2/16,
tabby 2/16

◄ **Weft color lime,
tabby color green**
Pattern weft 3x2/16,
tabby 2/16

Summer and Winter

The name is said to derive from blue and white bedcovers woven in this pattern with one side darker than the other. The dark side showing was for the winter when washing could not be done so frequently; the light for summer.

On four shafts it is a two-block weave, with the reverse of each block being the same as the opposite block. The blocks can be of any number of repeats as there are tie-downs every fourth thread, which makes Summer and Winter a very stable cloth.

The threading blocks are, (1, 3, 2, 3) and (1, 4, 2, 4).
Note: tabby is woven (1, 2) and (3, 4).

It is possible to weave pattern, and conversely background, all over across the entire width. Separate blocks of pattern can be placed within the overall background (and vice versa).

There are three main types of patterning: brick, columns, and pairs, with variations of each.

Bricks: Pattern lifts alternate 1:1.
Columns: The same pattern lift is repeated.
Pairs: Pairs of pattern lifts are repeated 2:2.

When there is only a single block, then the pairs can create a circular motif (Roseate) or crossed motif (Hourglass). The repeated lifts at the center of these motifs can be extended to more than two. Use of different or more than two colors produces other interesting variations.

NOTES FOR WEAVING SUMMER AND WINTER

Threads: See page 95.

Selvedges and sett: Thread the selvedges 1, 3, 2, 4. Use a floating selvedge to catch the pattern wefts. Use a sett suitable for tabby.

Reading the weaving draft: The tie-up grid has the two tabby picks at the left—remember these are (1, 2) and (3, 4). This makes it easier to see how the different lifting units are composed. A number within the color block for the picks shows how many times that shed has to be used, with tabby in between.

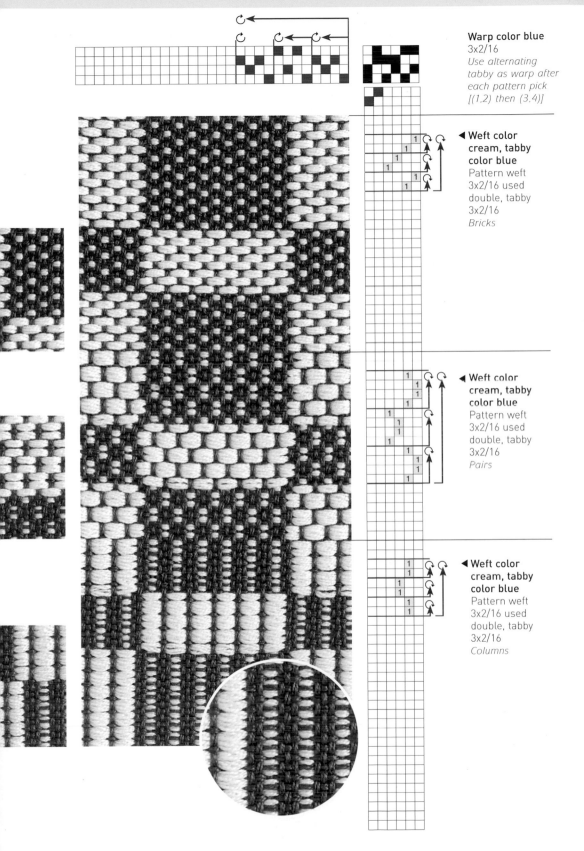

Warp color blue
3x2/16
*Use alternating
tabby as warp after
each pattern pick
[(1,2) then (3,4)]*

◀ Weft color
cream, tabby
color blue
Pattern weft
3x2/16 used
double, tabby
3x2/16
Bricks

◀ Weft color
cream, tabby
color blue
Pattern weft
3x2/16 used
double, tabby
3x2/16
Pairs

◀ Weft color
cream, tabby
color blue
Pattern weft
3x2/16 used
double, tabby
3x2/16
Columns

Summer and Winter

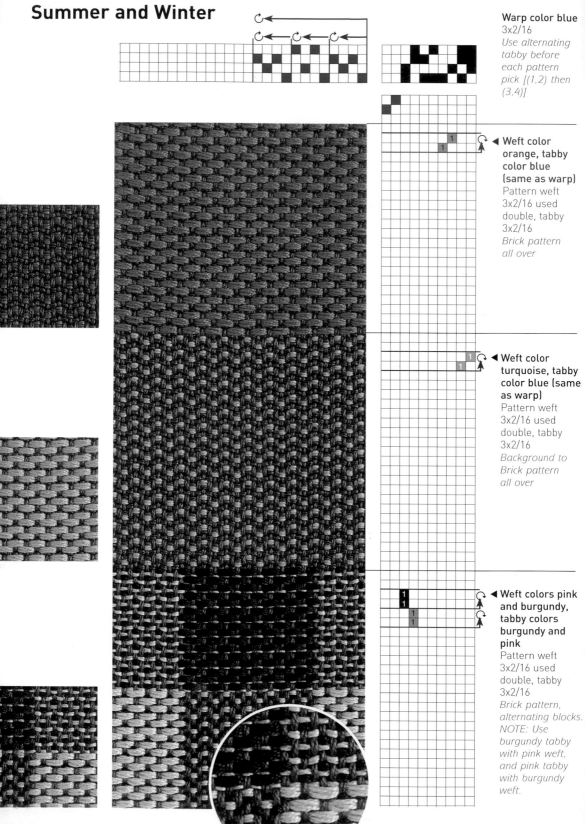

Warp color blue
3x2/16
*Use alternating
tabby before
each pattern
pick [(1,2) then
(3,4)]*

◄ **Weft color
orange, tabby
color blue
(same as warp)**
Pattern weft
3x2/16 used
double, tabby
3x2/16
*Brick pattern
all over*

◄ **Weft color
turquoise, tabby
color blue (same
as warp)**
Pattern weft
3x2/16 used
double, tabby
3x2/16
*Background to
Brick pattern
all over*

◄ **Weft colors pink
and burgundy,
tabby colors
burgundy and
pink**
Pattern weft
3x2/16 used
double, tabby
3x2/16
*Brick pattern,
alternating blocks.
NOTE: Use
burgundy tabby
with pink weft,
and pink tabby
with burgundy
weft.*

Summer and Winter

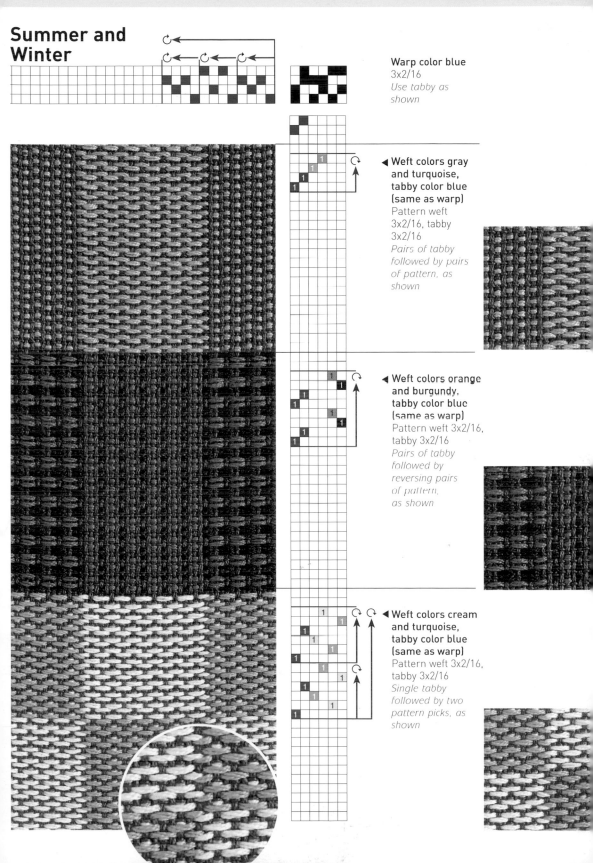

Warp color blue
3x2/16
*Use tabby as
shown*

◀ **Weft colors gray
and turquoise,
tabby color blue
(same as warp)**
Pattern weft
3x2/16, tabby
3x2/16
*Pairs of tabby
followed by pairs
of pattern, as
shown*

◀ **Weft colors orange
and burgundy,
tabby color blue
(same as warp)**
Pattern weft 3x2/16,
tabby 3x2/16
*Pairs of tabby
followed by
reversing pairs
of pattern,
as shown*

◀ **Weft colors cream
and turquoise,
tabby color blue
(same as warp)**
Pattern weft 3x2/16,
tabby 3x2/16
*Single tabby
followed by two
pattern picks, as
shown*

Summer and Winter

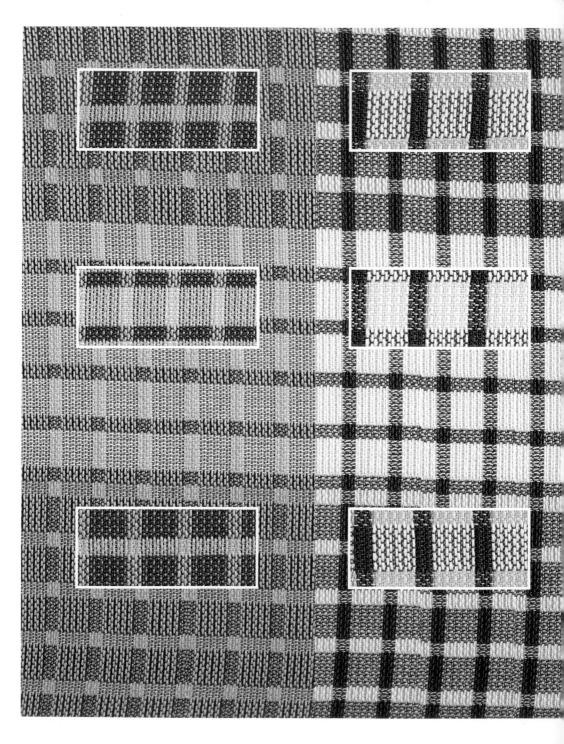

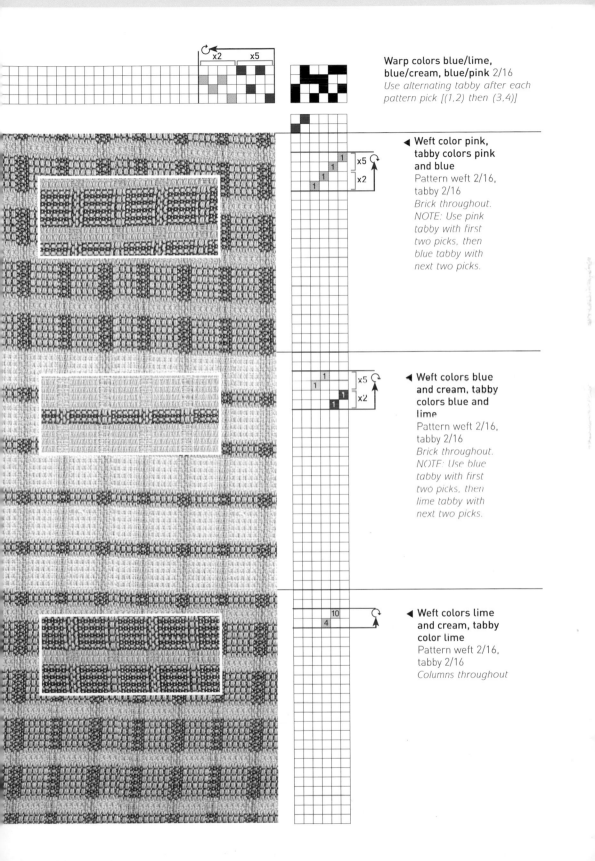

Warp colors blue/lime,
blue/cream, blue/pink 2/16
*Use alternating tabby after each
pattern pick [(1,2) then (3,4)]*

◄ Weft color pink,
tabby colors pink
and blue
Pattern weft 2/16,
tabby 2/16
*Brick throughout.
NOTE: Use pink
tabby with first
two picks, then
blue tabby with
next two picks.*

◄ Weft colors blue
and cream, tabby
colors blue and
lime
Pattern weft 2/16,
tabby 2/16
*Brick throughout.
NOTE: Use blue
tabby with first
two picks, then
lime tabby with
next two picks.*

◄ Weft colors lime
and cream, tabby
color lime
Pattern weft 2/16,
tabby 2/16
Columns throughout

Summer and Winter: Pairs

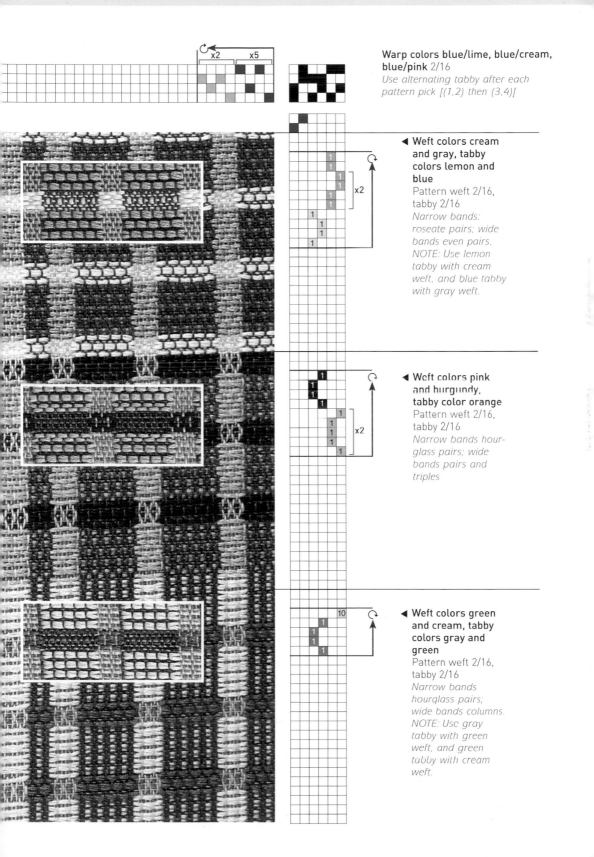

Warp colors blue/lime, blue/cream, blue/pink 2/16
Use alternating tabby after each pattern pick [(1,2) then (3,4)]

◀ **Weft colors cream and gray, tabby colors lemon and blue**
Pattern weft 2/16, tabby 2/16
Narrow bands: roseate pairs; wide bands even pairs.
NOTE: Use lemon tabby with cream weft, and blue tabby with gray weft.

◀ **Weft colors pink and burgundy, tabby color orange**
Pattern weft 2/16, tabby 2/16
Narrow bands hourglass pairs; wide bands pairs and triples

◀ **Weft colors green and cream, tabby colors gray and green**
Pattern weft 2/16, tabby 2/16
Narrow bands hourglass pairs; wide bands columns.
NOTE: Use gray tabby with green weft, and green tabby with cream weft.

Summer and Winter: Pairs

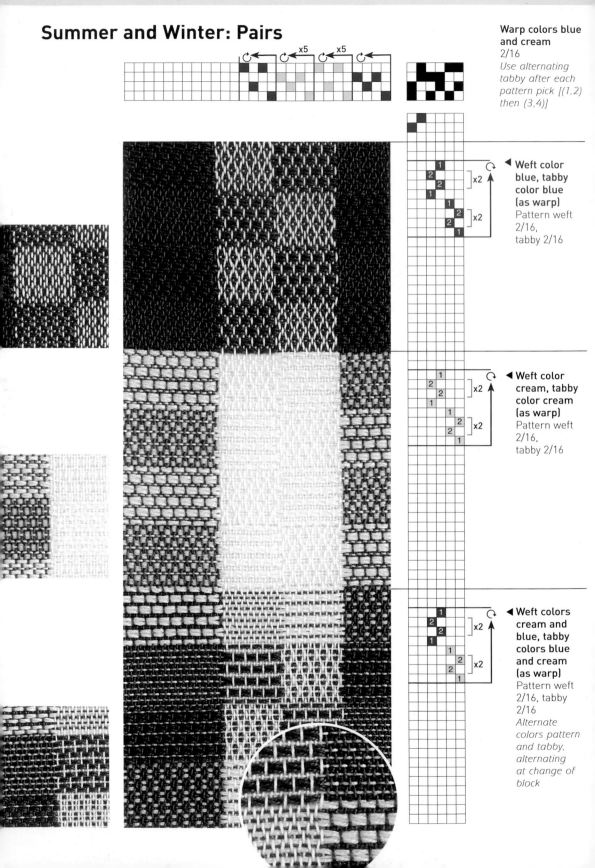

Warp colors blue and cream
2/16
Use alternating tabby after each pattern pick [(1,2) then (3,4)]

◄ **Weft color blue, tabby color blue (as warp)**
Pattern weft 2/16, tabby 2/16

◄ **Weft color cream, tabby color cream (as warp)**
Pattern weft 2/16, tabby 2/16

◄ **Weft colors cream and blue, tabby colors blue and cream (as warp)**
Pattern weft 2/16, tabby 2/16
Alternate colors pattern and tabby, alternating at change of block

Summer and Winter

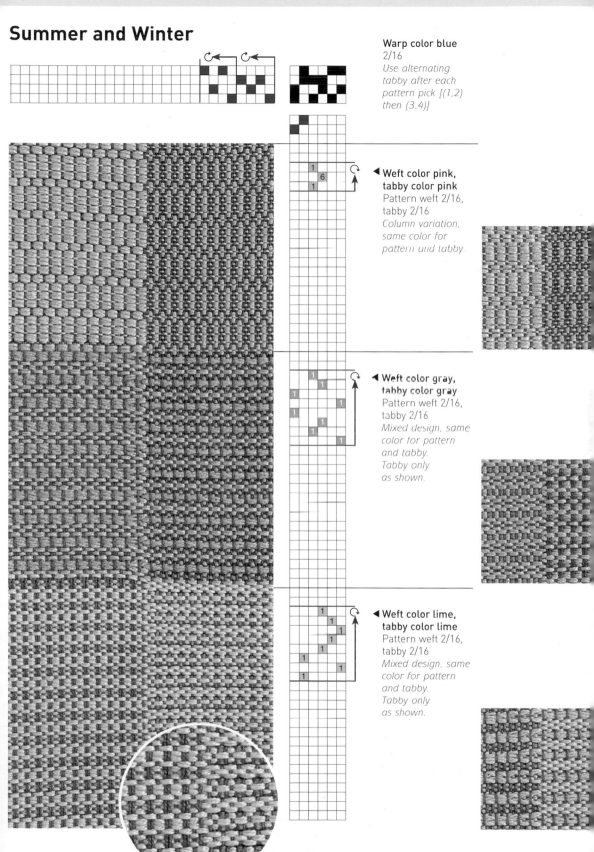

Warp color blue
2/16
*Use alternating
tabby after each
pattern pick [(1,2)
then (3,4)]*

◀ **Weft color pink,
tabby color pink**
Pattern weft 2/16,
tabby 2/16
*Column variation,
same color for
pattern and tabby.*

◀ **Weft color gray,
tabby color gray**
Pattern weft 2/16,
tabby 2/16
*Mixed design, same
color for pattern
and tabby.
Tabby only
as shown.*

◀ **Weft color lime,
tabby color lime**
Pattern weft 2/16,
tabby 2/16
*Mixed design, same
color for pattern
and tabby.
Tabby only
as shown.*

Honeycomb

Honeycomb resembles the curved cells in a bee's honeycomb. The name is also sometimes used for a straight-sided sunken pattern (see Waffle Variations, pages 228–229).

Thick threads curve around sunken areas of fine tabby. There can be two, three, or four blocks when using four shafts, but the most spectacular results appear when using only two opposing blocks. There will be long floats on the reverse so either use narrow blocks or line the fabric.

Here the opposing blocks are (1, 2) and (3, 4), although they could also be (2, 3) and (1, 4).

To Weave Honeycomb

First, two thick outline tabby picks are woven across the entire width. Then the blocks on (1, 2) are woven as tabby with a fine weft as many times as required. This fine weft thread floats under the opposite block.

When the repeated block is deep enough, then another two thick weft picks are woven across the entire width. These thick picks beat down around the woven blocks and join up with the first pair of thick outline tabby picks where there are floats on the back.

Then the opposite blocks are woven in the same way.

The ends at the edges of the blocks spread into the unwoven sections.

There is considerable take-up due to the fine blocks submerging themselves within the outlining thick tabby.

NOTES

Threads: The fine thread is usually the same type as the warp. Textured yarns are especially interesting when used as the thick thread.

Selvedges: The selvedge is a straight entry. Use a floating selvedge.

Sett: Use a sett suitable for a balanced weave using the warp and weft block threads.

The Honeycomb threading can be woven in other ways (page 149). Honeycomb can also be woven using other threading drafts, such as Overshot, producing three or four irregular-size blocks.

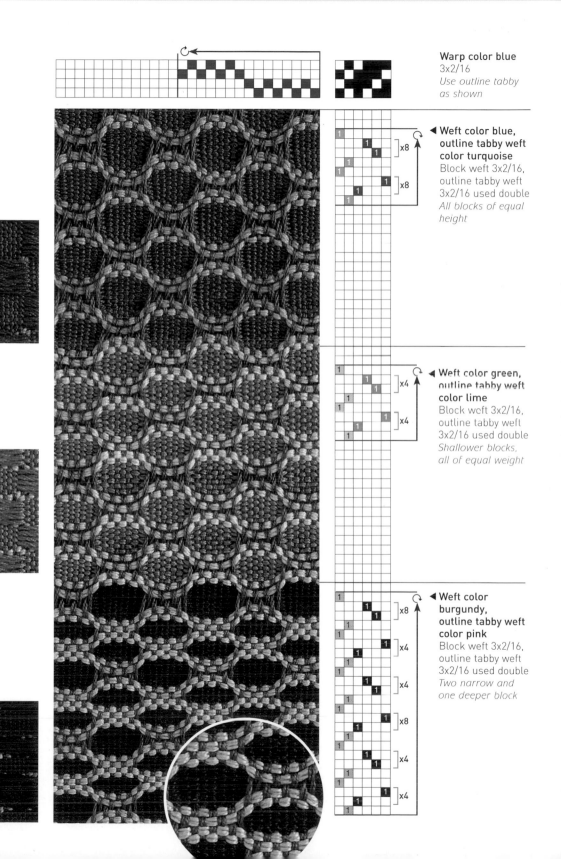

Warp color blue
3x2/16
Use outline tabby as shown

◀ **Weft color blue, outline tabby weft color turquoise**
Block weft 3x2/16, outline tabby weft 3x2/16 used double
All blocks of equal height

]x8

]x8

◀ **Weft color green, outline tabby weft color lime**
Block weft 3x2/16, outline tabby weft 3x2/16 used double
Shallower blocks, all of equal weight

]x4

]x4

◀ **Weft color burgundy, outline tabby weft color pink**
Block weft 3x2/16, outline tabby weft 3x2/16 used double
Two narrow and one deeper block

]x8

]x4

]x4

]x8

]x4

]x4

Honeycomb: Different Width Tabby Blocks

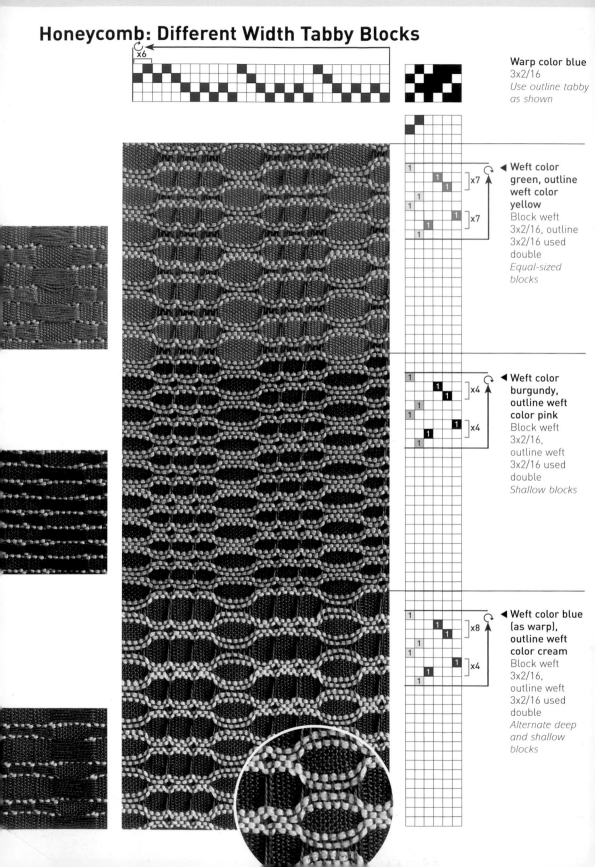

Warp color blue
3x2/16
Use outline tabby as shown

◄ **Weft color green, outline weft color yellow**
Block weft 3x2/16, outline 3x2/16 used double
Equal-sized blocks

◄ **Weft color burgundy, outline weft color pink**
Block weft 3x2/16, outline weft 3x2/16 used double
Shallow blocks

◄ **Weft color blue (as warp), outline weft color cream**
Block weft 3x2/16, outline weft 3x2/16 used double
Alternate deep and shallow blocks

Honeycomb Threading: Woven "As If"

Warp color blue
3x2/16
Using honeycomb threading in other ways. Use alternating tabby after each pattern pick.

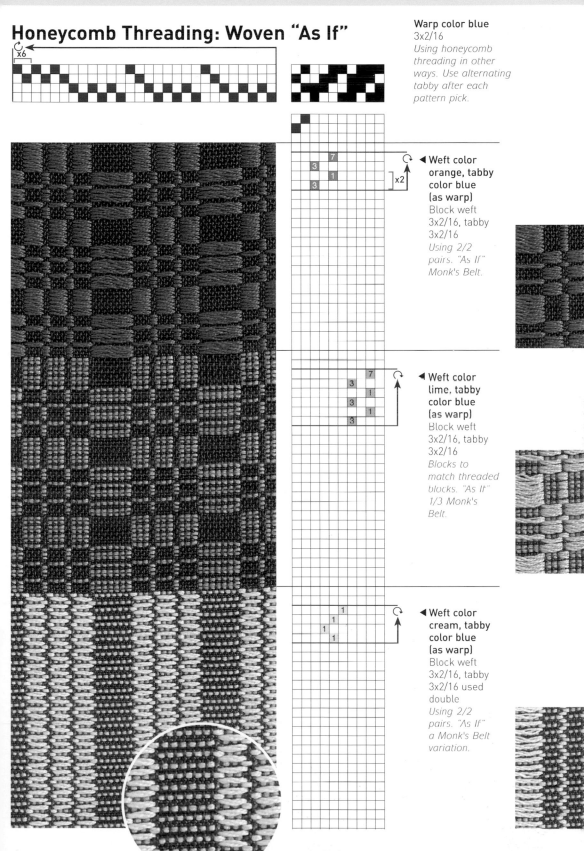

◄ **Weft color orange, tabby color blue (as warp)**
Block weft 3x2/16, tabby 3x2/16
Using 2/2 pairs. "As If" Monk's Belt.

◄ **Weft color lime, tabby color blue (as warp)**
Block weft 3x2/16, tabby 3x2/16
Blocks to match threaded blocks. "As If" 1/3 Monk's Belt.

◄ **Weft color cream, tabby color blue (as warp)**
Block weft 3x2/16, tabby 3x2/16 used double
Using 2/2 pairs. "As If" a Monk's Belt variation.

Lace Weaves

It is not possible to weave true lace on a loom, but lacy structures can be made, either using a very open weave and/or creating spaces within the cloth. There are two main ways in which this can be done: either hand-manipulated or loom-controlled.

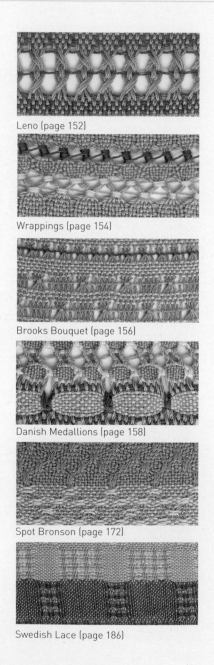

Leno (page 152)

Wrappings (page 154)

Brooks Bouquet (page 156)

Danish Medallions (page 158)

Spot Bronson (page 172)

Swedish Lace (page 186)

Hand-manipulated lace includes: Leno; Wrappings; Brooks Bouquet; and Danish Medallions. It can be worked on any threading draft, but more usually on one that can weave tabby so that a stabilizing tabby weft can be woven before and after the lace section. All the hand-manipulated laces here are shown using a straight threading draft.

Loom-controlled lace includes: Canvas; Huck; Spot Bronson; Lace Bronson; and Swedish lace. Each has its individual weave structures requiring specific threading and shedding drafts. Most only produce two separate threading blocks, although Spot Bronson can produce three. They rely on the creation of floats that allow both warp and weft threads to slide together or apart to form spaces.

Ruana (wrap) in
Bronson lace—
reversing spots,
using merino wool.

All lace needs to be fairly open and lightly beaten to create a balanced weave. When lit from behind the structure is shown to full advantage.

Lace has intense textural interest, and this shows to a certain extent when being woven. As soon as the tension is eased—such as when the cloth is removed from the loom—the floats begin to distort. For the full effect it is necessary to wash the lace, then both warp and weft threads can relax and distort into curves and spaces. All the lace examples in this section have been fully laundered.

Sett Generally as for a loose tabby.

Selvedges See the individual types for the threading for these. Maintaining the lace pattern completely to the edges is possible by entering the ends as suggested for selvedges on pages 16–17, but these require considerable care when weaving. Use a floating selvedge to help maintain a firm edge.

Threads Generally smooth threads show the structure best. Other suggestions are given for specific types. Thick threads are dramatic, fine threads that produce light, airy fabrics. The weft is usually the same weight as the warp unless otherwise suggested. Traditionally lace is white or cream; color has been used in the samples to highlight the structure.

Hand-manipulated Use fingers and/or a pick-up stick to work.

Beating Do this very gently, and confirm the weft (again, gently) into position when the next shed is open.

Leno: Hand-manipulated

Leno is worked with the fingers using a slightly relaxed closed shed. The warp ends are twisted around each other and a weft thread inserted to hold the twist. It is useful to use a thin pick-up stick or shuttle to make the twists. The number of threads in each group can vary.

Twists can be made to the right or left. The twist row can be followed by tabby or another twist row. The final tabby pick should not be positioned until the next pick is opened.

Two-end cross
The second end is brought under the first to the top and then taken over the first.

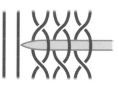

Six-end cross
Ends 5 and 6 are moved over and then under the shuttle; ends 1 and 2 are moved over 3 and 4, leaving ends 3 and 4 above and the others below the lace weft. Can also be worked 3 over 3.

Five-end cross
Only the outer ends on either side of the central one are moved across and down.

Sprang
NOTE: Worked on an open shed. You will need three thin pick-up sticks.
Open shed with first end raised. Use a pick-up stick. Work the first row of a two-end cross. When all the twists have been made, close the shed, turn the stick on edge and insert another stick in the same space. Push one stick to the fell and the other to the reed.
Using a third pick-up stick, ignore the first (lower) end and bring up the second lower above the [new] first upper. Continue across the row—there will be one extra upper left at the end of the row. Insert a weft thread into this space.

Remove the outer pick-up sticks and ease the twists into place before removing the last stick. There are many other movements in the Sprang technique.

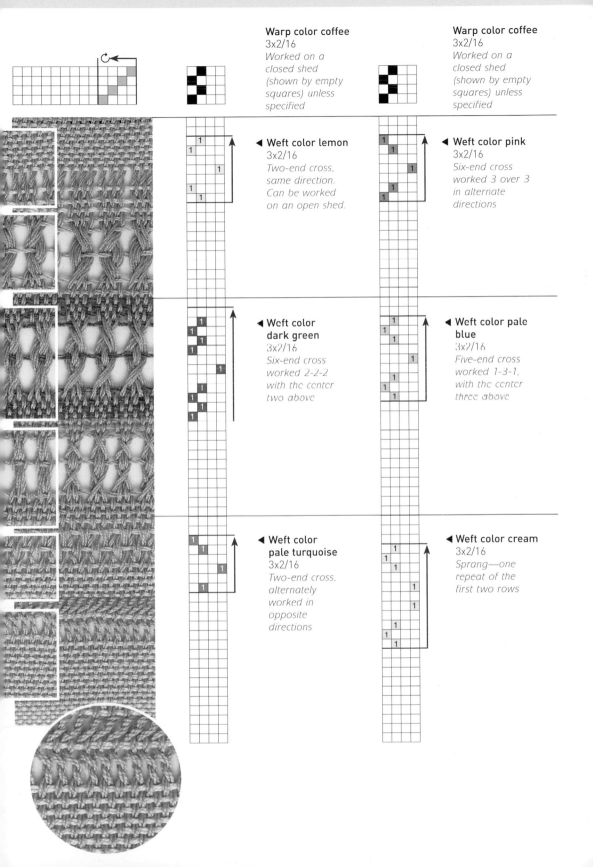

Warp color coffee
3x2/16
*Worked on a
closed shed
(shown by empty
squares) unless
specified*

Warp color coffee
3x2/16
*Worked on a
closed shed
(shown by empty
squares) unless
specified*

◄ **Weft color lemon**
3x2/16
*Two-end cross,
same direction.
Can be worked
on an open shed.*

◄ **Weft color pink**
3x2/16
*Six-end cross
worked 3 over 3
in alternate
directions*

◄ **Weft color
dark green**
3x2/16
*Six-end cross
worked 2-2-2
with the center
two above*

◄ **Weft color pale
blue**
3x2/16
*Five-end cross
worked 1-3-1,
with the center
three above*

◄ **Weft color
pale turquoise**
3x2/16
*Two-end cross,
alternately
worked in
opposite
directions*

◄ **Weft color cream**
3x2/16
*Sprang—one
repeat of the
first two rows*

Wrappings: Hand-manipulated

Instead of twisting and holding the twist in place, different bundles of ends are grouped together with a holding thread. The holding thread can be the normal weft or another contrasted yarn. This can wrap two or more times around the bundle in an upward direction. The wrapping thread can move from one bundle to the next either behind or in front of the fabric.

Instead of wrapping, a clove-hitch knot can also be used—this will hold even the slipperiest of yarns. The wrap or knot can be placed away from the fell or close to it. If using a different yarn for the wrapping or knotting this must be fixed securely in place before starting, otherwise it will unravel. Insert the wrapping yarn twice into the selvedge first outward and then inward.

Before starting the wrapping or knotting row, work at least three picks in the selvedge area only, and finish with an equal number of compensating picks in the selvedge at the other side. When a wrap or knot has been made, ease almost into place and use the beater to finally position when the "row" is completed. Insert the next pick, but open the next shed before finally positioning into place.

Small inserts of wrapped or knotted ends can be placed within normal woven sections. Insert a pick up to where the wrapping is to start; weave back another pick; weave a third pick up to where the wrapping is to start. Work the wrapping with as many bundles as required, work three picks after the wrapping to match the other side, and then continue weaving normally. If a deep wrap is required then more than three picks may need to be worked before and after each wrapping section.

Wraps and knotting can be worked in a twill weave more easily than leno. If the same weft is used for weaving and wrapping or knotting, use a narrow stick or netting shuttle for weaving and wrapping (this saves having to anchor the wrapping or knotting thread into position).

Wrapping: movement in front

Wrapping: movement behind

Clove hitch

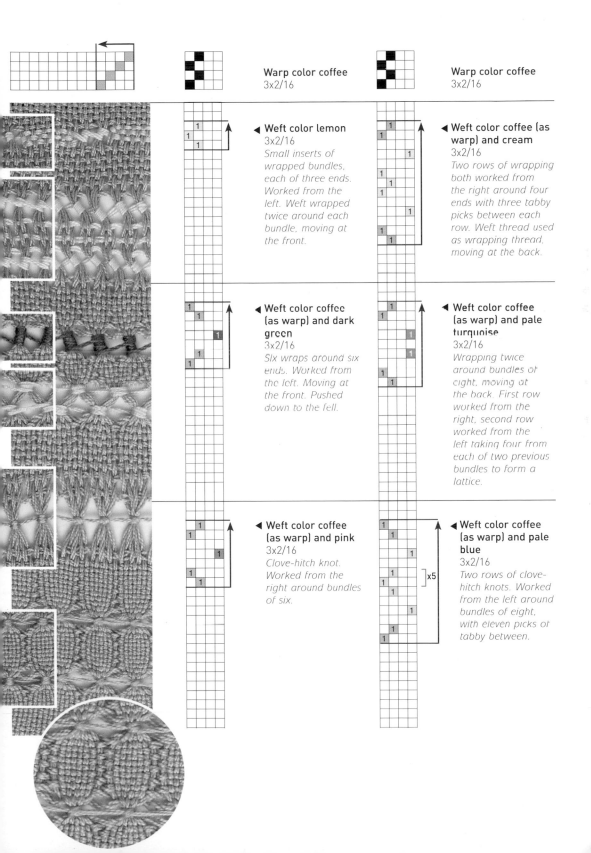

Warp color coffee
3x2/16

Warp color coffee
3x2/16

◀ Weft color lemon
3x2/16
*Small inserts of
wrapped bundles,
each of three ends.
Worked from the
left. Weft wrapped
twice around each
bundle, moving at
the front.*

◀ Weft color coffee (as
warp) and cream
3x2/16
*Two rows of wrapping
both worked from
the right around four
ends with three tabby
picks between each
row. Weft thread used
as wrapping thread,
moving at the back.*

◀ Weft color coffee
(as warp) and dark
green
3x2/16
*Six wraps around six
ends. Worked from
the left. Moving at
the front. Pushed
down to the fell.*

◀ Weft color coffee
(as warp) and pale
turquoise
3x2/16
*Wrapping twice
around bundles of
eight, moving at
the back. First row
worked from the
right, second row
worked from the
left taking four from
each of two previous
bundles to form a
lattice.*

◀ Weft color coffee
(as warp) and pink
3x2/16
*Clove-hitch knot.
Worked from the
right around bundles
of six.*

◀ Weft color coffee
(as warp) and pale
blue
3x2/16
*Two rows of clove-
hitch knots. Worked
from the left around
bundles of eight,
with eleven picks of
tabby between.*

Brooks Bouquet: Hand-manipulated

Brooks Bouquet can be worked on any threading draft that can weave tabby. Here it is shown on a straight draft.

Note: This is worked on an open shed.

The weft makes a single wrap around the upper threads of a bundle before moving to the next bundle. Ease into place and finally position with the beater. Whole rows or parts of a row can be worked.

When working with the same bundles, and with an odd number of picks between every time, it is very obvious that one lower end is not wrapped at all. This also happens when working lattice with an odd number of picks between, but the effect is not so noticeable.

The wrapping thread can be the same as the weft or different. If a different thread is used, anchor firmly into place before starting, by inserting twice into the selvedge using separate sheds (first outward and then inward).

Remember that the instructions specify the numbers of ends wrapped when the shed is open—the lower layer ends are not included in the numbers to be wrapped.

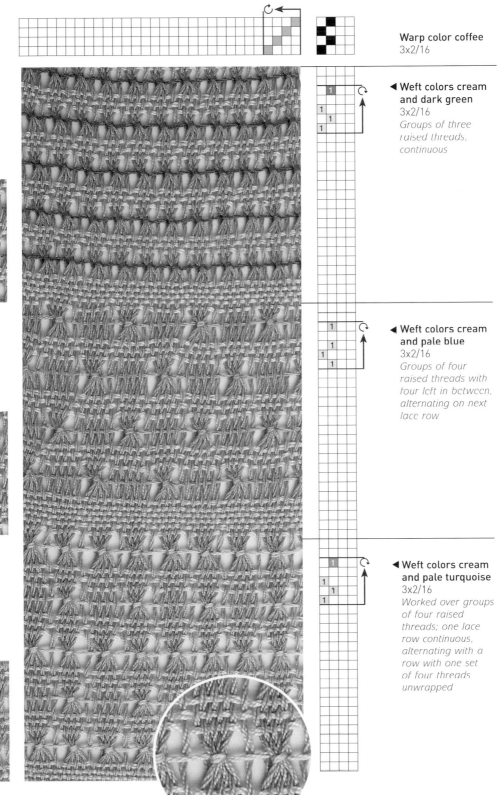

Warp color coffee
3x2/16

◀ Weft colors cream
and dark green
3x2/16
*Groups of three
raised threads,
continuous*

◀ Weft colors cream
and pale blue
3x2/16
*Groups of four
raised threads with
four left in between,
alternating on next
lace row*

◀ Weft colors cream
and pale turquoise
3x2/16
*Worked over groups
of four raised
threads; one lace
row continuous,
alternating with a
row with one set
of four threads
unwrapped*

Danish Medallions: Hand-manipulated

Danish Medallions can be worked on any warp that can weave tabby. It can be very useful to have missed dents between blocks of threading so that it is clear where the looping is to take place.

A single pick of outline tabby is woven, followed by a number of "filler" tabby picks, and then the second outline tabby is inserted. For each medallion weave with the outline thread as far as the first position for the loop; place a hook under all the tabby picks and pick up the last outline thread; bring this under and then up to the surface below all the picks and insert the outline shuttle through the loop; pull down to close the loop and then up firmly to draw all the picks into a medallion. Keeping the weft under tension, insert the shuttle into the next section as far as required and repeat the looping.

If the medallions are worked on an unspaced warp, take care to insert the hook directly under where the pick emerged. It is essential that the outline thread is on a separate shuttle, such as a small stick or netting shuttle. The outline thread can also be worked with just the fingers.

The outline thread can be a contrast or the same as warp or weft, but is usually of at least the same thickness as the normal weft and can be thicker. It needs to be strong enough to withstand the tugging into place.

These samples are worked with an empty dent between each group of eight ends. The first two samples are worked into every space in the warp, with a separate wrapping thread placed between each row of medallions in the second sample. The last sample here works over two groups in a lattice fashion. After washing, the other weft threads fill the empty space.

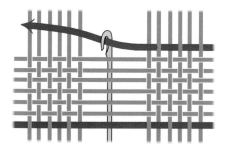

Stage 1

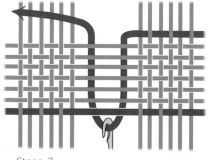

Stage 2

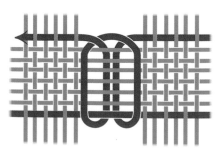

Stage 3

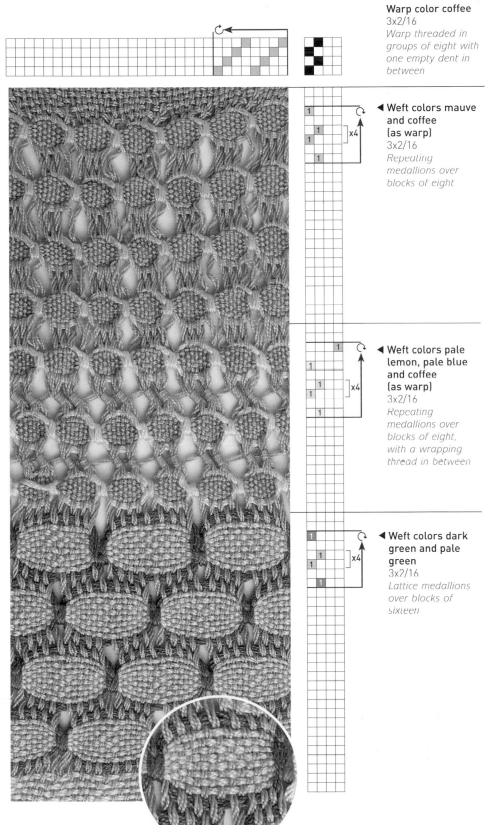

Warp color coffee
3x2/16
*Warp threaded in
groups of eight with
one empty dent in
between*

◀ **Weft colors mauve
and coffee
(as warp)**
3x2/16
*Repeating
medallions over
blocks of eight*

x4

◀ **Weft colors pale
lemon, pale blue
and coffee
(as warp)**
3x2/16
*Repeating
medallions over
blocks of eight,
with a wrapping
thread in between*

x4

◀ **Weft colors dark
green and pale
green**
3x2/16
*Lattice medallions
over blocks of
sixteen*

x4

Canvas

Canvas weave resembles the cloth used for some counted-thread embroidery, with easily observable spaces between doubled center threads.

Two different blocks can be woven on a four-shaft loom. There are usually four threads per block, threaded: 1, 2, 2, 1 and 4, 3, 3, 4, but five-thread blocks can be made with three identically threaded ends rather than two at the center of each block. It is best to keep the center ends together in one dent, adjusting the other dentage accordingly.

Plain weave can be threaded between lace blocks—these are threaded 4, 1, 4, 1, adapting the order to fit in with adjacent lace areas. Only the centers of the lace blocks have doubled threads.

Areas threaded in plain weave will weave as tabby when the tabby sheds are used: (1, 3) and (2, 4). They will weave as mock tabby with horizontal doubled threads when woven with the lace sheds.

Lace areas will weave as lace when the lace sheds are used but as mock tabby with vertical doubled lines when the tabby sheds are used.

What you can do:
- Weave each lace block with either warp or weft floats.
- Weave large sections of lace by alternating and repeating both threading and weaving sequences.
- Use color and/or yarn variations to emphasize structure.
- Create patterning based on sections of mock tabby, tabby, and lace.

What you can't do:
- Repeat identical blocks without plain weave between.
- Weave true tabby across the whole cloth.

NOTES

Selvedges: Thread 4, 1, 4, 1. Use a floating selvedge.

Sett: As for loose tabby.

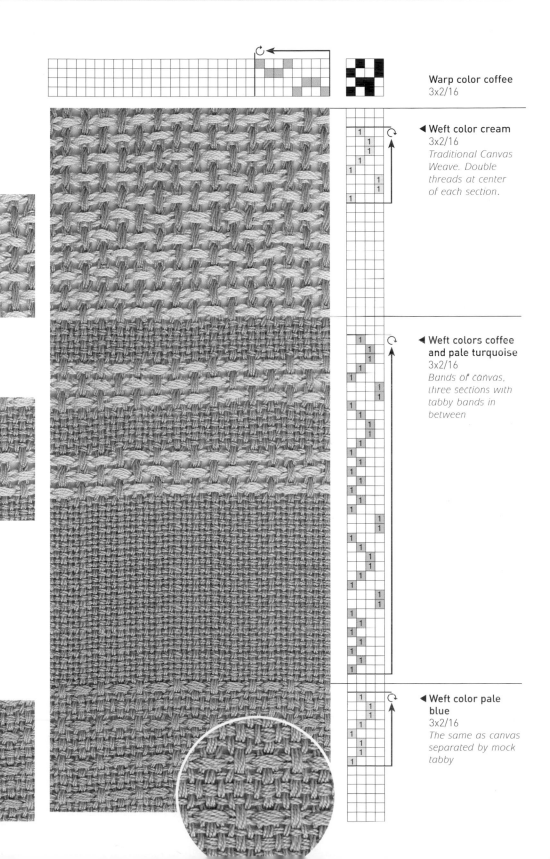

Warp color coffee
3x2/16

◀ **Weft color cream**
3x2/16
Traditional Canvas Weave. Double threads at center of each section.

◀ **Weft colors coffee and pale turquoise**
3x2/16
Bands of canvas, three sections with tabby bands in between

◀ **Weft color pale blue**
3x2/16
The same as canvas separated by mock tabby

Canvas

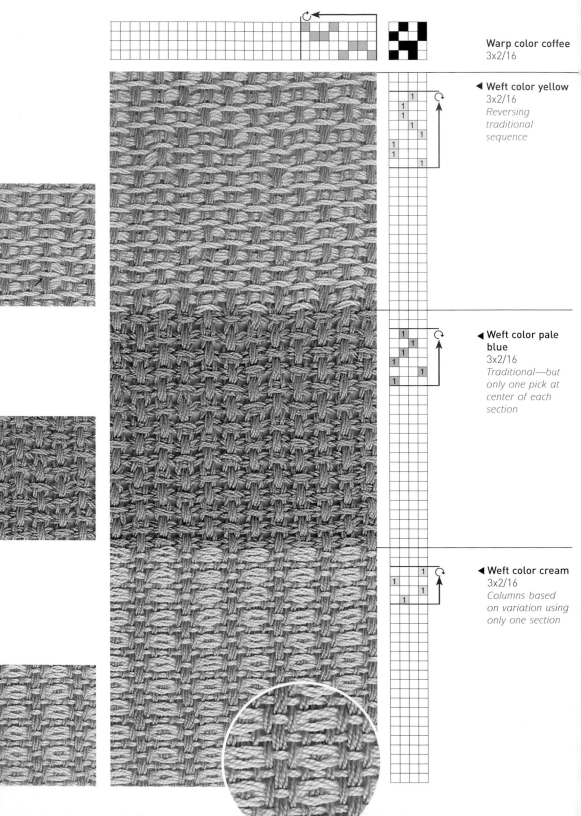

Warp color coffee
3x2/16

◀ **Weft color yellow**
3x2/16
*Reversing
traditional
sequence*

◀ **Weft color pale
blue**
3x2/16
*Traditional—but
only one pick at
center of each
section*

◀ **Weft color cream**
3x2/16
*Columns based
on variation using
only one section*

Canvas

Warp colors coffee and turquoise
Coffee 2/16,
turquoise 3x2/16

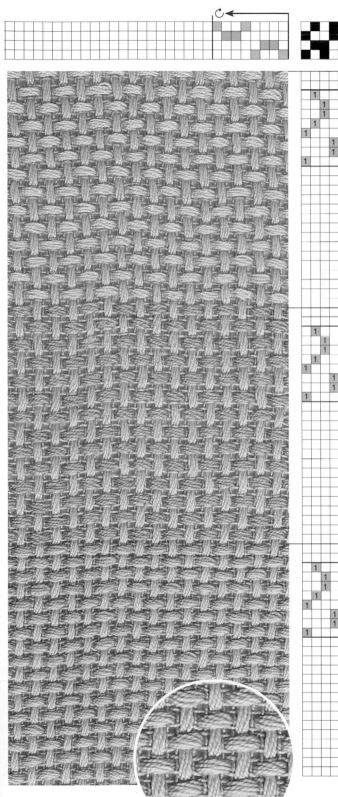

◀ **Weft colors coffee and turquoise (both as warp)**
Coffee 2/16,
turquoise 3x2/16
Weft same colors and thicknesses of threads as warp

◀ **Weft colors coffee and turquoise (both as warp)**
Coffee 3x2/16,
turquoise 2/16
Weft colors opposite thicknesses to warp and on different sheds

◀ **Weft colors turquoise and coffee (both as warp)**
Wefts in alternating thicknesses in both colors: 3x2/16 (thick) and 2/16 (thin)
Weave thin, thick, thick, thin. Colors in twos so that both thick and thin wefts are of opposite colors. Juggling with four shuttles!

Huck

Huck can also be referred to as Huckaback. Two different blocks can be woven when using four shafts. The blocks are always of an odd number of ends beginning and finishing on the same shaft. The most usual number of ends per block is five, but blocks of three and seven can be used—possibly even nine with very fine threads! The weft picks follow the same restrictions.

Often the five-thread blocks are threaded 1, 2, 1, 2, 1 and 4, 3, 4, 3, 4. Here the five-thread blocks are threaded 1, 3, 1, 3, 1 and 2, 4, 2, 4, 2, with plain weave threaded 2, 1, 2, 1, this adjusting to fit in with adjacent lace blocks. Other threading sequences can be used, but this one places the largest number of ends on the front shafts and the least on the back.

The ends on the upper shafts of each block float either over or under the weft floats in the lace areas. The other ends in the block weave as tabby. A block with warp floats on the upper cloth surface is referred to as a warp spot, and one with weft floats on the upper surface is referred to as a weft spot. Warp and weft spots switch to the opposite configuration on the reverse of the cloth.

The blocks must be threaded in opposition—it is not possible to repeat a block as then there would be doubled threads and the floats would be too long.

What you can do:
- Thread two different blocks, each of which can be woven as warp or weft spots.
- Thread and weave warp and weft spots adjacent.
- Thread for plain weave.
- Weave lace areas as tabby.

What you can't do:
- Have adjacent blocks as both warp or weft spots, either in the threading or weaving.

> **NOTES**
>
> **Selvedges**: Thread 1, 2, repeat. Use a floating selvedge.
>
> **Sett**: As for loose tabby.

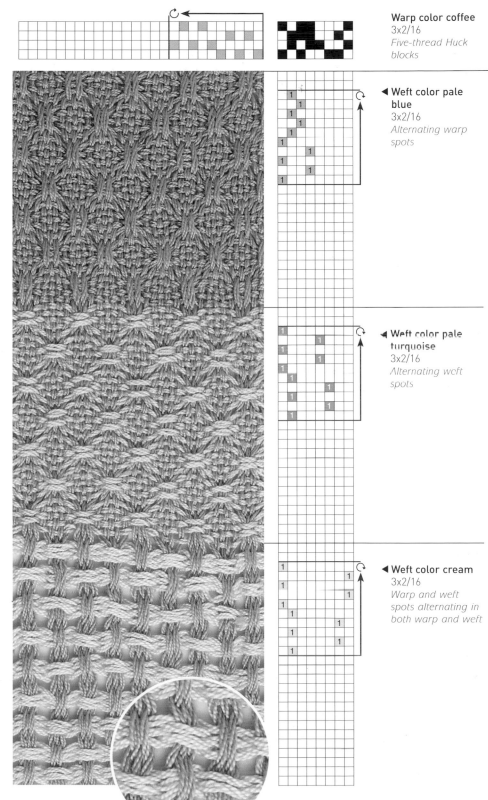

Warp color coffee
3x2/16
Five-thread Huck blocks

◀ **Weft color pale blue**
3x2/16
Alternating warp spots

◀ **Weft color pale turquoise**
3x2/16
Alternating weft spots

◀ **Weft color cream**
3x2/16
Warp and weft spots alternating in both warp and weft

Huck: Color Variation

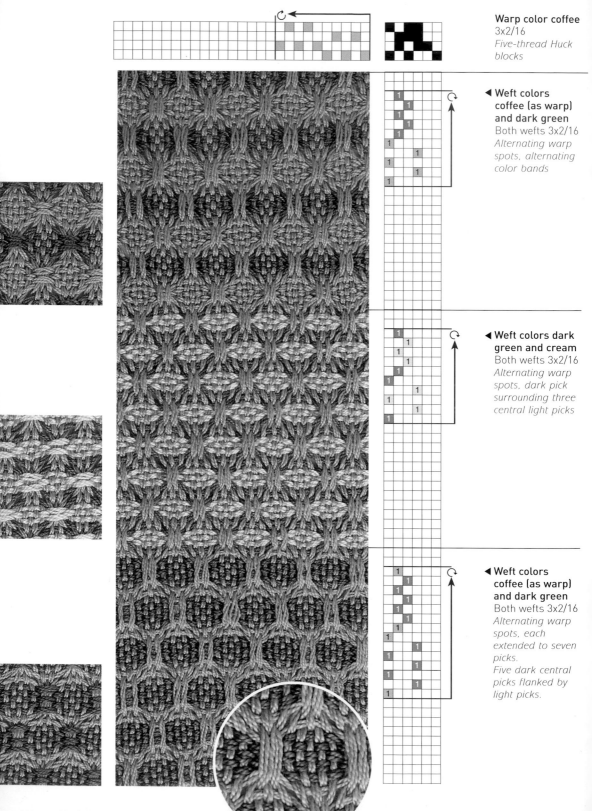

Warp color coffee
3x2/16
Five-thread Huck blocks

◀ **Weft colors coffee (as warp) and dark green**
Both wefts 3x2/16
Alternating warp spots, alternating color bands

◀ **Weft colors dark green and cream**
Both wefts 3x2/16
Alternating warp spots, dark pick surrounding three central light picks

◀ **Weft colors coffee (as warp) and dark green**
Both wefts 3x2/16
Alternating warp spots, each extended to seven picks.
Five dark central picks flanked by light picks.

Huck

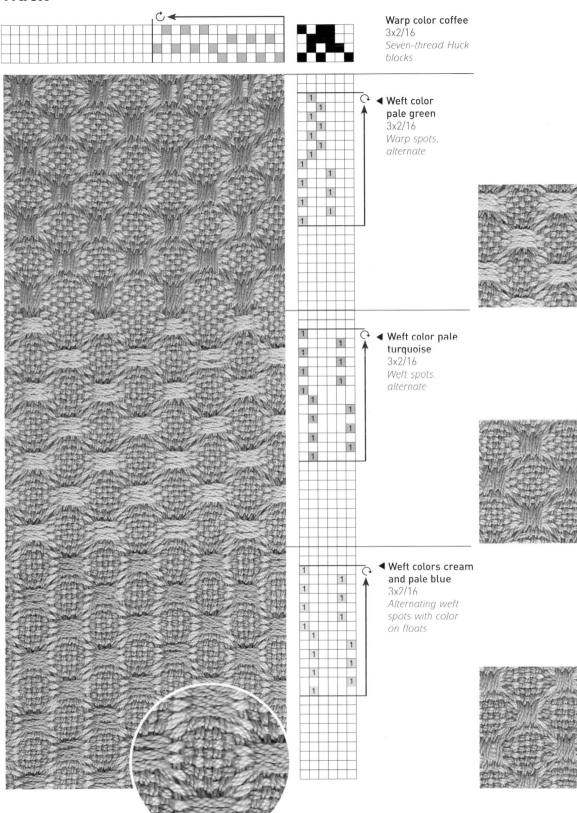

Warp color coffee
3x2/16
*Seven-thread Huck
blocks*

◀ **Weft color
pale green**
3x2/16
*Warp spots.
alternate*

◀ **Weft color pale
turquoise**
3x2/16
*Weft spots.
alternate*

◀ **Weft colors cream
and pale blue**
3x2/16
*Alternating weft
spots with color
on floats*

Huck

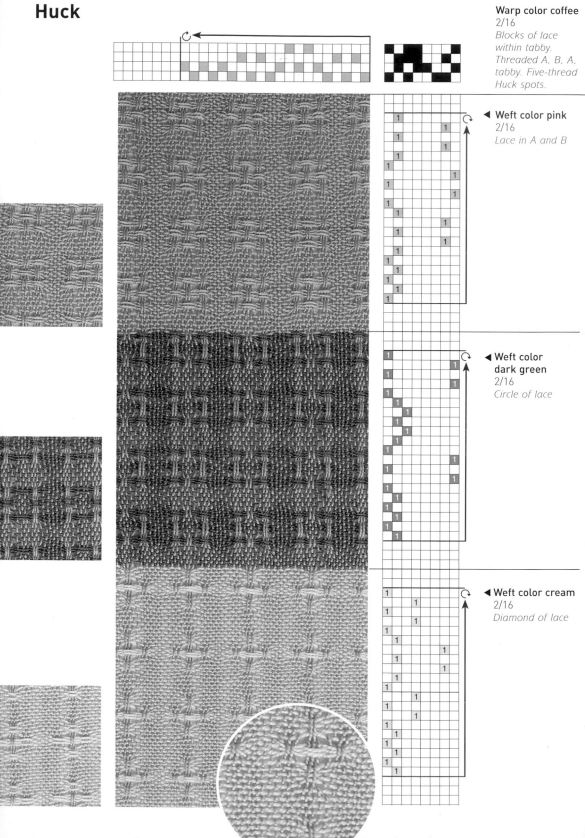

Warp color coffee
2/16
*Blocks of lace
within tabby.
Threaded A, B, A,
tabby. Five-thread
Huck spots.*

◀ **Weft color pink**
2/16
Lace in A and B

◀ **Weft color
dark green**
2/16
Circle of lace

◀ **Weft color cream**
2/16
Diamond of lace

Huck

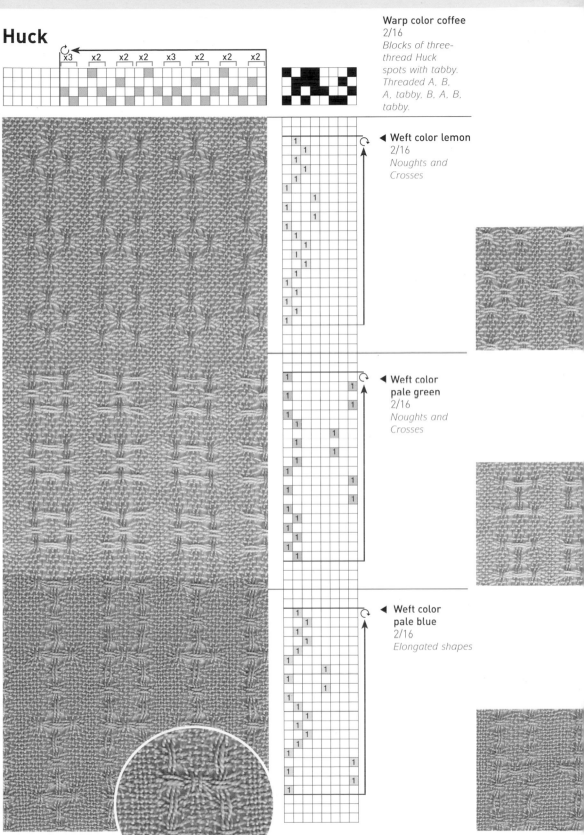

Warp color coffee
2/16
Blocks of three-thread Huck spots with tabby. Threaded A, B, A, tabby, B, A, B, tabby.

◄ **Weft color lemon**
2/16
Noughts and Crosses

◄ **Weft color pale green**
2/16
Noughts and Crosses

◄ **Weft color pale blue**
2/16
Elongated shapes

Huck

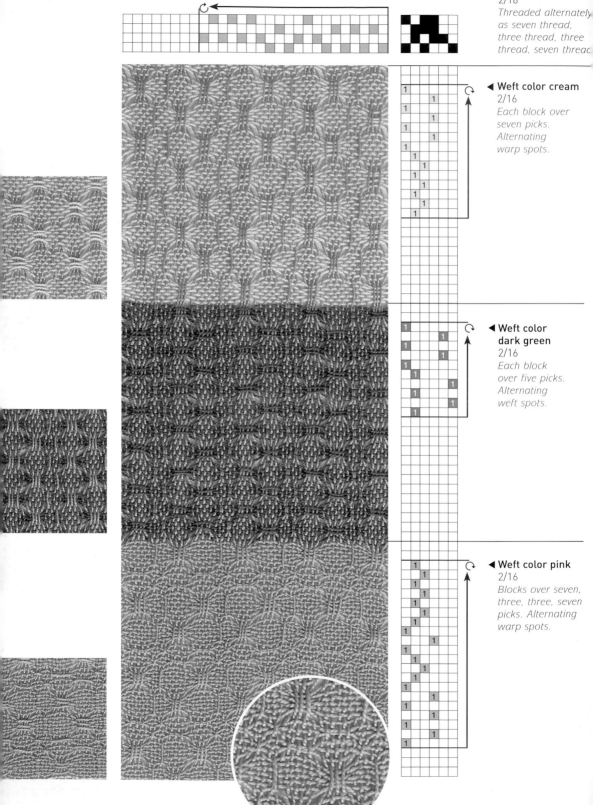

2/16
*Threaded alternately
as seven thread,
three thread, three
thread, seven thread*

◀ **Weft color cream**
2/16
*Each block over
seven picks.
Alternating
warp spots.*

◀ **Weft color
dark green**
2/16
*Each block
over five picks.
Alternating
weft spots.*

◀ **Weft color pink**
2/16
*Blocks over seven,
three, three, seven
picks. Alternating
warp spots.*

Huck

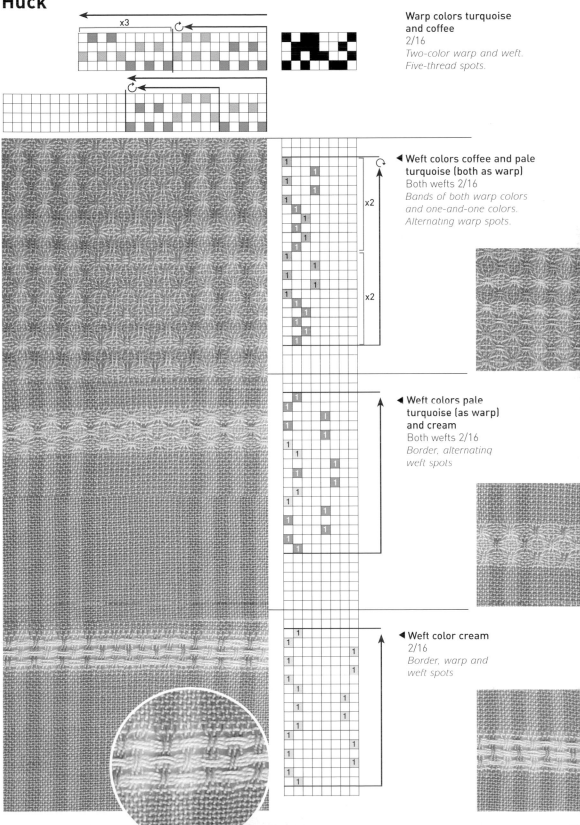

Warp colors turquoise and coffee
2/16
Two-color warp and weft. Five-thread spots.

◄ **Weft colors coffee and pale turquoise (both as warp)**
Both wefts 2/16
Bands of both warp colors and one-and-one colors. Alternating warp spots.

◄ **Weft colors pale turquoise (as warp) and cream**
Both wefts 2/16
Border, alternating weft spots

◄ **Weft color cream**
2/16
Border, warp and weft spots

Spot Bronson

Spot Bronson produces a delightfully delicate textured cloth. It is usually a four-thread block lace weave, and on four shafts, three different blocks can be woven. Instead of the usual four threads per block there can be six or even eight, or just two—always an even number.

Every alternate end is threaded on shaft one. It is best to use shaft one for this, especially if using a floor loom, as it will need the most effort to treadle and this is easiest if the most heavily loaded shaft is closest to the weaver.

Obviously it is important to ensure that there are enough heddles on shaft one before starting to thread the loom. It is possible that the necessity of alternating with just a single shaft is the reason for the large number of old five-shaft Spot Bronson designs. These, probably woven on eight shafts, could have used four shafts instead of one for the alternating base shaft, with the other four shafts used for the spot patterns— in effect, a five-shaft weave.

As in Huck, warp spots reverse to weft and vice versa. If using a loom that lifts the shafts, then theoretically weft spots are easier to weave than warp spots, but traditionally warp spots are shown in many pattern books. Here both are shown in the samples.

The lace threading groups can weave as either lace or plain. Each "spot" must be surrounded on all sides by plain weave with no repeat, or adjacently.

What you can do:
- Arrange spots in any order.
- Weave tabby totally across the whole cloth.
- Use only two spots for lace and use the third block entirely for tabby.
- Weave designs comparative to a three-shaft straight or point draft.

What you can't do:
- Weave spots adjacent either vertically or horizontally.

NOTES

Selvedge: 4, 1 / 3, 1/ 2, 1 in any sequence that will fit in with the adjacent threading. Always use a floating selvedge.

Selvedge areas threaded in this way will not weave a true tabby as ends on the pattern shafts will produce single floats when that block is woven as lace.

The three blocks, or spots, are single blocks only and must be used independently of adjacent spots. They cannot be repeated in weft either.

There is no threading for tabby if all three spots are threaded. The best tabby is 1, 2, 1, 3, 1, 4—but even this will produce long weft floats at the sides. If it is vital that there is a dedicated tabby edging then one of the spots must be sacrificed.

Sett: As for loose tabby.

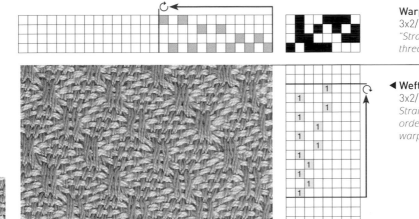

Warp color coffee
3x2/16
*"Straight entry"
threading for blocks*

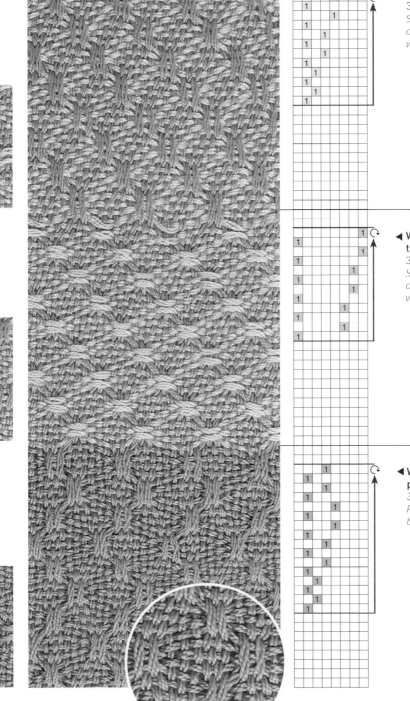

◀ **Weft color cream**
3x2/16
*Straight diagonal
order for blocks;
warp spots*

◀ **Weft color pale
turquoise**
3x2/16
*Straight diagonal
order for blocks;
weft spots*

◀ **Weft color pale
pink**
3x2/16
*Point order for
blocks; warp spots*

Spot Bronson: Point Order

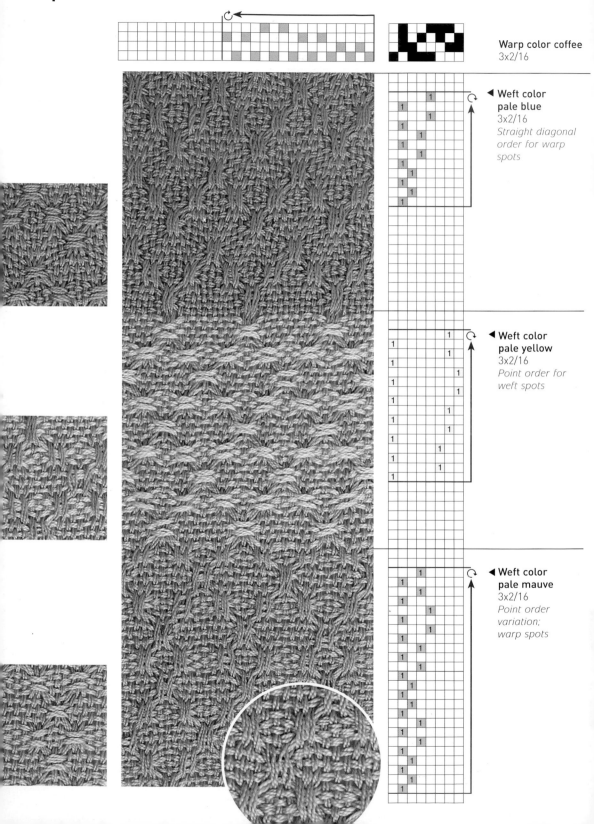

Warp color coffee
3x2/16

◀ Weft color
pale blue
3x2/16
*Straight diagonal
order for warp
spots*

◀ Weft color
pale yellow
3x2/16
*Point order for
weft spots*

◀ Weft color
pale mauve
3x2/16
*Point order
variation;
warp spots*

Spot Bronson: Point Order

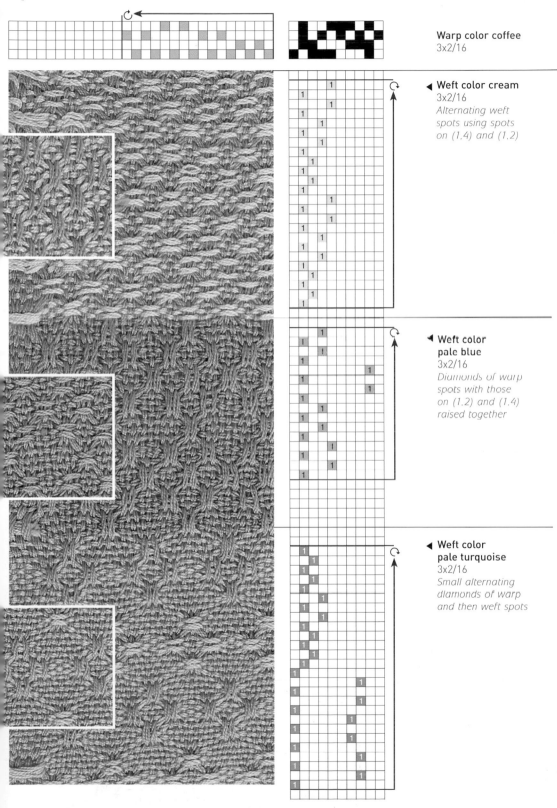

Warp color coffee
3x2/16

◀ **Weft color cream**
3x2/16
*Alternating weft
spots using spots
on (1,4) and (1,2)*

◀ **Weft color
pale blue**
3x2/16
*Diamonds of warp
spots with those
on (1,2) and (1,4)
raised together*

◀ **Weft color
pale turquoise**
3x2/16
*Small alternating
diamonds of warp
and then weft spots*

Spot Bronson

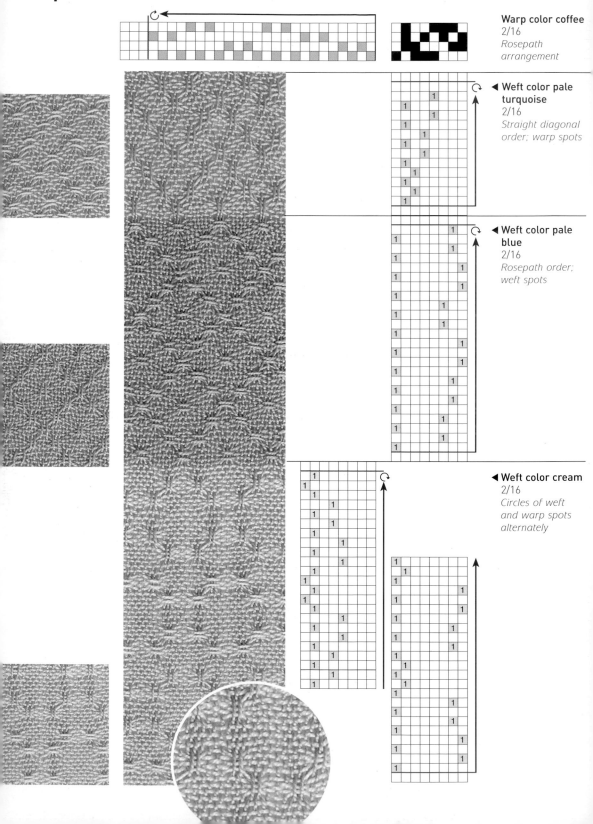

Warp color coffee
2/16
*Rosepath
arrangement*

◀ **Weft color pale
turquoise**
2/16
*Straight diagonal
order; warp spots*

◀ **Weft color pale
blue**
2/16
*Rosepath order;
weft spots*

◀ **Weft color cream**
2/16
*Circles of weft
and warp spots
alternately*

Spot Bronson

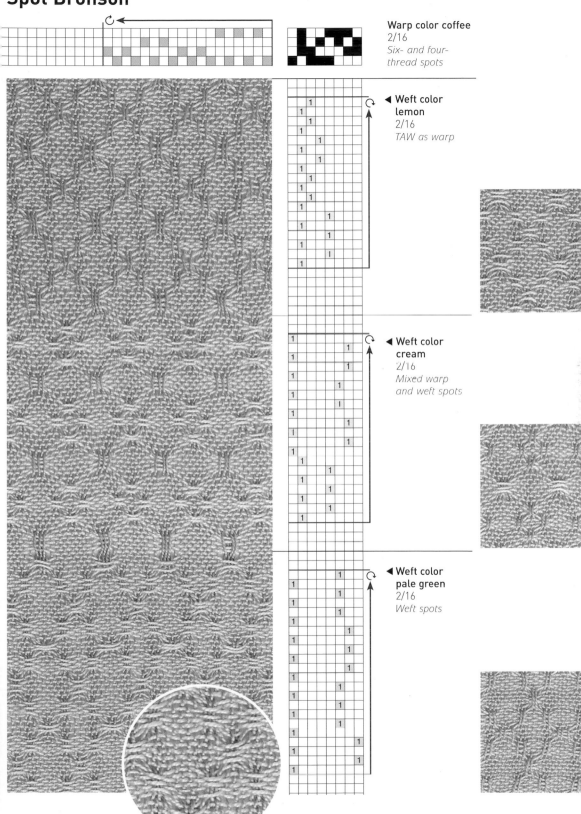

Warp color coffee
2/16
*Six- and four-
thread spots*

◄ **Weft color
lemon**
2/16
TAW as warp

◄ **Weft color
cream**
2/16
*Mixed warp
and weft spots*

◄ **Weft color
pale green**
2/16
Weft spots

Spot Bronson

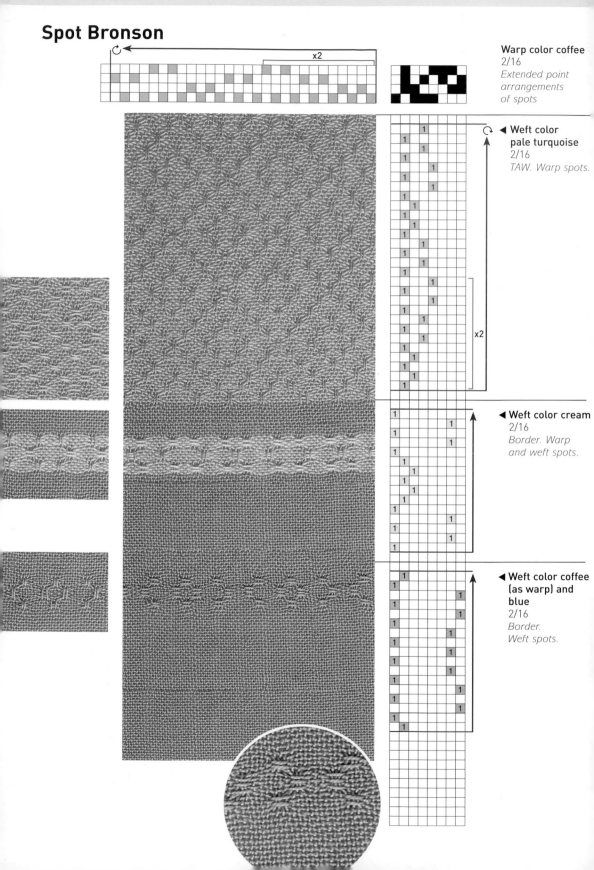

x2

Warp color coffee
2/16
*Extended point
arrangements
of spots*

◀ **Weft color
pale turquoise**
2/16
TAW. Warp spots.

x2

◀ **Weft color cream**
2/16
*Border. Warp
and weft spots.*

◀ **Weft color coffee
(as warp) and
blue**
2/16
*Border.
Weft spots.*

Spot Bronson

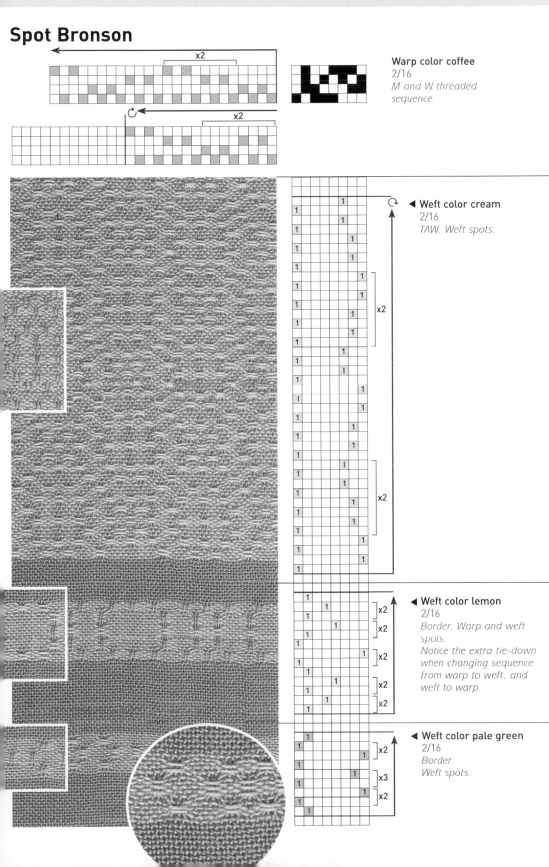

Warp color coffee
2/16
*M and W threaded
sequence*

◀ **Weft color cream**
2/16
TAW. Weft spots.

◀ **Weft color lemon**
2/16
*Border. Warp and weft
spots.
Notice the extra tie-down
when changing sequence
from warp to weft, and
weft to warp.*

◀ **Weft color pale green**
2/16
*Border.
Weft spots.*

Bronson Lace

Bronson Lace is an old lace weave, recorded by the weavers J and R
Bronson and popularized by Mary Meigs Atwater. Apparently originally
called Spot Weave it is now referred to as Bronson Lace, Lace Bronson,
or Atwater–Bronson Lace.

Each lace block has an even number of ends—usually six, but four
and (more rarely) eight are also used—always an even number.

The sequence resembles that of Huck, with the addition of an extra
thread on a third shaft. This additional shaft and the base shafts are the
same for each of the lace blocks, which means there are just two shafts
available on a four-shaft loom, to create the pattern floats. The base
ends are usually threaded on shaft 1 with the final (additional) end on
shaft 2. Thus, the lace blocks on shaft 3 or 4 are: (1, 3, 1, 3, 1, 2) and
(1, 4, 1, 4, 1, 2) for the six-thread blocks. The four-thread blocks are
(1, 3, 1, 2) and (1, 4, 1, 2).

The lace pattern floats are "framed" by tabby threads, in both warp
and weft, which means that the same block can be repeated both
vertically and horizontally, and the open lace weave shows at its best
when at least two lace blocks are adjacent, although single blocks are
perfectly possible.

Both blocks can be woven as either warp or weft spots
simultaneously, or woven as separate blocks.

Plain weave blocks are threaded on 2, 1 repeat, using weft picks: (1),
(2, 3, 4).

What you can do:
- Thread separately for tabby areas.
- Repeat the spots both horizontally and vertically.
- Weave both units as warp or weft spots at the same time.

What you can't do:
- Weave different spots as warp and weft at the same time.
(Theoretically, this is so, but see the last weave on page 183 where
adjacent spot-areas are slightly out of true alignment that enables them
to be different.)

NOTES

Selvedges: Threaded 2, 1, 2, 1. Use a floating selvedge.

Sett: As for loose tabby.

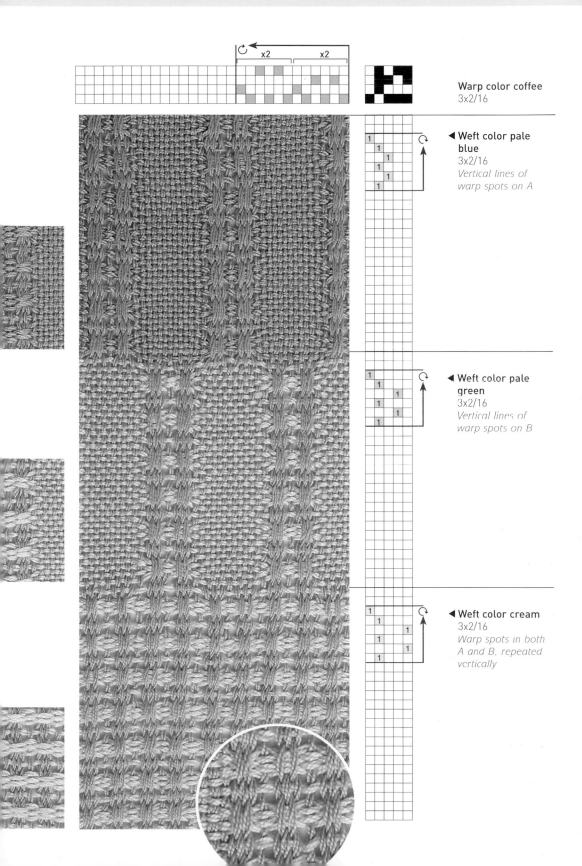

Warp color coffee
3x2/16

◀ **Weft color pale blue**
3x2/16
Vertical lines of warp spots on A

◀ **Weft color pale green**
3x2/16
Vertical lines of warp spots on B

◀ **Weft color cream**
3x2/16
Warp spots in both A and B, repeated vertically

Bronson Lace

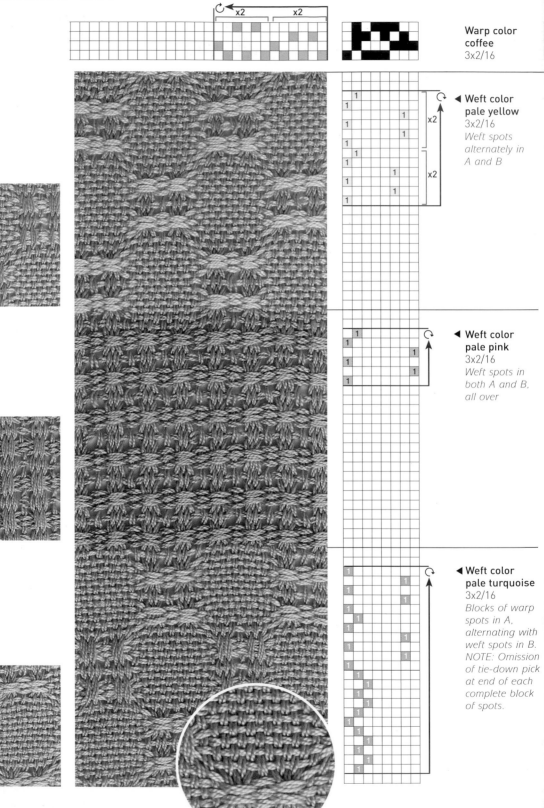

Warp color coffee
3x2/16

◀ **Weft color pale yellow**
3x2/16
Weft spots alternately in A and B

◀ **Weft color pale pink**
3x2/16
Weft spots in both A and B, all over

◀ **Weft color pale turquoise**
3x2/16
Blocks of warp spots in A, alternating with weft spots in B. NOTE: Omission of tie-down pick at end of each complete block of spots.

Bronson Lace

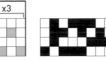

Warp color coffee
3x/216
Blocks of four-thread spots

◀ **Weft color pale green**
3x2/16
Alternating blocks of weft spots

◀ **Weft color pale blue**
3x2/16
Alternating blocks of warp spots

◀ **Weft color cream**
3x2/16
Weft spots in both blocks throughout

Bronson Lace

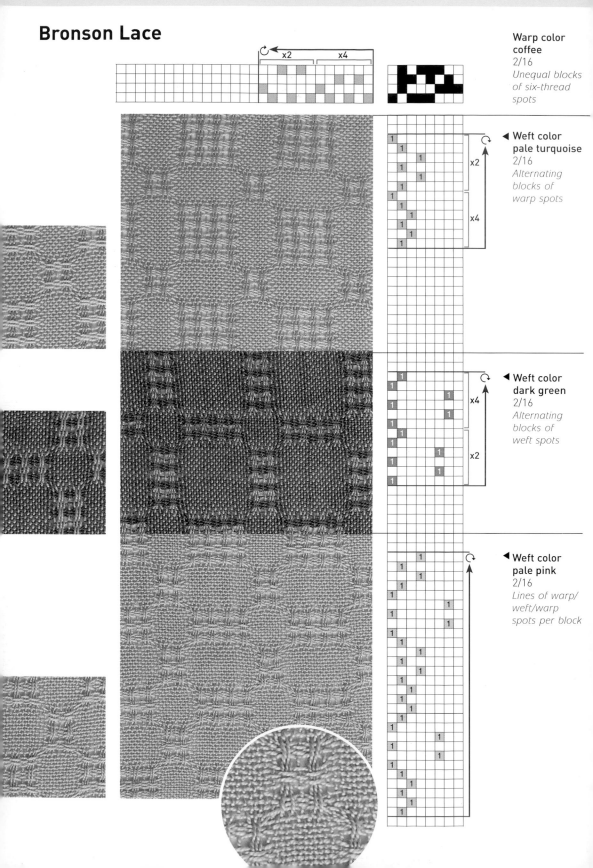

x2　x4

Warp color coffee
2/16
Unequal blocks of six-thread spots

◀ **Weft color pale turquoise**
2/16
Alternating blocks of warp spots

x2

x4

◀ **Weft color dark green**
2/16
Alternating blocks of weft spots

x4

x2

◀ **Weft color pale pink**
2/16
Lines of warp/ weft/warp spots per block

Bronson Lace

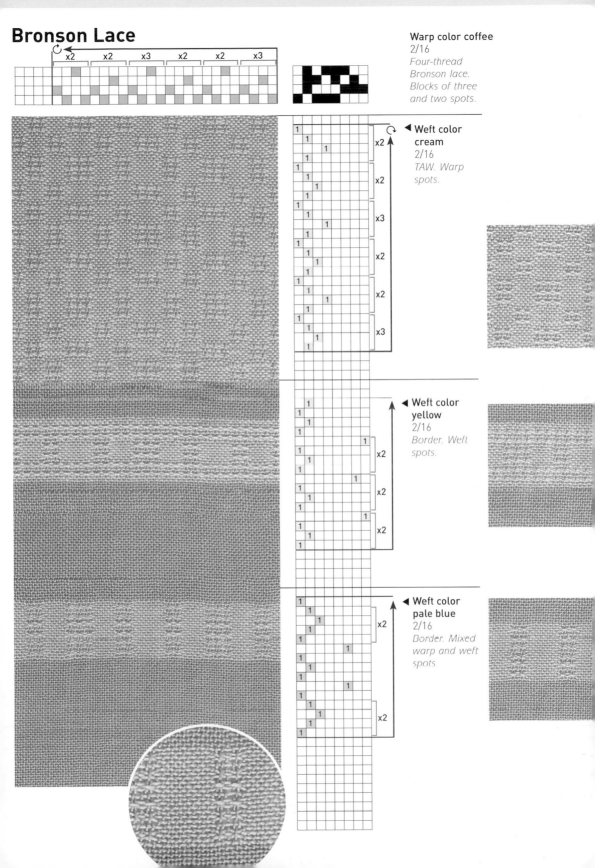

Warp color coffee
2/16
*Four-thread
Bronson lace.
Blocks of three
and two spots.*

◀ Weft color
cream
2/16
*TAW. Warp
spots.*

◀ Weft color
yellow
2/16
*Border. Weft
spots.*

◀ Weft color
pale blue
2/16
*Border. Mixed
warp and weft
spots.*

Swedish Lace

Another very old lace weave, dating back to the early first millennium A.D., and, as its name suggests, of Scandinavian origin.

On four shafts, two separate blocks plus tabby are possible. Each lace unit is composed of an odd number of ends—three, five, or seven, with the odd number of ends on **one** of the tabby shafts. But there is an additional end threaded on the opposing tabby shaft finishing each lace block **except** when a repeat of the same lace blocks is completed. In effect, this means each lace block is composed of six ends except for the final block, which has only five. The reason for this is that the next block of lace threading starts on the opposing tabby shaft so there is no need to duplicate an end on that shaft. Five-thread blocks are thus (1, 4, 1, 4, 1) with two repeated blocks threaded (1, 4, 1, 4, 1, 2, 1, 4, 1, 4, 1, 4)—note the addition of an end on shaft two between the blocks, and (2, 3, 2, 3, 2) with two repeated blocks threaded (2, 3, 2, 3, 2, 1, 2, 3, 2, 3, 2)—note the addition of an end on shaft one between the blocks.

Because there are frequent ends and picks weaving tabby, this lace structure is very stable. It also means that adjacent lace blocks, both horizontally and vertically, can be woven.

Tabby areas are threaded (1, 2, 1, 2) repeat.

What you can do:
- Thread and weave tabby areas.
- Repeat lace spots horizontally and vertically.
- Weave opposing spot blocks as warp and weft simultaneously.

What you can't do:
- Weave opposing spot blocks as all warp (or weft) spots simultaneously.

NOTES

Selvedges: Either use the pattern sequence, with adjustments for selvedge threading (see pages 16–17) or thread as tabby. Use a floating selvedge.

Sett: As for loose tabby.

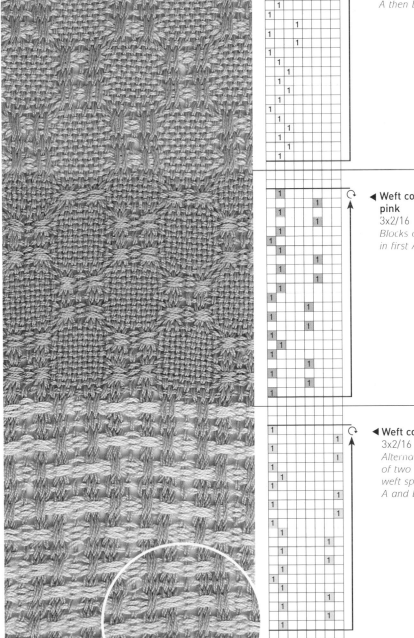

Warp color coffee
3x2/16
*Note omission of
extra thread at end
of repeated blocks*

◀ **Weft color yellow**
3x2/16
*Blocks of warp
spots in first
A then B*

◀ **Weft color pale
pink**
3x2/16
*Blocks of weft spots
in first A then B*

◀ **Weft color cream**
3x2/16
*Alternating blocks
of two warp and
weft spots in both
A and B*

Swedish Lace

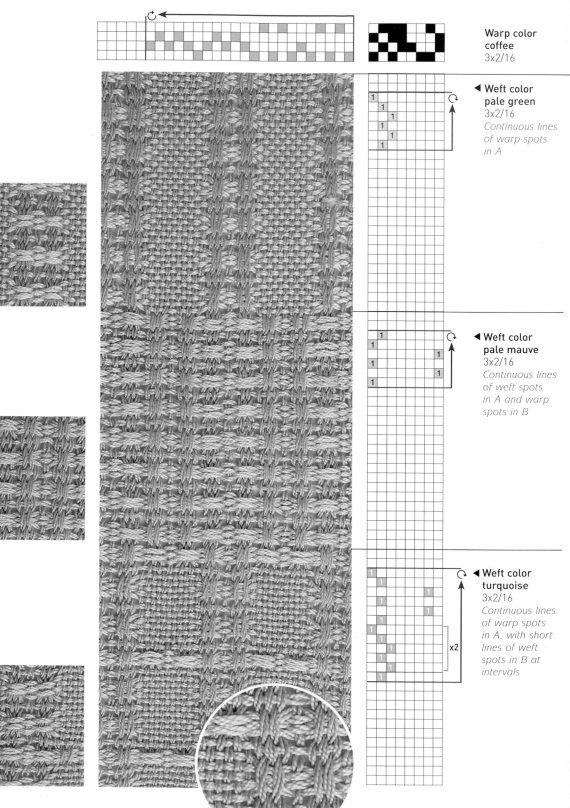

Warp color
coffee
3x2/16

◀ Weft color
pale green
3x2/16
*Continuous lines
of warp spots
in A*

◀ Weft color
pale mauve
3x2/16
*Continuous lines
of weft spots
in A and warp
spots in B*

◀ Weft color
turquoise
3x2/16
*Continuous lines
of warp spots
in A, with short
lines of weft
spots in B at
intervals*

x2

Swedish Lace

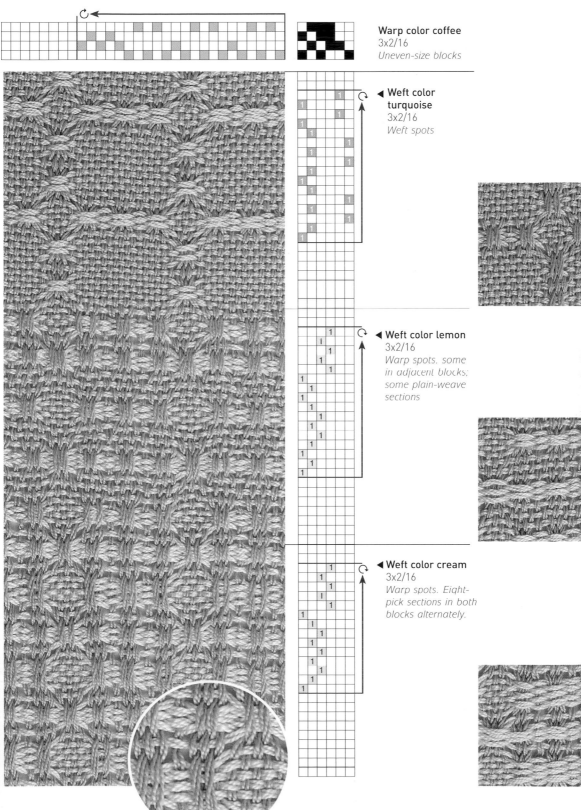

Warp color coffee
3x2/16
Uneven-size blocks

◀ **Weft color turquoise**
3x2/16
Weft spots

◀ **Weft color lemon**
3x2/16
Warp spots, some in adjacent blocks; some plain-weave sections

◀ **Weft color cream**
3x2/16
Warp spots. Eight-pick sections in both blocks alternately.

Swedish Lace

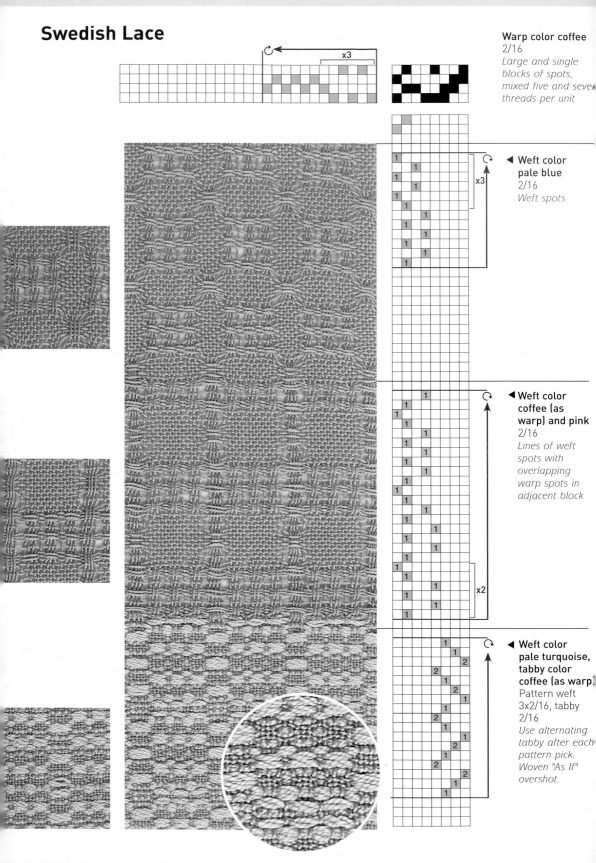

Warp color coffee
2/16
*Large and single
blocks of spots,
mixed five and seven
threads per unit*

◄ **Weft color
pale blue**
2/16
Weft spots

◄ **Weft color
coffee (as
warp) and pink**
2/16
*Lines of weft
spots with
overlapping
warp spots in
adjacent block*

◄ **Weft color
pale turquoise,
tabby color
coffee (as warp).**
Pattern weft
3x2/16, tabby
2/16
*Use alternating
tabby after each
pattern pick.
Woven "As If"
overshot.*

Swedish Lace

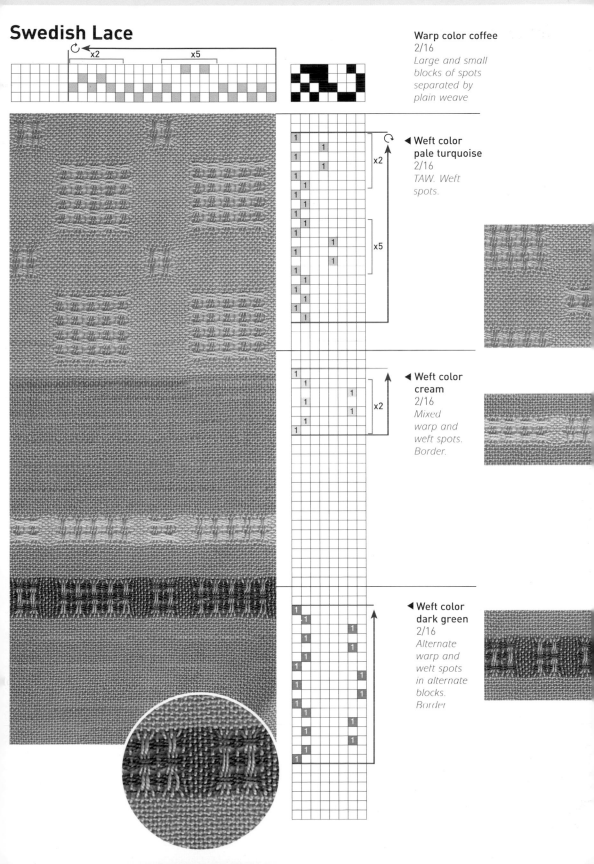

Warp color coffee
2/16
*Large and small
blocks of spots
separated by
plain weave*

◀ Weft color
pale turquoise
2/16
*TAW. Weft
spots.*

◀ Weft color
cream
2/16
*Mixed
warp and
weft spots.
Border.*

◀ Weft color
dark green
2/16
*Alternate
warp and
weft spots
in alternate
blocks.
Border.*

Special Threadings

In this section are those threadings that are specific for unique techniques. In reality all threadings are special, but (to misquote George Orwell), some are more special than others.

Some techniques—such as Crammed and Spaced, Undulating Twill, and Three-shaft drafts—are based on a simple threading draft, but there is a singular feature that defines the technique. Others, such as Skip Twill and Syncopated Threading drafts are more complicated, following specific rules.

A method of turning the weaving draft into the threading draft, and vice versa, is demonstrated in Turned Monk's Belt.

Distorted weft and supplementary warp techniques provide an opportunity to use fancy yarns that are mostly on the surface of the fabric.

Waffle Weave, with the same surface appearance as the waffle, is one of the most deeply textured techniques, and can also use fancy yarn types.

Warp-faced and weft-faced are also just as they sound, demonstrating that weaving does not have to always be balanced.

Finally, some techniques require ends or picks to be manipulated with the fingers. These are of course slower to weave than the loom-operated weaves, but can be used decoratively to produce definition to an article.

Scarf, crammed and spaced; rayon with high-twist bouclé-wool weft.

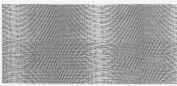

Crammed and Spaced (page 194)

Undulating Twill (page 198)

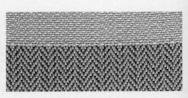

Three-shaft Drafts (page 204)

Crammed and Spaced

This threading is just as it sounds: Some of the warp ends are crammed together with a higher than normal e.p.i./e.p.c.m., while others are spaced out with a lower than normal e.p.i./e.p.c.m. The change from crammed to spaced can be gradual or abrupt. When washed, and even before removing from the loom, the ends just at the edges of the crammed areas will slide toward the spaced areas. If woven as twill, the angle of the twill lines varies from steep in the crammed areas to shallow in the spaced, creating a waved effect.

Sett No hard and fast rule, but a useful criteria is to make the overall sett equal to the normal.

Threads Wool is useful as it clings together, but all types work well. If a high-twist weft yarn is used, then the finished fabric will collapse in upon itself.

Selvedges Straight entry. Use a floating selvedge.

Undulating Twill

This threading also produces a waved effect, which is entirely dependent upon the nature of the threading. There are repeat threadings of adjacent ends on the same shafts, interspersed with single (normal) threadings. The repeats can be of two or three ends, but rarely more. The repeated ends must be threaded separately otherwise they will bunch together. The angle of the twill lines in the repeated areas is shallower.

Sett A little closer than normal because there are fewer interlacements.

Threads Most smooth yarns work very well.

Selvedges Straight entry. Use a floating selvedge.

Three-Shaft Threading

These drafts are of great antiquity, especially in Northern Europe and areas where the vertical rather than the horizontal loom developed. Three-shaft blocks are also the basis of many pattern drafts. Unless the threading is a direct point return, then tabby is not possible.

The fabric produced is either 1/2 or 2/1 twill, or a combination of both. It is an extremely stable fabric because the interlacement is more frequent than a 2/2 twill. There is a marked difference of warp-dominance and weft-dominance on the two faces of the fabric.

Sett About 10% closer than a tabby sett.

Threads Any.

Selvedges Straight three-shaft entry but using the same quantities and double threads as a four-shaft weave: e.g.,

(float) RHS

		2			1			1
	2			2			1	
		2			1			

The other specialized techniques featured in this section have instructions immediately preceding the samples.

Crammed and Spaced: Straight Draft

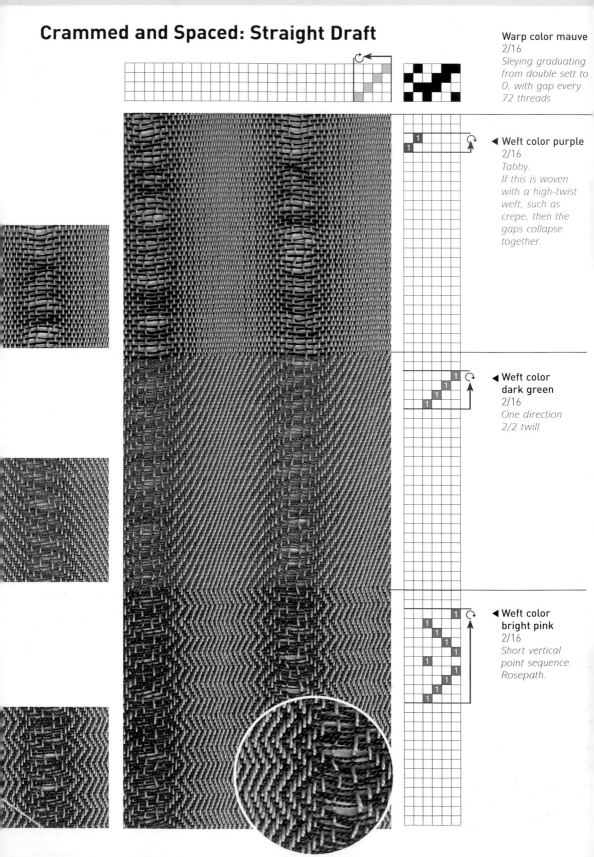

Warp color mauve
2/16
Sleying graduating from double sett to 0, with gap every 72 threads

◀ **Weft color purple**
2/16
Tabby.
If this is woven with a high-twist weft, such as crepe, then the gaps collapse together.

◀ **Weft color dark green**
2/16
One direction 2/2 twill

◀ **Weft color bright pink**
2/16
Short vertical point sequence. Rosepath.

Crammed and Spaced: Straight Draft

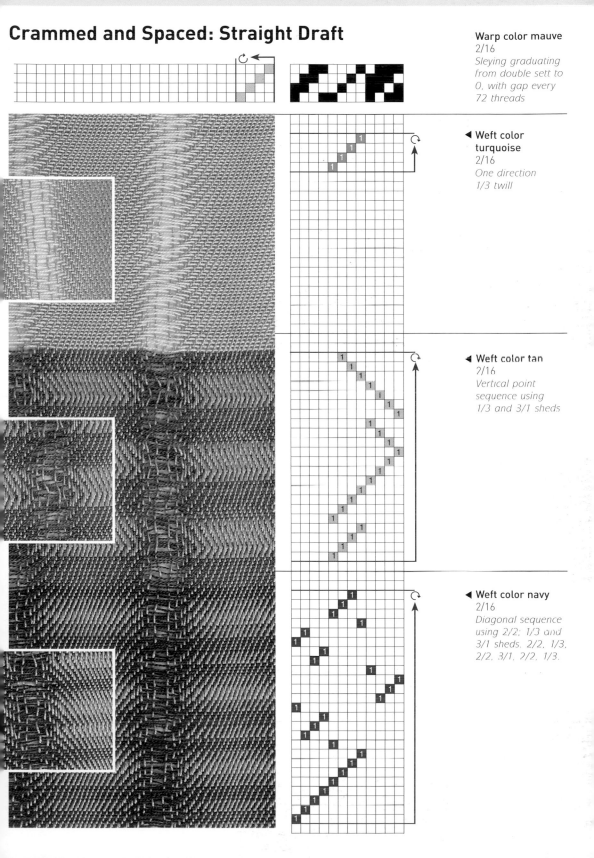

Warp color mauve
2/16
*Sleying graduating
from double sett to
0, with gap every
72 threads*

◀ Weft color
turquoise
2/16
*One direction
1/3 twill*

◀ Weft color tan
2/16
*Vertical point
sequence using
1/3 and 3/1 sheds*

◀ Weft color navy
2/16
*Diagonal sequence
using 2/2; 1/3 and
3/1 sheds. 2/2, 1/3,
2/2, 3/1, 2/2, 1/3.*

Crammed and Spaced: Point Draft; 2/2 Twill

Warp color mauve
2/16
*Sleying graduating
from double sett to
0, with gap after
each threading
repeat*

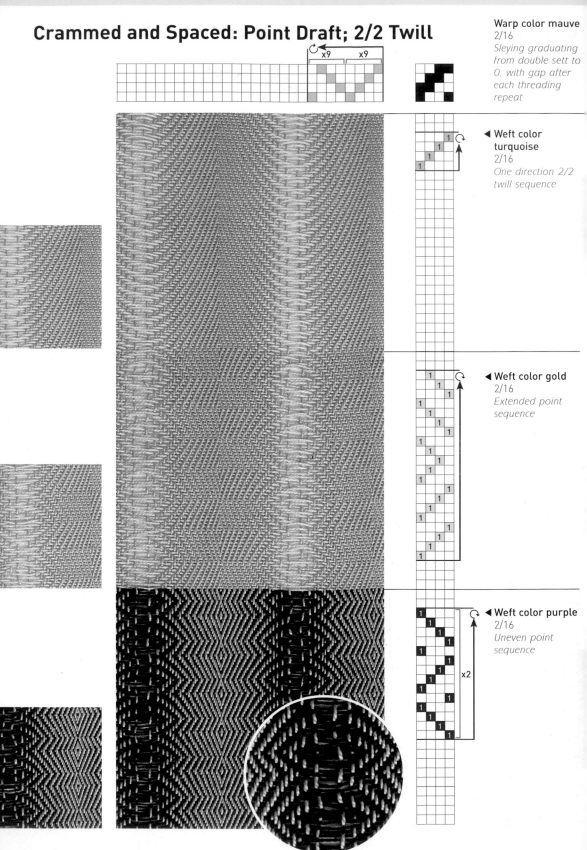

◄ Weft color
turquoise
2/16
*One direction 2/2
twill sequence*

◄ Weft color gold
2/16
*Extended point
sequence*

◄ Weft color purple
2/16
*Uneven point
sequence*

Crammed and Spaced: Point Draft

Warp color mauve
2/16
Sleyed 24 ends at double sett, with corresponding number of empty dents between groups. Points arranged to occur alternately in the center of each crammed area.

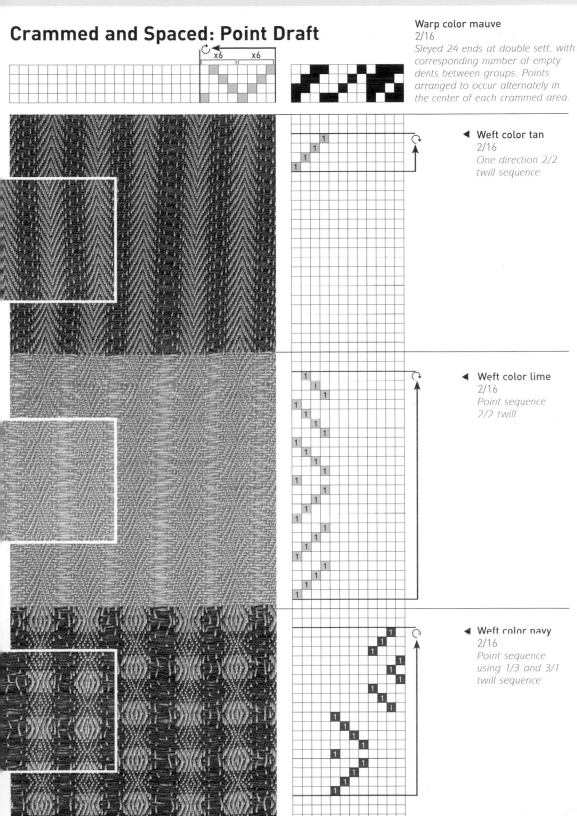

◄ Weft color tan
2/16
One direction 2/2 twill sequence

◄ Weft color lime
2/16
Point sequence 2/2 twill

◄ Weft color navy
2/16
Point sequence using 1/3 and 3/1 twill sequence

Undulating Twill: Straight Draft; 2/2 Twill

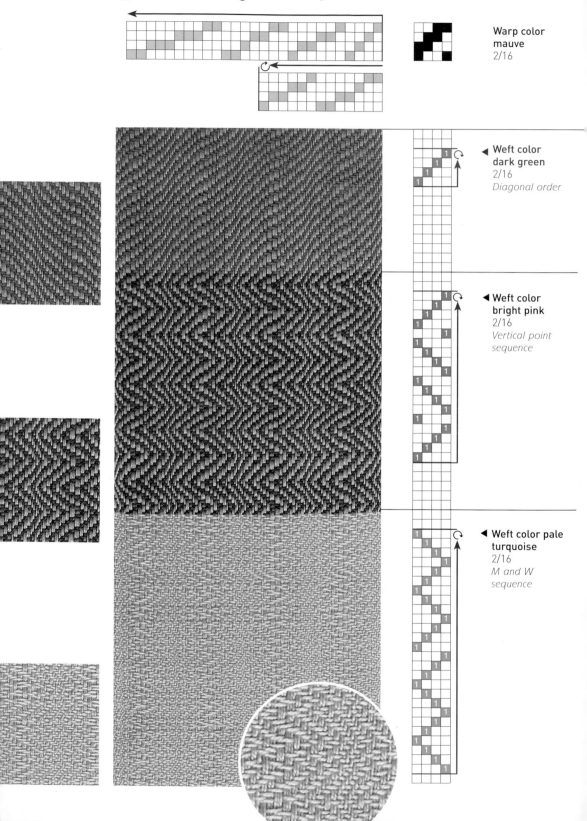

Warp color
mauve
2/16

◄ Weft color
dark green
2/16
Diagonal order

◄ Weft color
bright pink
2/16
*Vertical point
sequence*

◄ Weft color pale
turquoise
2/16
*M and W
sequence*

Undulating Twill: Point Draft; 2/2 Twill

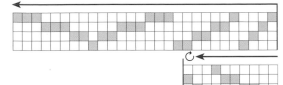

Warp color
mauve
2/16

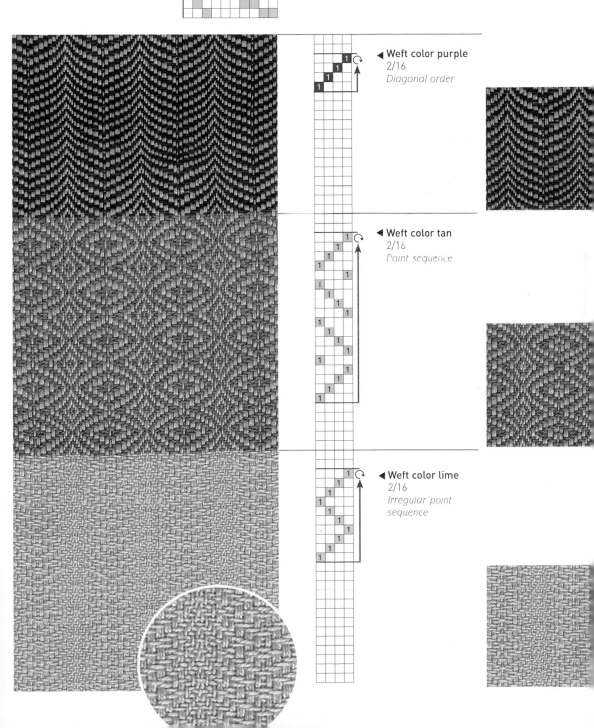

◄ Weft color purple
2/16
Diagonal order

◄ Weft color tan
2/16
Point sequence

◄ Weft color lime
2/16
*Irregular point
sequence*

Undulating Twill: Point Draft; 2/2 Twill

Warp color
mauve
2/16

◄ Weft color navy
2/16
*An extended point
sequence*

◄ Weft color tan
2/16
*The same point
sequence, but
woven as a High
Twill. Note the
repetition of the
tabby picks at the
reversal points.*

◄ Weft color
bright pink
2/16
*The same point
sequence, woven
as a High Twill
with the tabby
picks reversed*

Undulating Twill: Point Draft; 2/2 Twill

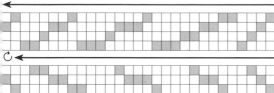

Warp color
mauve
2/16

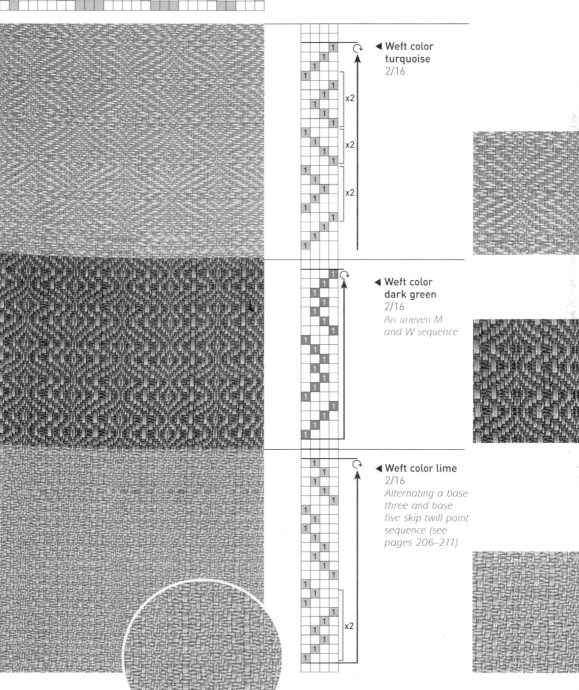

◀ Weft color
turquoise
2/16

◀ Weft color
dark green
2/16
*An uneven M
and W sequence*

◀ Weft color lime
2/16
*Alternating a base
three and base
five skip twill point
sequence (see
pages 206–211)*

Three-shaft Straight Threading: 1/2 and 2/1 Twill

Warp color mauve
3x2/16
Tabby not possible

◄ **Weft color tan**
3x2/16
Straight diagonal 1/2 twill

◄ **Weft color gold**
3x2/16
Straight diagonal 2/1 twill

◄ **Weft color lime and purple**
3x2/16
Straight diagonal order. Mixed 1/2 and 2/1 twill.

Three-shaft Straight Threading: 1/2 and 2/1 Twill

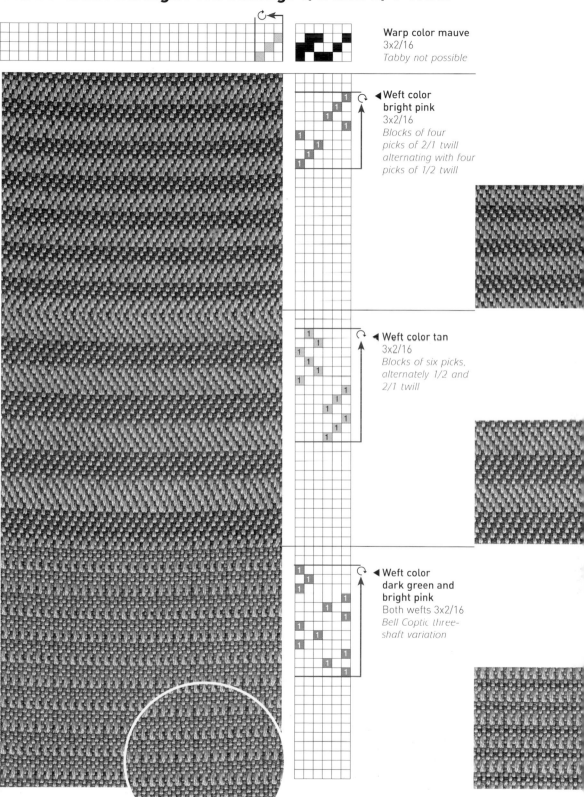

Warp color mauve
3x2/16
Tabby not possible

◀ **Weft color
bright pink**
3x2/16
*Blocks of four
picks of 2/1 twill
alternating with four
picks of 1/2 twill*

◀ **Weft color tan**
3x2/16
*Blocks of six picks,
alternately 1/2 and
2/1 twill*

◀ **Weft color
dark green and
bright pink**
Both wefts 3x2/16
*Bell Coptic three-
shaft variation*

Three-shaft Extended Point Threading: 1/2 and 2/1 Twill

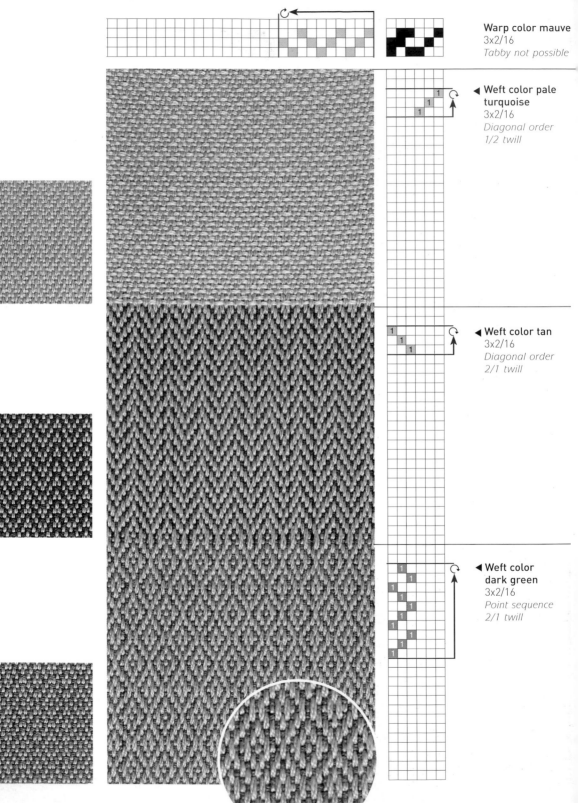

Warp color mauve
3x2/16
Tabby not possible

◄ Weft color pale turquoise
3x2/16
*Diagonal order
1/2 twill*

◄ Weft color tan
3x2/16
*Diagonal order
2/1 twill*

◄ Weft color dark green
3x2/16
*Point sequence
2/1 twill*

Three-shaft Extended Point Threading: 1/2 and 2/1 Twill

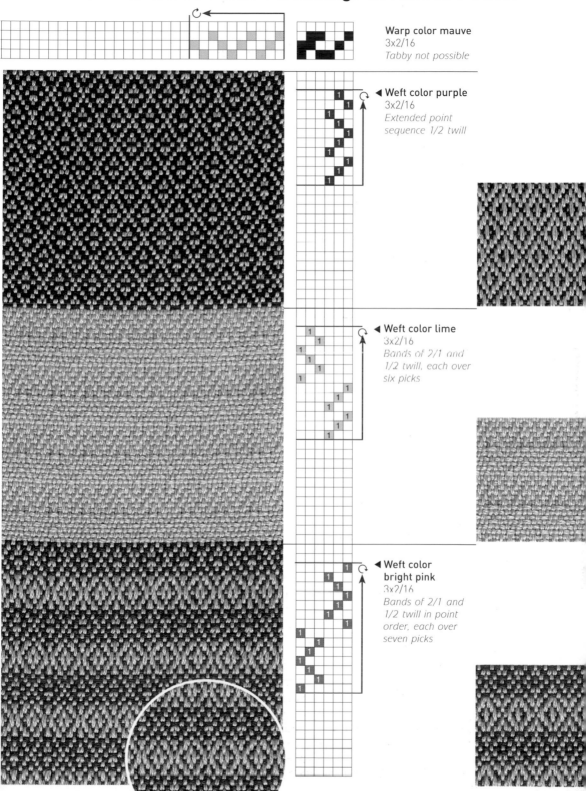

Warp color mauve
3x2/16
Tabby not possible

◀ **Weft color purple**
3x2/16
*Extended point
sequence 1/2 twill*

◀ **Weft color lime**
3x2/16
*Bands of 2/1 and
1/2 twill, each over
six picks*

◀ **Weft color
bright pink**
3x2/16
*Bands of 2/1 and
1/2 twill in point
order, each over
seven picks*

Advancing 2/2 Twill

In "Advancing Twill" or "Incremental Twill" the threading "skips" or "advances" out of the normal by a set number of ends or increments. It is most often seen as or within multishaft patterns, but can also be used with great effect on four shafts.

A short straight draft entry is threaded in the usual way, and then the threading "skips" or leaves out a number of shafts before recommencing. On a four-shaft loom the skip is usually over two, although it can be over one. If the skip is over three, the last end of the threading would be repeated. Obviously if no shafts are skipped the threading continues as normal. Here, all the samples show skips over two, as then tabby can be woven if required.

The length of the straight entry before the skips can be of any number from three upward. Repeated sequences of these can be referred to as "Base 3," "Base 4," "Base 5," etc.

With a normal straight entry on four shafts, the repeat is spread over four ends. By skipping a set number of ends, the repeat can be extended considerably. Using a skip of two, with Base 3 (1, 2, 3, 2, 3, 4, 3, 4, 1, 4, 1, 2) this extends to twelve ends. Base 5 (1, 2, 3, 4, 1, 4, 1, 2, 3, 4, 3, 4, 1, 2, 3, 2, 3, 4, 1, 2) could seem to be even more dramatic, extending as it does over twenty ends, but the twill lines are less defined than with Base 3. Base 4 actually only extends to eight ends because of the nature of the repeat (1, 2, 3, 4, 3, 4, 1, 2). By using a skip of one, Base 4 extends to sixteen ends (1, 2, 3, 4, 2, 3, 4, 1, 3, 4, 1, 2, 4, 1, 2, 3), and Base 5 extends to ten (1, 2, 3, 4, 1, 3, 4, 1, 2, 3). Base 3 just repeats on three shafts.

Alternatively, it can be thought of as a straight run of threading recommencing a set number of shafts further on than the last run began. Thus a three-thread run of (1, 2, 3) advancing 1 recommences on 2 to become the next run of (2, 3, 4). A five-thread run of (1, 2, 3, 4, 1) advancing 3 is followed by a run of (4, 1, 2, 3, 4).

The base sequences, both threaded and shedded, can be constant or mixed, overall or small scale, repeating or random. When both threading and lifting are extended to a point sequence the possible patterns are stunning.

When reversing a sequence, the skip can continue to follow the same method as above, or the threading/lifting can mirror the previous section.

NOTES

Sett: As for usual 2/2 twill.

Threads: Any, but fine silks especially, with warp and weft either close in color or of the same tonal value, show an added shimmer.

Selvedges: Either straight four-shaft entry, or use the pattern threading, doubling where necessary to maintain format. Use a floating selvedge.

In the one-directional woven samples shown, the sequences all start from shaft 4 but adhere to the same rules as above.

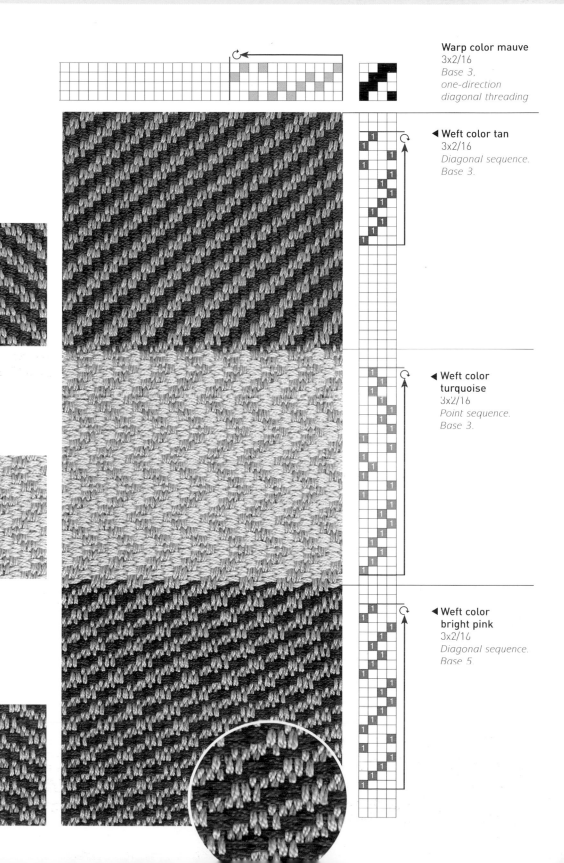

Warp color mauve
3x2/16
*Base 3,
one-direction
diagonal threading*

◀ **Weft color tan**
3x2/16
*Diagonal sequence.
Base 3.*

◀ **Weft color
turquoise**
3x2/16
*Point sequence.
Base 3.*

◀ **Weft color
bright pink**
3x2/16
*Diagonal sequence.
Base 5*

Advancing 2/2 Twill

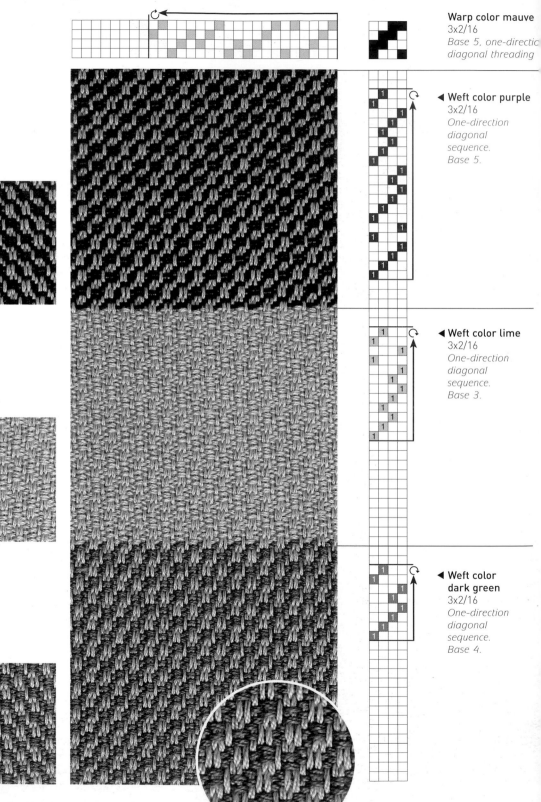

Warp color mauve
3x2/16
*Base 5, one-directic
diagonal threading*

◀ **Weft color purple**
3x2/16
*One-direction
diagonal
sequence.
Base 5.*

◀ **Weft color lime**
3x2/16
*One-direction
diagonal
sequence.
Base 3.*

◀ **Weft color
dark green**
3x2/16
*One-direction
diagonal
sequence.
Base 4.*

Advancing 2/2 Twill

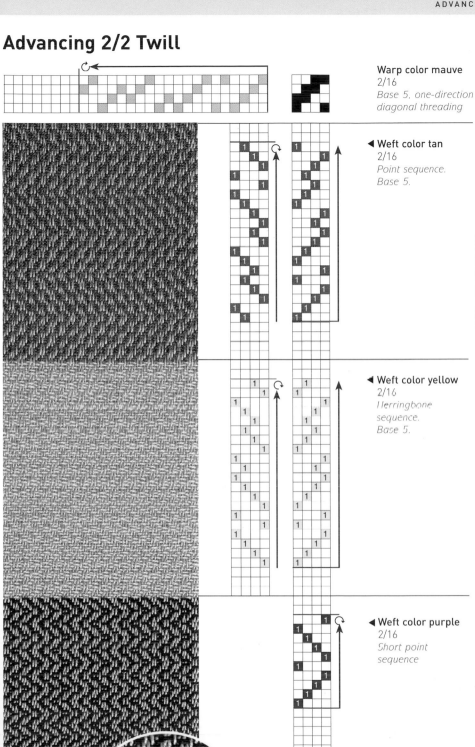

Warp color mauve
2/16
Base 5, one-direction diagonal threading

◀ **Weft color tan**
2/16
*Point sequence.
Base 5.*

◀ **Weft color yellow**
2/16
*Herringbone
sequence.
Base 5.*

◀ **Weft color purple**
2/16
*Short point
sequence*

Advancing 2/2 Twill

Warp color mauve
2/16
Base 3. Point threading sequence.

◀ Weft color bright pink
2/16
TAW. Base 3.

◀ Weft color purple
2/16
Picks in base 5

◀ Weft color pale turquoise
2/16
Picks in mixed bases 3 and 5

Advancing 2/2 Twill

Warp color mauve
2/16
*Base 4. Point
threading sequence.*

◀ **Weft color lime**
2/16
*Base 4. Point
sequence TAW.*

◀ **Weft color tan**
2/16
M and W sequence

x2

x2

◀ **Weft color
dark green**
2/16
*Mixed 5, 4, and
3 sequences*

Advancing 2/2 Twill

Warp color mauve
2/16
*Base 3. M & W
threading sequence.*

◀ **Weft color tan**
2/16
*Base 3, point
sequence*

◀ **Weft color lime**
2/16
*Border. Base 3,
point sequence.*

◀ **Weft color purple**
2/16
*Border. Base 3,
point sequence.*

Advancing 2/2 Twill

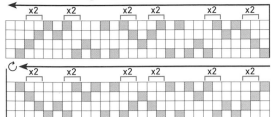

Warp color mauve
2/16
*Base 3. M & W
threading sequence
(same as page 212).*

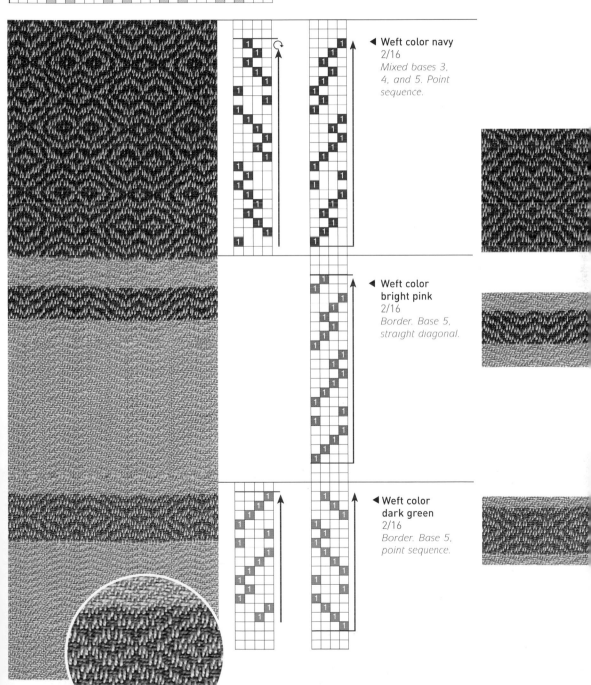

◀ **Weft color navy**
2/16
*Mixed bases 3,
4, and 5. Point
sequence.*

◀ **Weft color
bright pink**
2/16
*Border. Base 5,
straight diagonal.*

◀ **Weft color
dark green**
2/16
*Border. Base 5,
point sequence.*

Syncopated Threading

This threading can be thought of as a threading draft on opposites. The pattern looks far more textured than it actually is; it also appears more complicated than a usual four-shaft pattern.

The traditional method is to use alternate colors in the warp, but equally interesting patterns result from a single-color threading.

Any threading draft suitable for a 2/2 twill can be used, with each threading followed by its opposite:

1 followed by 3
2 followed by 4
3 followed by 1
4 followed by 2

When threaded using two alternating colors, the first pattern "leads" its opposite across the weaving.

Great care needs to be taken when threading as each group of four threads uses one heddle from each of the four shafts. It is easier to use alternating colors, which define the patterning. Alternating colors are also useful when designing, again defining the "lead" pattern, then, if wished, a single-color warp can be threaded using this draft.

The lifting sequence can be with or without the opposite shed; and with or without alternating the sheds with the other two pairs of shafts: (1, 3) & (2, 4). It is useful to use at least one of the colors in a two-color warp as a weft color. Experimentation can produce some interesting combinations.

NOTES

Tabby is not possible, but all six paired lifts can be used.

Threads: Any.

Sett: As for 2/2 twill.

Selvedges: Continue the pattern sequence to the edges, using the rules for selvedges on pages 16–17.

Warp colors mauve and dark green
All warp threads 3x2/16
Warp threaded in straight order with alternate syncopated ends, using two colors also in alternate order

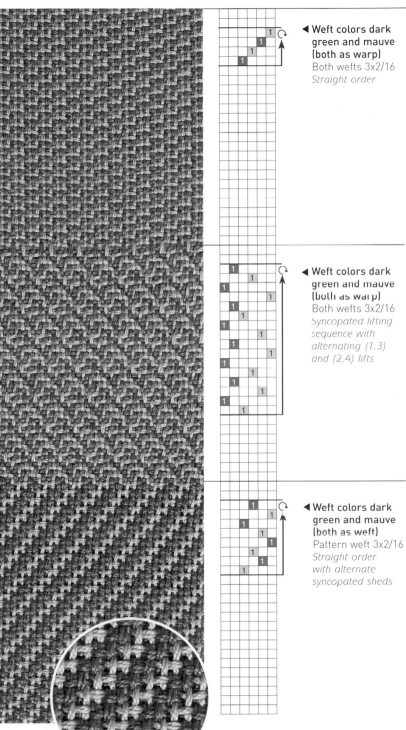

◀ **Weft colors dark green and mauve (both as warp)**
Both wefts 3x2/16
Straight order

◀ **Weft colors dark green and mauve (both as warp)**
Both wefts 3x2/16
Syncopated lifting sequence with alternating (1,3) and (2,4) lifts

◀ **Weft colors dark green and mauve (both as weft)**
Pattern weft 3x2/16
Straight order with alternate syncopated sheds

Syncopated Threading: Point

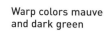

**Warp colors mauve
and dark green**
All warp threads 3x2/16
*Warp threaded in point
order with alternate
syncopated ends, using
two colors*

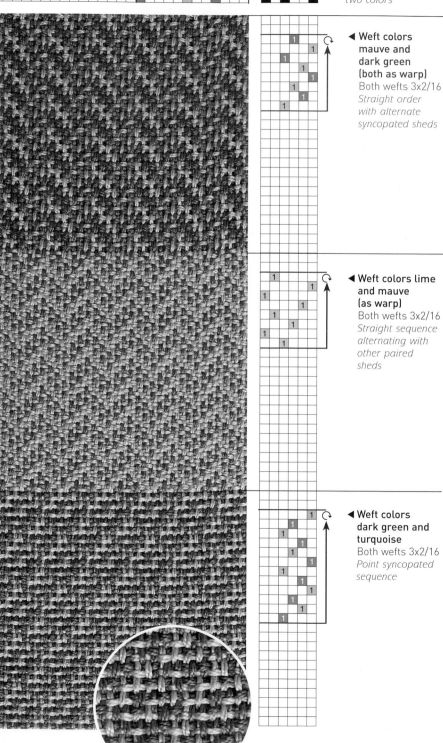

◀ **Weft colors
mauve and
dark green
(both as warp)**
Both wefts 3x2/16
*Straight order
with alternate
syncopated sheds*

◀ **Weft colors lime
and mauve
(as warp)**
Both wefts 3x2/16
*Straight sequence
alternating with
other paired
sheds*

◀ **Weft colors
dark green and
turquoise**
Both wefts 3x2/16
*Point syncopated
sequence*

Syncopated Threading: Rosepath

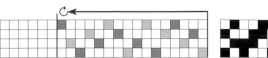

Warp color mauve
and dark green
All warp threads 3x2/16
*Warp threaded in Rosepath
order with alternate syncopated
ends, using two colors also in
alternate order*

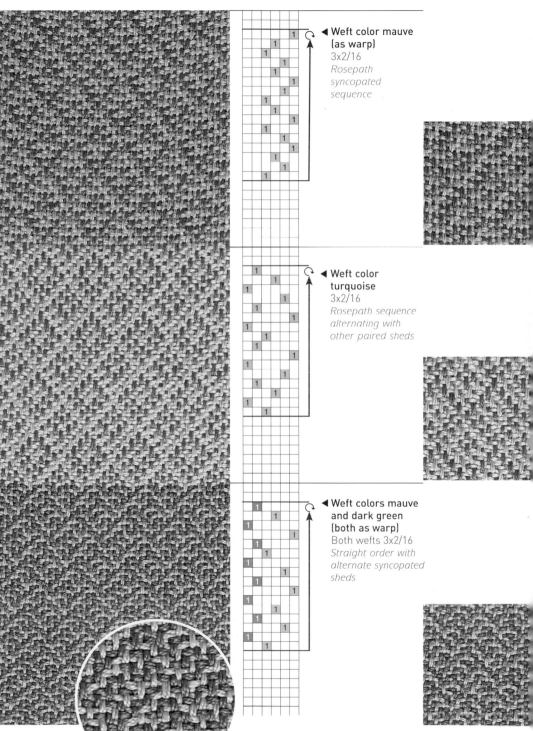

◀ **Weft color mauve
(as warp)**
3x2/16
*Rosepath
syncopated
sequence*

◀ **Weft color
turquoise**
3x2/16
*Rosepath sequence
alternating with
other paired sheds*

◀ **Weft colors mauve
and dark green
(both as warp)**
Both wefts 3x2/16
*Straight order with
alternate syncopated
sheds*

Syncopated Threading: Rosepath

Warp color mauve
3x2/16
Warp threaded in Rosepath order with alternate syncopated ends, as page 217, but in a single color

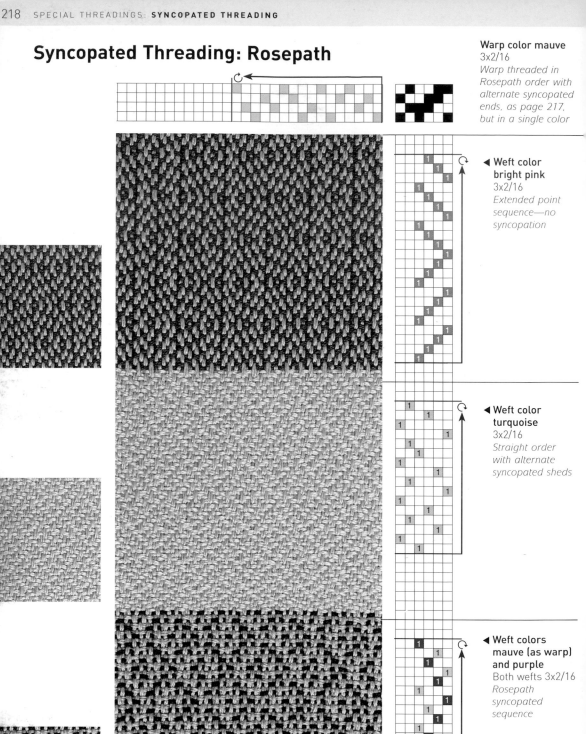

◀ **Weft color bright pink**
3x2/16
Extended point sequence—no syncopation

◀ **Weft color turquoise**
3x2/16
Straight order with alternate syncopated sheds

◀ **Weft colors mauve (as warp) and purple**
Both wefts 3x2/16
Rosepath syncopated sequence

Syncopated Threading: M and W

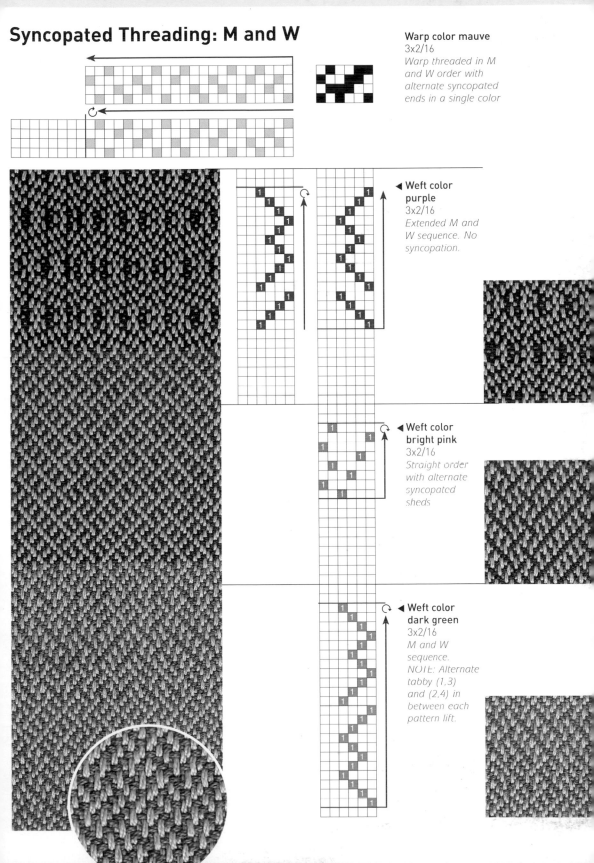

Warp color mauve
3x2/16
Warp threaded in M and W order with alternate syncopated ends in a single color

◄ **Weft color purple**
3x2/16
Extended M and W sequence. No syncopation.

◄ **Weft color bright pink**
3x2/16
Straight order with alternate syncopated sheds

◄ **Weft color dark green**
3x2/16
M and W sequence. NOTE: Alternate tabby (1,3) and (2,4) in between each pattern lift.

Threaded Monk's Belt

Also referred to as "turned Monk's Belt." The "turned" threading method is frequently used for overshot, but this requires six or more shafts. Monk's Belt can be "turned" or threaded using only four shafts. Even the simplest threading has several possibilities.

The usual pattern threads are in the warp, and the weft weaves as tabby, using just one shuttle, with different sections of the pattern threads remaining above or below the cloth for chosen intervals. The pattern threads thus act as a supplementary warp.

Traditional Monk's Belt needs to have the pattern threads tied down by the warp threads at sufficient intervals so that the weft floats do not become too long. Here the weaving sequence needs to have a change of sheds at intervals so that the warp floats do not become too long. In traditional Monk's Belt, the vertical lines can be as long as desired; here the horizontal lines can be as long as required.

Traditional Monk's Belt allows you to use the "linking" sheds with the pairs of adjacent shafts not used for the pattern. Instead of this, threaded Monk's Belt allows you to raise or lower all pattern threads together across the cloth. An advantage is that you can use just one shuttle.

The main drawback is that there are three times as many warp threads as normal—requiring extra time spent making the warp and threading the loom, as well as extra heddles. Another drawback is that if the woven length is long, then the tension of the pattern threads will gradually become looser. Either use a second back beam for warping the pattern threads, or, if your loom does not have two back-beams, wind on as one warp, weave a short length, raise all the pattern threads and insert a warp stick under these behind the shafts. Lower the pattern threads and push the warp stick right back to the farthest it can go just under the back beam. Hang heavy weights at intervals along this warp stick so that the tension of the pattern threads depends on the weighted warp stick. You will need to check the position of the weighted warp stick every time you wind forward.

If using two adjacent threads for the pattern, rather than a single thicker pattern thread, it is vital to thread these separately so that they lie smoothly and don't bunch together. This will require even more heddles. Make sure you have enough; if you need more, consider string or polyester heddles, which will not add to the weight on the shafts.

NOTES

Threads: Any, but remember that there will be more threads through the reed so smooth yarns work best.

Sett: The ground warp thread is sett at the normal tabby sett for the yarn, with the pattern warp ends as extras. This means that if you are using two adjacent threads together alternately with the ground thread, there will be three times as many ends through the reed as normal.

Selvedges: Make a narrow separate selvedge of 14 ends. Use two for the floating selvedge. It is important to remember that these ends will be sleyed as usual at twice the number per dent as the background threads (i.e., not including the pattern threads!).

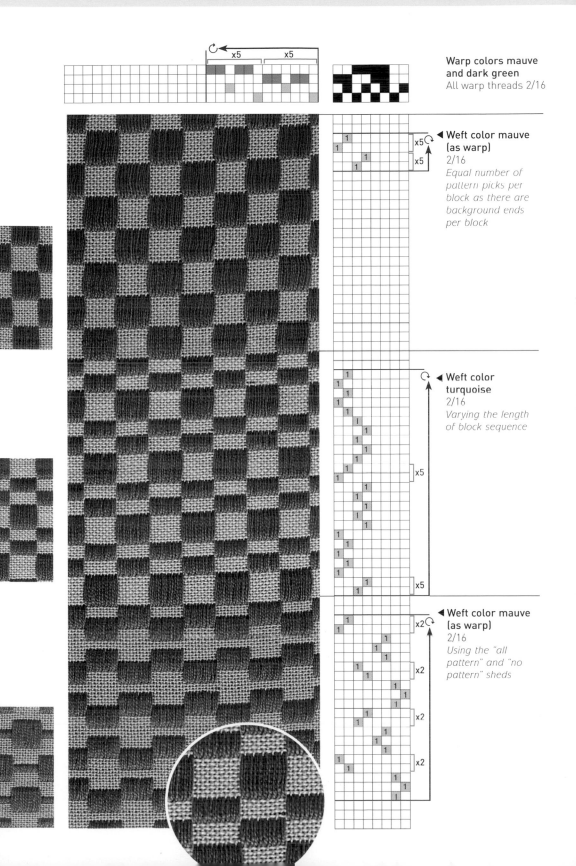

Warp colors mauve and dark green
All warp threads 2/16

◄ **Weft color mauve (as warp)**
2/16
Equal number of pattern picks per block as there are background ends per block

◄ **Weft color turquoise**
2/16
Varying the length of block sequence

◄ **Weft color mauve (as warp)**
2/16
Using the "all pattern" and "no pattern" sheds

Threaded Monk's Belt

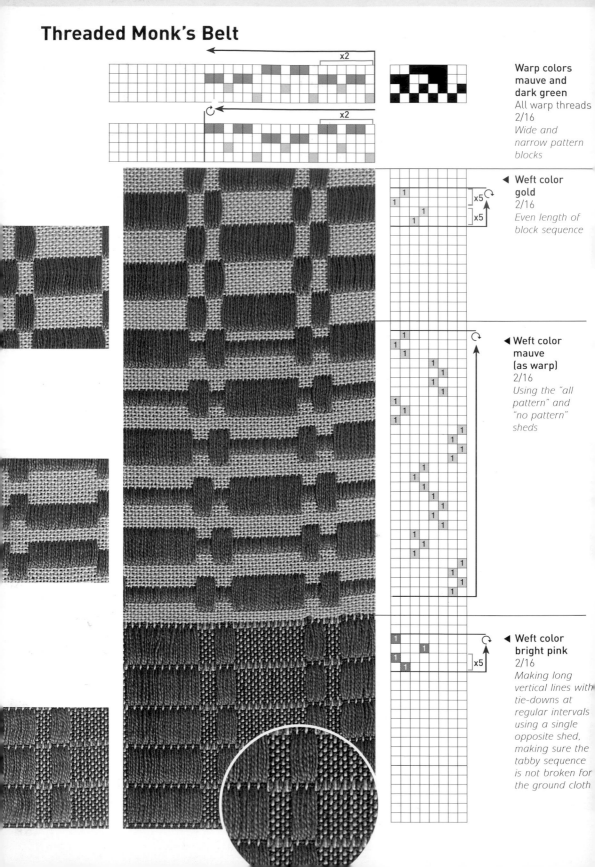

Warp colors mauve and dark green
All warp threads 2/16
Wide and narrow pattern blocks

◀ **Weft color gold**
2/16
Even length of block sequence

◀ **Weft color mauve (as warp)**
2/16
Using the "all pattern" and "no pattern" sheds

◀ **Weft color bright pink**
2/16
Making long vertical lines with tie-downs at regular intervals using a single opposite shed, making sure the tabby sequence is not broken for the ground cloth

Threaded Monk's Belt

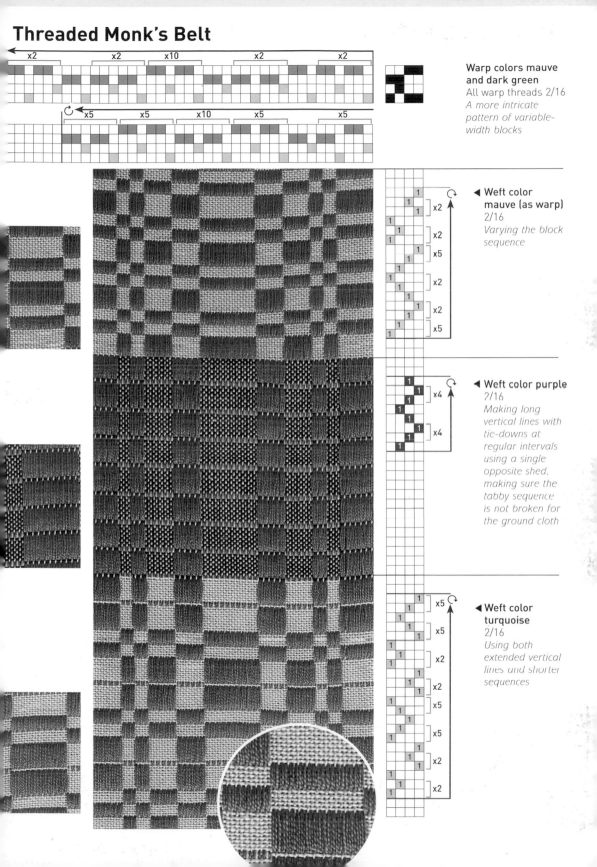

Warp colors mauve and dark green
All warp threads 2/16
A more intricate pattern of variable-width blocks

◄ **Weft color mauve (as warp)** 2/16
Varying the block sequence

◄ **Weft color purple** 2/16
Making long vertical lines with tie-downs at regular intervals using a single opposite shed, making sure the tabby sequence is not broken for the ground cloth

◄ **Weft color turquoise** 2/16
Using both extended vertical lines and shorter sequences

Distorted Weft

For a distorted weft, when using four shafts, the ground fabric is tabby on shafts 1 and 2, leaving shafts 3 and 4 free to carry extra threads that can float above or below the surface. If these extra threads are raised alternately then a pattern weft, thrown between the raised shafts on 3 and 4, will distort into waves or lozenges. The ends on shafts 3 and 4 can be single, double, or several in sequence between the ground fabric. These ends can either be woven to intersect with the ground fabric when not raised during weaving, or be left below when not required.

   If the number of tabby picks between the pattern wefts is not too great, then the distorted wefts can slide together to create lozenges when the waves are created in the opposite directions.

   NOTE: If a long piece of cloth is to be woven, then the distort pattern ends should be beamed separately because there will be less take-up due to the fewer intersections. If your loom does not have two warp beams, then beam normally and when the work has progressed a little way a warp stick can be inserted behind the shafts with the distort pattern ends above. The stick is then moved to the back beam and hanging weights added at intervals along the stick to tension this part of the warp separately from the rest. Alternatively each distort pattern warp end can be weighted separately without the need for the warp stick. (See also Supplementary Warp Ends, pages 226–227.)

   NOTE: "Ground weave/cloth" is specified because with more than four shafts the ground can be any type as long as it leaves enough spare shafts to carry the interlacing ends that control the distorted weft.

NOTES

Threads: Any can be used. The distorted weft is really impressive if worked in a fabulous textured yarn. It also enables the weaver to show such a yarn to its full advantage as almost all of it is above the surface.

Sett: Normal tabby sett.

Selvedges: Normal for the ground cloth. Use a floating selvedge— this is essential for catching the distorted weft correctly.

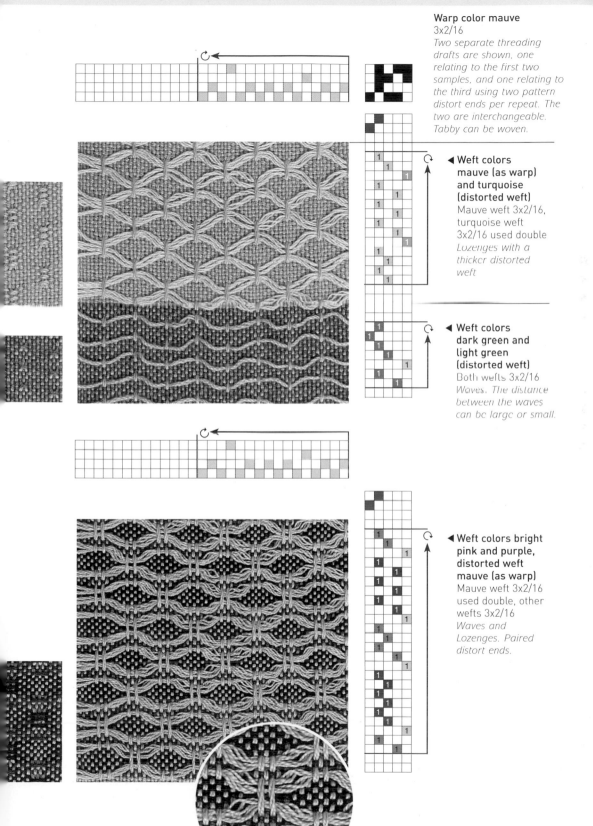

Warp color mauve
3x2/16
Two separate threading drafts are shown, one relating to the first two samples, and one relating to the third using two pattern distort ends per repeat. The two are interchangeable. Tabby can be woven.

◄ **Weft colors mauve (as warp) and turquoise (distorted weft)**
Mauve weft 3x2/16, turquoise weft 3x2/16 used double
Lozenges with a thicker distorted weft

◄ **Weft colors dark green and light green (distorted weft)**
Both wefts 3x2/16
Waves. The distance between the waves can be large or small.

◄ **Weft colors bright pink and purple, distorted weft mauve (as warp)**
Mauve weft 3x2/16 used double, other wefts 3x2/16
Waves and Lozenges. Paired distort ends.

Supplementary Warp Ends

Supplementary warps are additional warp ends added into an existing warp, but not necessarily needed for the basic weave structure. They can be placed in the threading from the start or during weaving. They are usually tensioned separately with the use of a second beam or weighted separately in some other way.

One way of weighting separately has been described on pages 220 and 224. Another is to have the supplementary warp ends weighted individually. A small container is filled with weighting material; the length of the supplementary warp is attached to it, and then hung over the back of the loom.

The easiest method is to first warp the ground warp on the loom as usual without the supplementary ends. Make the supplementary ends separately and then insert into position within the warp as required. It will be necessary to leave empty heddles at the correct points for this when threading the ground warp. The extra warp ends can be tied to the front beam if used from the start, or each wound around a pin. The pin is inserted into the woven fabric, some way back along the weaving, at the required point within the width. With the weight supported, the extra end is threaded through the heddles and reed, and then wound around the pin two or three times. Then the weight is hung over the back of the loom to tension. The weight inside the container can be adjusted to suit the particular weave—some require a light weight; others a very heavy weight to tension the supplementary ends to at least the same tension as the ground warp. Weaves such as pique require a well-weighted end; others, such as "scribbling" (see opposite), require only a light weight. Holding ends of a different color can be used.

The weft-distorted technique can be used with the distort pattern end passing under the cloth when not above to hold the distorted weft.

The cloth can be automatically prepared for pleating—so much easier than doing counted-thread work. The supplementary ends work together over and then under the cloth at set intervals. The cloth is pleated off the loom by pulling the supplementary ends, and can be used for shibori dyeing. The pleats can be regular or random. If the supplementary ends are set much closer together and strongly tensioned, then a pique cloth can be woven, which distorts off the loom. In this case the pleating threads can work in opposition.

NOTES

Threads: Any. If different types of yarn are used for supplementary and ground warp, be aware of any shrinkage differences when washing. (Differences can also be used to advantage.)

Sett: The supplementary ends have very little impact upon the sett, so whatever is normal for the ground cloth.

Selvedges: A normal threaded selvedge. Use a floating selvedge.

NOTE: If starting a pattern weft in the main part of the cloth rather than at the selvedge, pass the thread around a warp end that is to be used and then work double for one or two rows—this will anchor it firmly. If the thread is to be used double throughout, then pass it around the warp end almost at the center. Then if the thread proves to be too short, the joins will occur at different places.

Warp color mauve, supplementary ends purple, lime, or dark green as shown
All warp threads 3x2/16, except purple used double
Straight entry threading. For tabby ground with supplementary ends below.

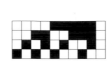

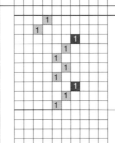

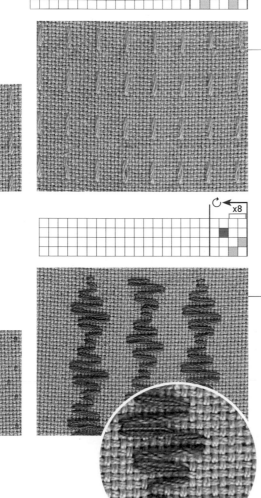

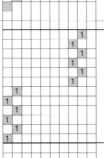

◄ **Weft color mauve, distorted weft purple (both as warp)**
Weft 3x2/16, distort weft 3x2/16 used double
Distorted weft, but the supplementary end only shows above the cloth when holding the weft

For tabby ground with supplementary ends below

◄ **Weft color mauve (as warp)**
3x2/16
Preparation for pleating—so much easier than counted thread work

For tabby ground with supplementary ends below

◄ **Weft color mauve (as warp)**
3x2/16
Scribbling. When "scribbling end" is above cloth, position by hand into required place so that next pick weaves over it.

Waffle Variations

Waffle produces textured fabric, resembling the ridged outlines of small square pockets of the waffle. Traditional waffle is worked on a six-thread point draft: 2, 3, 4, 3, 2, 1. However, by extending the center portion of threading (on 1 and 2), an extended sunken pocket can be produced.

The number of threads used for the ridged outline and the number of threads used in the small squares can be varied, but both ridges and squares always use an odd number in their sequence.

It is usual to thread the ridges on shafts 3 and 4 as there are normally fewer threads than for the square pockets, which are threaded on 1 and 2.

The color can be the same throughout, or the ridges can be in a different (usually lighter) color in both warp and weft. A deeper color or shade in the pockets further deepens the visual appearance.

The ridge is usually threaded (3, 4, 3), but can be extended to (3, 4, 3, 4, 3) but rarely more. The end on shaft 4 only intersects twice within each sequence with the weft picks (once under and then raised for the rest of the sequence). The end on shaft 3 intersects six times.

The small pockets are threaded (2, 1, 2, 1, 2), or (2, 1, 2), or (2, 1, 2, 1, 2, 1, 2).

In the samples the threading is (3, 4, 3, / 2, 1, 2, 1, 2, 1, 2). The weaving sequence mirrors the warp. Sometimes it is necessary to insert two extra picks within the pocket section in order to "square-up" the pocket.

The samples are shown with the number of ends and picks used, but the * and ** show where these can be adjusted to suit.

If wool is used, together with a fairly loose sett, then the take-up in both warp and weft can be about 25 percent. It is necessary to wash the fabric for the full amount of reduction to occur. (See Finishings, page 247.)

Apart from waffle, it is not possible to weave in many other ways using the same draft—and the take-up will be very different. The central sample shows a small warp float sequence using shafts 3 and 4. The lower sample uses only shaft 4 as the long float.

NOTES

Threads: Any, but wool gives the greatest texture. Soft cotton and linen is great for towels. Acrylic and similar are easily washable and good for baby blankets. The ridges can be in a thicker thread than the pockets.

Sett: Normal tabby or looser.

Selvedges: A straight draft and a floating selvedge must be used.

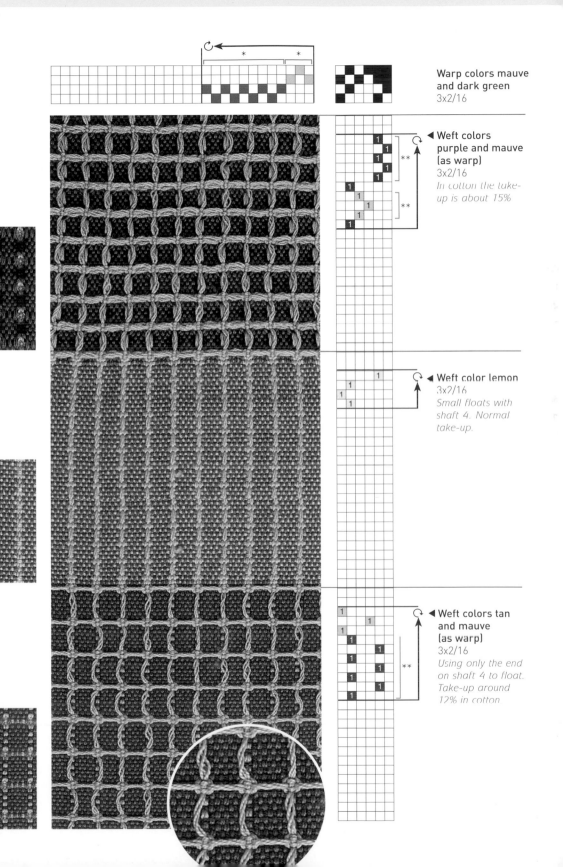

Warp colors mauve
and dark green
3x2/16

◀ Weft colors
purple and mauve
(as warp)
3x2/16
*In cotton the take-
up is about 15%*

◀ Weft color lemon
3x2/16
*Small floats with
shaft 4. Normal
take-up.*

◀ Weft colors tan
and mauve
(as warp)
3x2/16
*Using only the end
on shaft 4 to float.
Take-up around
12% in cotton*

Warp Face

Warp face is the opposite of weft face. As the name suggests, only the warp shows on the surface. The weft, which is completely covered, remains straight in the pick, rather than intersecting with the warp ends. The warp ends curve above and below the straight weft and so the take-up is considerably more than with a balanced weave. Any patterns have to be threaded in the warp. Various color patterns can be threaded.

The patterns on the opposite page show three of the possibilities using color patterning. The center sample shows how to raise alternate (dark) ends to create a visual one-color block. The lower sample shows how to create a dark-dominant block using alternate thick and thin weft threads. This is also known as Rep Weave.

Rep, Ripsmatta, Matta, Warp Rib—these are all alternative names for the same weave structure. If the warp is threaded with alternate colors and woven with alternate thick and thin wefts, then the fabric will have one color dominant on one side and the other color on the reverse.

Threading the two colors in a block of color A, color B repeat, and then a block of B, A repeat can exchange the dominant colors across the width.

Two successive thick picks will change the dominant color lengthwise. (Two successive thin picks will also change the order but are not quite so clean cut.) Interchanging blocks can be woven on just two shafts. If the threading is extended to four shafts however (by altering both the color sequence of the blocks on 1 and 2, and 3 and 4, and also by using the four pairs, rather than two, of possible picks: (1, 3); (2, 4); (1, 4); (2, 3), then there is a much larger range of possibilities.

NOTES

Threads: Any.

Sett: About three times as close as a normal tabby.

Selvedges: No special selvedge. With two shafts there is no need for a floating selvedge; with four shafts it will be necessary.

NOTE 1: When weaving with both thick and thin weft threads, the thin weft can be inserted into each pick. The thick weft will make small loops along the two sides alternately. If a doubled weft is used for the thick weft, this can be inserted as a double thread in the usual way, making alternating thick loops at the selvedges. Alternatively, place a length of (thick) yarn as a single thread centrally into the first pick, then weave this from both directions across the warp in subsequent thick picks (thus doubling the thread); this makes thinner loops along both selvedges.

NOTE 2: Keep weft under tension when beating, and tug gently to release the buckling at the edges before inserting the next pick.

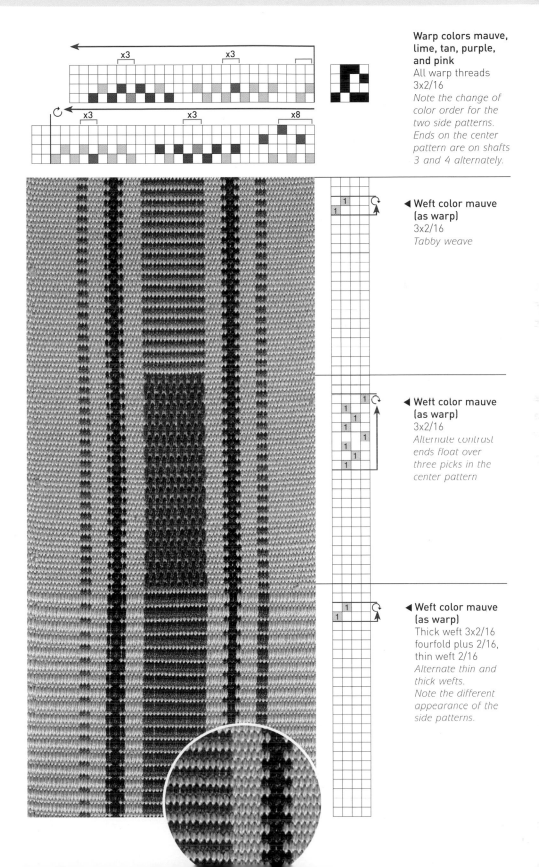

Warp colors mauve, lime, tan, purple, and pink
All warp threads 3x2/16
Note the change of color order for the two side patterns. Ends on the center pattern are on shafts 3 and 4 alternately.

◄ **Weft color mauve (as warp)**
3x2/16
Tabby weave

◄ **Weft color mauve (as warp)**
3x2/16
Alternate contrast ends float over three picks in the center pattern

◄ **Weft color mauve (as warp)**
Thick weft 3x2/16 fourfold plus 2/16, thin weft 2/16
Alternate thin and thick wefts.
Note the different appearance of the side patterns.

Warp Face: Rep; Two Color

Warp colors navy and mauve
2/16
Warp colors threaded alternately. Blocks using four shafts.

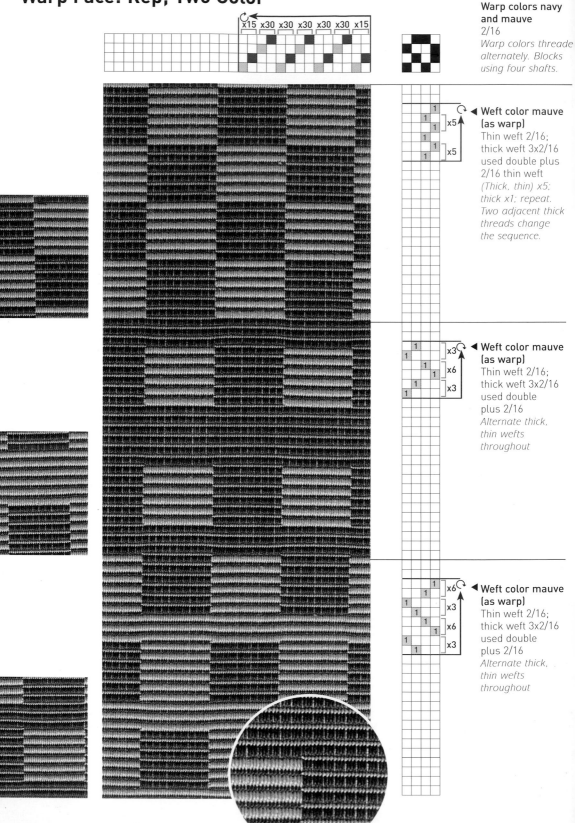

◄ Weft color mauve (as warp)
Thin weft 2/16; thick weft 3x2/16 used double plus 2/16 thin weft
(Thick, thin) x5; thick x1; repeat. Two adjacent thick threads change the sequence.

◄ Weft color mauve (as warp)
Thin weft 2/16; thick weft 3x2/16 used double plus 2/16
Alternate thick, thin wefts throughout

◄ Weft color mauve (as warp)
Thin weft 2/16; thick weft 3x2/16 used double plus 2/16
Alternate thick, thin wefts throughout

Warp Face: Rep; Two Color

x15 x15 x15 x15 x15 x15

Warp colors mauve
and navy
2/16
*Warp colors changing
sequence as well as
blocks*

◀ Weft color mauve
(as warp)
Thin weft 2/16;
thick weft 3x2/16
used double
plus 2/16
*Alternate thick, thin
wefts throughout*

◀ Weft color mauve
(as warp)
Thin weft 2/16;
thick weft 3x2/16
used double
plus 2/16
*Thick, thin (x3, x2,
x2), thick (x1), thick,
thin (x3, x2, x2),
thick (x1).
Note where the
order of thick and
thin changes*

◀ Weft color mauve
(as warp)
Thin weft 2/16;
thick weft 3x2/16
used double
plus 2/16
*Alternate thick, thin
wefts throughout*

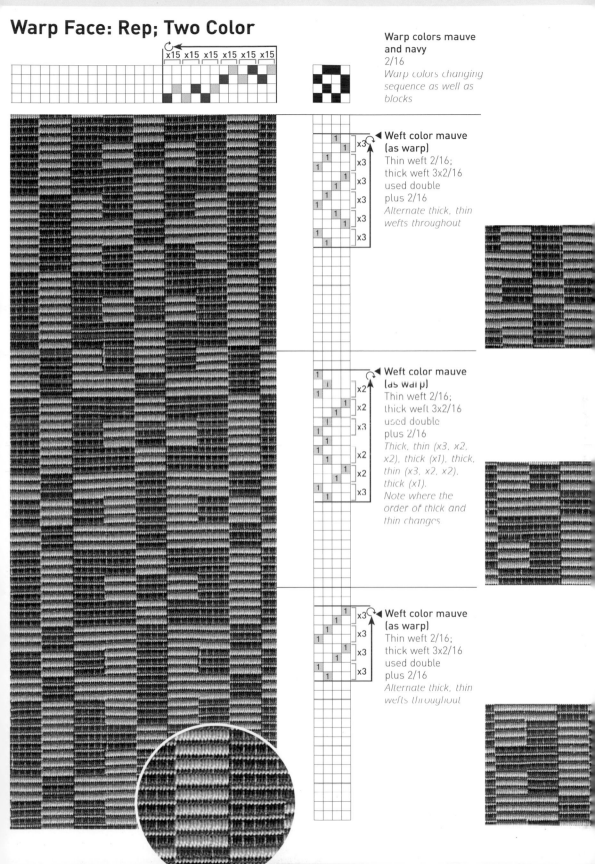

Warp Face: Rep; Two Color

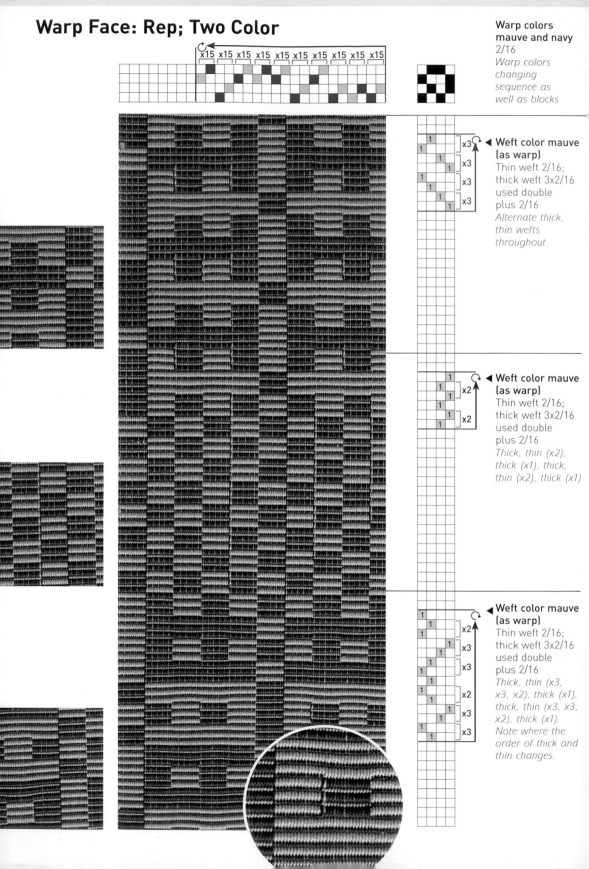

Warp colors
mauve and navy
2/16
*Warp colors
changing
sequence as
well as blocks*

◄ Weft color mauve
(as warp)
Thin weft 2/16;
thick weft 3x2/16
used double
plus 2/16
*Alternate thick,
thin wefts
throughout*

◄ Weft color mauve
(as warp)
Thin weft 2/16;
thick weft 3x2/16
used double
plus 2/16
*Thick, thin (x2),
thick (x1), thick,
thin (x2), thick (x1)*

◄ Weft color mauve
(as warp)
Thin weft 2/16;
thick weft 3x2/16
used double
plus 2/16
*Thick, thin (x3,
x3, x2), thick (x1),
thick, thin (x3, x3,
x2), thick (x1).
Note where the
order of thick and
thin changes.*

x15 x15 x15 x15 x15 x15 x15 x15 x15 x15

Warp Face: Rep; Three Color

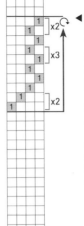

Warp colors navy, mauve, and tan 2/16
Far more possibilities. More suitable for large-scale work.

◄ **Warp color mauve (as warp)**
Thin weft 2/16; thick weft 3x2/16 used double plus 2/16
Thick, thin (x2), thick, thin, thick (x1), thick, thin (x3), thick (x1), thick, thin (x2). Note where the order of thick and thin changes.

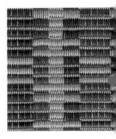

◄ **Warp color mauve (as warp)**
Thin weft 2/16; thick weft 3x2/16 used double plus 2/16
Thick, thin (x2), thick, thin, thick (x1), thick, thin (x3), thick (x1), thick, thin (x2). Note where the order of thick and thin changes.

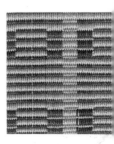

◄ **Warp color mauve (as warp)**
Thin weft 2/16; thick weft 3x2/16 used double plus 2/16
Alternate thick, thin wefts throughout

Weft Face

Weft face is the opposite of warp face, with the weft entirely dominating and covering the warp. The warp is kept under strong tension throughout, with the weft curving over and under the completely straight warp. The weft needs to be inserted with plenty of slack otherwise the edges of the piece will be pulled inward. On wider pieces a series of waves is created with the weft across the width by inserting at an angle and then pulling the thread downwards at frequent intervals. This can be done in the open shed or on a closed shed—but not the next shed. Hold the weft thread loosely and make the waves starting from the woven side and working toward the shuttle. Beat this weft into place, then open the next shed and beat hard, before inserting the next pick.

If the piece is very wide then a temple or stretcher, moved along frequently, will keep the width constant. For fine work and tapestry, a small beater or fork can be used for each narrow section.

Weft-face weaving is used extensively for tapestry weaving. It can be used for floor rugs with heavy-duty yarns, with medium yarn for bags, cushion covers, and tablemats, and finer yarns for tapestry.

NOTE: Always overlap or splice weft joins within the width rather than at the edges, as this will ensure that the edges are kept stable. Overlap old and new weft for only two or three ends. Stitch in the loose threads downwards within the weft threads—this can be done on the loom after a few more picks have been woven.

Various threading drafts can be employed. The most comprehensive book on the subject is Peter Collingwood's *The Techniques of Rug Weaving*. There are also many excellent manuals that deal specifically with tapestry weaving.

The three samples shown opposite are all on a straight four-shaft entry, which gives some idea of the range of possibilities.

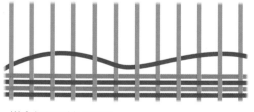

Weft inserted in waves

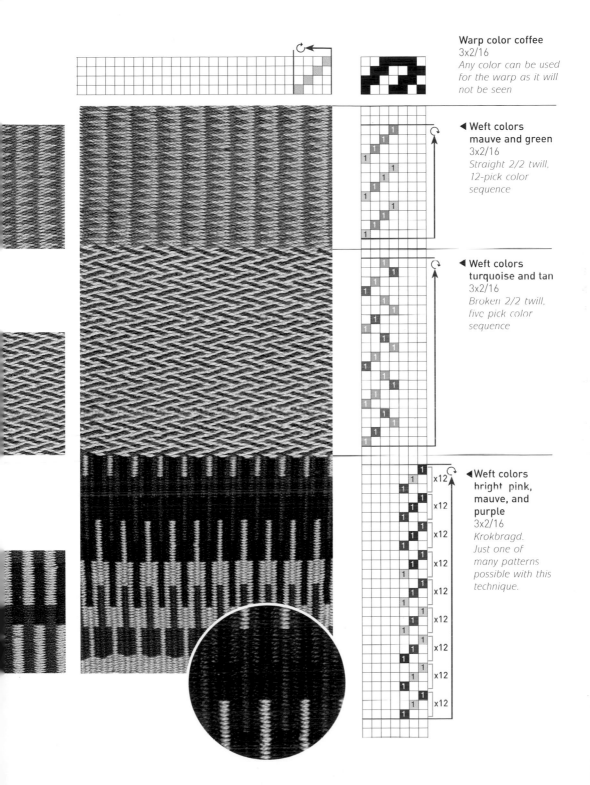

Warp color coffee
3x2/16
*Any color can be used
for the warp as it will
not be seen*

◀ **Weft colors
mauve and green**
3x2/16
*Straight 2/2 twill,
12-pick color
sequence*

◀ **Weft colors
turquoise and tan**
3x2/16
*Broken 2/2 twill,
five pick color
sequence*

◀ **Weft colors
bright pink,
mauve, and
purple**
3x2/16
*Krokbragd.
Just one of
many patterns
possible with this
technique.*

Twining, Loops, and Soumak

Warp color mauve
Warp and background weft 3x2/16
Straight diagonal threading draft

◀ **Twining,** all worked on a closed shed.
[i] Three color, worked from right; over 2 and under 4 in color rotation. Twining threads—all 3x2/16 (single).

[ii] Single color, worked from left, around four ends, reversing twist at center. Twining threads—both 3x2/16 used double.

[iii] Two-color Maori adaptation. Twined around same two ends each row. Color not on surface pulled to back after each twist. Twining angle reversed at center. Twining threads—both 3x2/16 (single).

[iv] Three-color Maori adaptation. Twined around two ends, but move to different pairing for each successive row, same angle throughout. Color not on surface pulled to back after each twist. Twining threads—all 3x2/16 (single).

◀ **Loops,** all worked on an open shed. Use a rod or knitting needle to hold the separate looping thread.
[i] Pulled loops, between every raised end on alternate sheds. Two rows looping thread 3x2/16 (single).

[ii] Wrapped loops between pair of ends; the looping thread wraps around the previous end after the loop is made (use a netting shuttle!); two picks tabby between; second looping row worked between alternate pairs. Looping thread 3x2/16 used double.

[iii] Deep pulled loops at intervals, after a number of tabby picks subsequent rows vertically chained through the previous loops. Looping thread 3x2/16 (single).

◀ **Soumak,** diagonal, all worked on an open shed, all from left each worked over 4 and back under 2 after every 0, 2, 4, 6, 8 tabby picks between.
Soumak threads all 3x2/16 used double.

Inlay

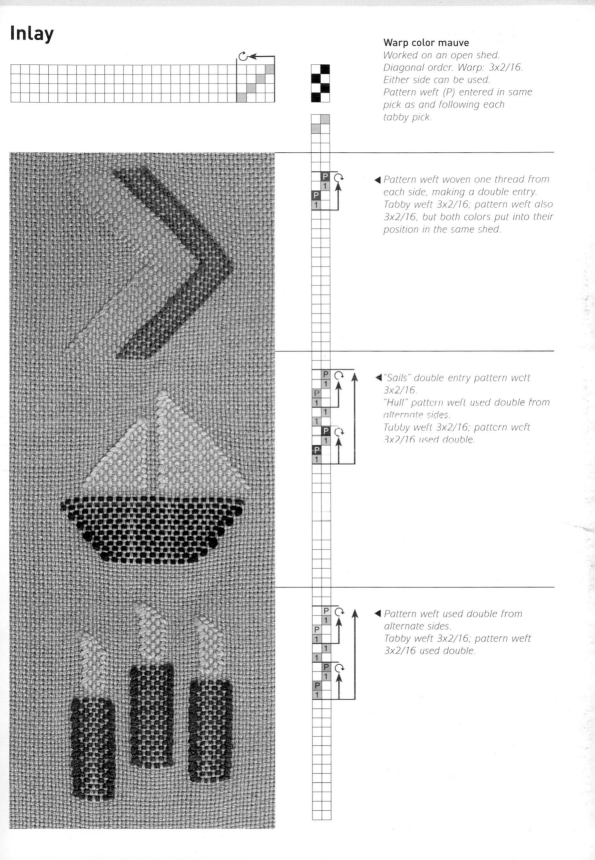

Warp color mauve
Worked on an open shed.
Diagonal order. Warp: 3x2/16.
Either side can be used.
Pattern weft (P) entered in same
pick as and following each
tabby pick.

◀ *Pattern weft woven one thread from*
each side, making a double entry.
Tabby weft 3x2/16; pattern weft also
3x2/16, but both colors put into their
position in the same shed.

◀ *"Sails" double entry pattern weft*
3x2/16.
"Hull" pattern weft used double from
alternate sides.
Tabby weft 3x2/16; pattern weft
3x2/16 used double.

◀ *Pattern weft used double from*
alternate sides.
Tabby weft 3x2/16; pattern weft
3x2/16 used double.

Brocade

Warp color mauve
*Straight entry. Warp: 3x2/16.
Worked from back of fabric.
Pattern weft (P) inserted
on closed shed after every
alternate tabby pick.
Long floats are avoided
by use of tie-down ends.*

◀ *Point diagonal
motifs with tie-
downs for wider
pattern.
Tabby weft
3x2/16; pattern
weft 3x2/16 used
double. Both
colors put into
position at the
same time.*

◀ *Self-color motif,
worked in
separate areas to
avoid long floats.
Tabby weft
3x2/16; pattern
weft 3x2/16 used
double.*

◀ **Weft color
turquoise**
*Single-color motif
worked as one.
Tabby weft
3x2/16; pattern
weft 3x2/16 used
double.*

Dukagang

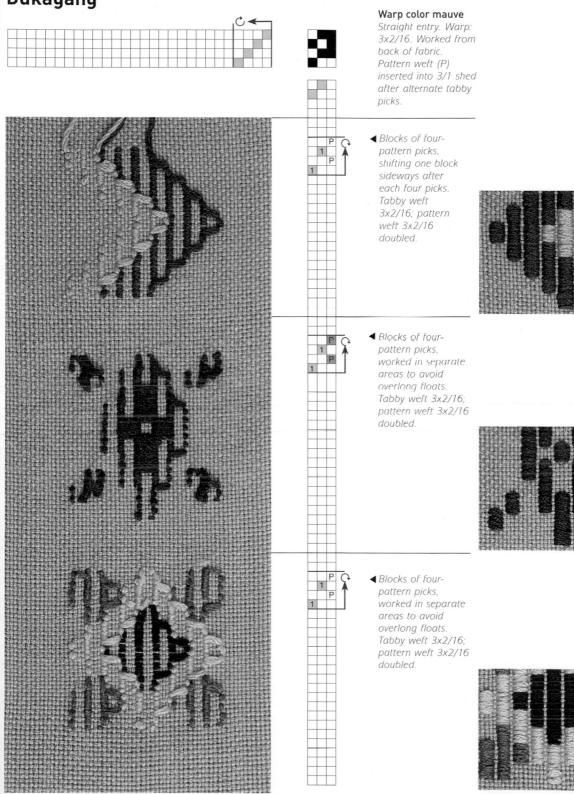

Warp color mauve
Straight entry. Warp: 3x2/16. Worked from back of fabric. Pattern weft (P) inserted into 3/1 shed after alternate tabby picks.

◄ *Blocks of four-pattern picks, shifting one block sideways after each four picks. Tabby weft 3x2/16; pattern weft 3x2/16 doubled.*

◄ *Blocks of four-pattern picks, worked in separate areas to avoid overlong floats. Tabby weft 3x2/16; pattern weft 3x2/16 doubled.*

◄ *Blocks of four-pattern picks, worked in separate areas to avoid overlong floats. Tabby weft 3x2/16; pattern weft 3x2/16 doubled.*

Finishing Your Piece

Once you've woven your piece, there are several things you'll need to do to secure and finish it. You may also choose to enhance an item by adding embellishments.

You'll need to secure the start and end of the piece, so that it does not ravel when taken from the loom. You must also check the structure for loose ends—or "tails"—of yarn. Additionally, you may want to decorate your piece using techniques such as hemstitching, adding fringes, and whipping. Consider all of this during the design stage, so that you can add extra warp length if necessary and work any techniques that must be carried out on the loom, at the right time.

Preparation Against Raveling

All weaving needs to include a woven "heading" before and after the rest of the piece. The depth of this depends upon the type of edging you are planning to add. If you are not going to use any decorative finishing techniques, weave a fairly deep heading, which can have a hem lightly turned and tacked to protect it during wet finishing (see page 247). Deep headings are used for finishing cloth lengths that are to be cut for garments.

If you are planning on adding a decorative edge, you don't need to weave such a deep heading at the start and end of the item, as this will only remain in place until you start work on the edging.

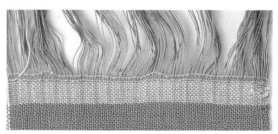

Heading at end of piece

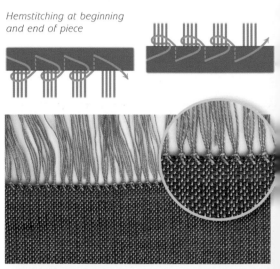

Hemstitching at beginning and end of piece

Hemstitching using warp color

Preparation for Edgings

You can either do this while the cloth is on the loom or once it has been taken off, but you must do it before any wet finishing. It is useful to use same thread as the weft, so that any shrinkage during wet finishing will be of the same amount.

Hemstitching

At the start of weaving, after weaving the heading, weave about ¼ inch (6 mm) in very smooth yarn of a contrasting color and with a separate weft length for each pick. Start to weave the cloth a little way. Before winding on, draw out the smooth auxiliary weft threads, one at a time, and then hemstitch upward into the woven cloth. If the hemstitching is to be permanent, use the same color as the warp or weft, unless you wish it to be a color decoration. You can leave a weft length of about four times the width of the cloth at the start to work the hemstitching.

Hemstitching using weft color

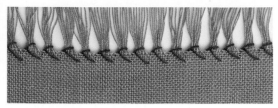

At the end of weaving, hemstitch downward into the cloth when the final pick has been woven. Weave a heading to stabilize the work before cutting it off the loom. If the hemstitching is to be removed later (see Fringes, page 245), use a contrasting smooth yarn. If you are weaving a series of items (scarves, perhaps), you can do the hemstitching at the start and end of each piece, weaving a short heading before and after each and leaving sufficient unwoven warp between the pieces for any fringing required.

Cutting mark between fringe lengths

When weaving pieces that all need to be fringed, weave a small section at the middle of the two fringe lengths, with three separate smooth and contrasting weft lengths at the center. When you remove the pieces from the loom, pull out these three weft threads and cut along the space. You can leave hemstitching until you remove the weaving from the loom. To do this you will need to weave about ¼ inch (6 mm) in smooth yarn and

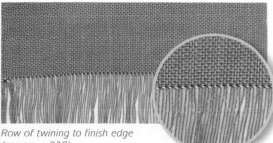

Row of twining to finish edge (see page 238)

with a separate weft length for each pick just before the final heading—the reverse of the hemstitching you did at the start.

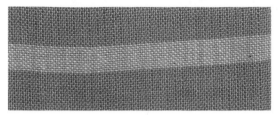

Separate weft threads (yellow) to draw out

Twining
You can secure the edge of the weaving by working a row of fine twining just after the initial heading and just before the final heading.

Preparation for Drawn Threads
Insert enough very smooth and separate weft threads in subsequent picks to fill the space required. It is best to do the hemstitching while on the loom. The hemstitching can be a decorative horizontal section within the cloth, or you can use it as a guide for hemming (see Hemming, next page). It can be worked with the same groups of threads or staggered.

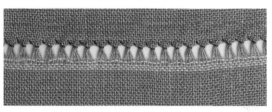

One row of hemstitching, other threads to be drawn out

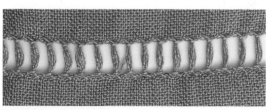

Ladder hemstitching

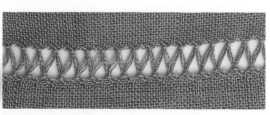

Staggered hemstitching

Preparation for Hemming

Place one pick of fine, smooth yarn of a contrasting color in the pick with the normal weft to act as a guide for turning hems. Remove the contrast yarn after pressing and tacking the hem into place.

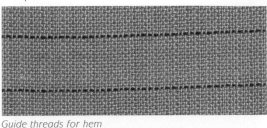

Guide threads for hem

Hem tacked into position

Guide thread removed

Completed hem

Instead of temporarily marking the hemline, you can insert a decorative permanent marker, such as a row of one- or two-color twining, or a row of soumak. Off loom, you can hemstitch down the end of the weaving using a drawn-thread band.

Hem with twined edge

Hem with soumak edging

Preparation for Smocking

Place separate picks of fine, smooth yarn at regular intervals in the cloth. (This is far more accurate than sewing!) Insert the smocking yarn on a closed shed, unless there are suitable small groups of thread at the required distance that you can use. Pick up 3–5 ends at each point. The picked-up threads must be the same each time. Make large, firm knots in the smocking weft at each end, because they will need to remain in the cloth until it is laundered.

Marking for Fringe Bundles

This is easiest to see while the warp is taut on the loom. Work as for the preparation for edges at both the start and finish of the piece, but work the hemstitching loosely and in a bold contrasting color. Work the hemstitching around the correct number of threads for each braid or twisted cords, and oversew the ends loosely. When you have removed the weaving from the loom make the cords or braids and then carefully remove the hemstitching thread—this need not be taken out in one piece.

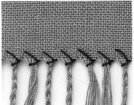

Twisted fringe during construction

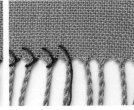

Hemstitch thread partly removed

Mending (or Burling)

Work with the cloth on a table, not bunched in your hand. Darn lengths of warp ends for broken ends into the fabric in the correct sequence. Trim the weft joins closely to the fabric if this has not been done during weaving. Check the reverse of the cloth to ensure that the structure is correct.

Pick out and correct any faults: insert a weft thread into the correct path, overlapping at the fault edge. It is sometimes possible to move variations in beat carefully with a bodkin.

Securing the Headings

If the cloth is to be cut for use as clothing, then machine-stitch a zigzag row along the edges of the heading. Alternatively tack a single-turn hem.

Loose Fringe

If you have secured the edges of the cloth properly, you can leave the warp ends as a loose fringe. You can cut the edges of the fringe straight or shape them.

Knotted Fringe

This can be temporary or permanent.

Temporary Loosely tie small bundles of warp threads, starting at each side, then at the middle, and then in between. Take the loose knot up to the cloth. Not all bundles need to be tied, just enough to hold the weft in place.

Permanent The best practice is to mark for the fringe bundles on the loom, although it can be done off loom. Again start at each of the sides, and then the middle, using a predetermined

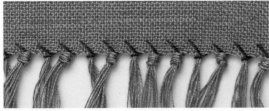
Initial knotting in progress

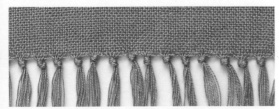
Single row of knotting

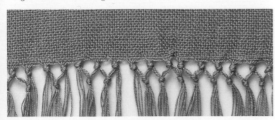
Second row of trellis in progress

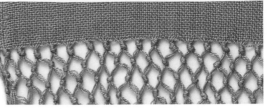
Completed trellis

number of threads for each bundle. First tie all the knots loosely and then work again, taking each knot firmly up to the cloth. An extension of this is to work more rows of knots, taking half from each side of a pair of knots, and creating a knotted trellis. Knot around a narrow strip of card to keep the space between the knots even.

Twisted Fringe

A minimum of two threads—or two sets of threads—can be twisted together. Take the fringe bundle and separate into equal sets. Twist one set in the direction in which the yarn is twisted (S or Z—see Spinning, page 13) until tight. Secure by taping or pinning to a surface while twisting the other set/sets in the same direction. When you have twisted all the threads hold the ends of the sets together and twist, as one, in the opposite direction to ply together. Knot loosely at the end to secure until all bundles are twisted. Finally, secure the ends at the desired length by whipping (see below), or with a tight knot.

Braided Fringe

There is a huge variety of braided fringes. Two types are outlined below.

Three-group flat braid

This is the most commonly known. Secure cloth, e.g., by weighting it on a table and divide fringe bundle into three groups. Hold the two right-hand groups together between thumb and forefinger. Place left-hand group over center group, and hold together. Repeat until braid is the desired length, and secure. When all braids have been made, finish permanently.

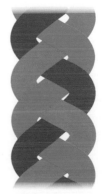

Four-group round braid

It doesn't matter which way this braid hangs because it is round. Secure the cloth and divide the fringe bundle into four groups, two at the right and two at the left. Take the extreme right-hand group behind two groups to the left, up (between these two and the extreme left group), then back to the right over one group. (It returns to its own side but is now nearer to the center.)

Repeat with the extreme left-hand group: behind two groups to the right, up, back to the left over one group. Continue until the desired length is reached and knot loosely to secure. When all braids have been made, finish permanently as desired.

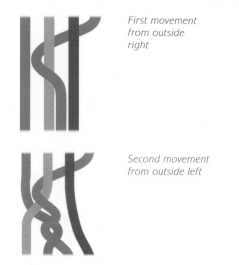

First movement from outside right

Second movement from outside left

Hemstitching Off the Loom

It is best to secure weaving on a table with a weight, rather than bunched up in the hand.
Edges Draw out spacer threads and work as above (see Hemstitching, page 242).
Hemstitched hem Fold the hem so that the top fold sits at the lower edge of the drawn-thread section. Tack in place. Pull out the spacer threads. Hemstitch into three layers to the hem, catching in a set number of vertical threads. On

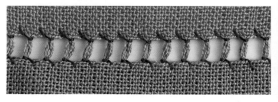

Hem with hemstitched border

the other side of the drawn threads work another row of hemstitching, working into the single layer.

Whipping

You can do this after laundering because any yarn shrinkage will tighten the whipping but not distort the weaving. For short lengths of whipping, use one of the threads in the bundle; for longer lengths, use a separate thread.

Using one of the threads in the bundle Separate one thread at the whipping point. Position a suitably sized sewing needle with the eye away from the loose ends. Wind the thread around the needle and all other ends together, working toward the eye. When you have made four to eight wraps, thread the whipping thread through the needle and pull back down through the whipping.

Hidden style Suitable for whipping with a contrasting thread. Fold back a short length of the whipping thread to make a loop, and place it along the bundle. Start to whip around the loop and bundle toward the loop. When the desired length of whipping has been reached, hold the whipping securely in one hand and insert the end of the whipping thread loosely through the loop.

Pull the short end of thread emerging at the other end until the clasped join is in the center of the whipping. Snip off both ends of the thread.

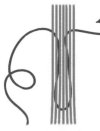

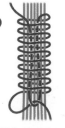

Loop in whipping thread

Whipping thread through loop

Both loops pulled to center

Wet Finishing

When the woven piece is taken from the loom it is called "gray cloth," probably because originally it would have been gray in color due to dirt. The wet finishing process combines heat and pressure to finish the cloth. There are various techniques used within this phase.

Crabbing Setting by steaming before washing. Done with a very wet cloth and hot iron. Cover fabric with a wet cloth, place iron on cloth until steam rises, and lift iron into the next position. Do not slide the iron across. Crab until the cloth is dry and then wash and wind on a roller.
Use for wool; wool mixes; tabby; special effects yarns (lightly).

Scouring Removing oil and dirt by soaking. If the length to be scoured is short, use a sink or bowl, otherwise use the bathtub. Soak the cloth in water as hot as the fiber can stand (see Fibers, pages 12–15), using a mild detergent. Keep changing the water until it remains clear of any dirt or oil. Do not scrub or rub.
Use for wool; wool mixes.

Fulling (or Milling) Working the cloth so that the structure melds together. Put cloth in a shallow amount of water—of the same temperature as for scouring—with enough mild detergent to make a lather. (Soap can produce a scum that is difficult to remove from the scales of natural fibers.) Either squeeze the cloth repeatedly in the sink, or "walk" the cloth with bare feet in the tub! If the lather subsides before fulling is complete, replace both water and detergent at the same temperature. (Changes of temperature will felt rather than full the cloth.) Check the cloth constantly to see if it has reached the correct texture. Fulling can't be undone. Once ready, rinse using the same temperature of water. Set to dry on a roller.
Use for wool; wool mixes.

Winding on a roller A slatted roller is best, although a cardboard tube can be used. Cover the roller with sheeting to prevent any staining. Wind the fabric around the roller, keeping it smooth and flat, with the selvedges straight, and the weft at right angles across the width.
Use for wool; wool mixes.

Laundering For fabrics that do not require scouring or fulling. Use a mild detergent—or hair shampoo if you feel that detergent is too harsh. Handwashing is best.
Washing Use for cotton and linen (hot); silk (hand-hot); man-made (warm); special effects yarns (test first).
Rinsing Cotton and linen (cool); wool, wool mixes, and special effects yarns (at washing temperature); silk (add teaspoon of vinegar to next-to-last rinse).
Drying (all types) Do not wring—squeeze (smaller pieces can be rolled in a towel). Dry naturally.

Pressing Use a wet cloth and dry iron, or a dry cloth and a steam iron. Place cloth on the fabric and press with iron. Lift iron to move to next section. Do not move iron across the fabric.
Use for all.

Ironing Done after the other finishing techniques. As the structure of the cloth will have been secured, you can move the iron across it. Ironing too soon in the finishing process can move threads out of position in the weave structure.
Use for all. Temperature to suit yarn type.
Note: Iron cotton on wrong side while damp; linen on both sides to polish.

Glossary

Apron
A length of sturdy cloth or series of cords attached to the back and front beams of the loom.

Balanced weave
When there are the same number of warp ends per unit of measurement as there are weft picks over the same unit of measurement.

Bast
From plant stems (see Fibers, page 13).

Batten see Beater

Beam
The back (or front) roller on the loom.

Beaming
Winding the warp threads onto the back beam under tension.

Beat
The confirming of a pick into position using a beater.

Beater
The swinging frame at the front of the loom that holds the reed, which is swung forward to set the pick into place. Can be overslung (pivoting from the castle) or underslung (pivoting from the lower framework of the loom).

Block
One pattern or threading unit, or one area forming a separate section. As a verb it means to set a piece of work into shape.

Bobbin (quill)
Small spool wound with thread, used with a boat shuttle.

Bobbin winder
Device for winding weft thread onto the bobbin (see Basic Equipment, page 11).

Bodkin
A needle with a blunt end.

Boll
Seedpod of the cotton plant.

Boundweave
Each pick is "bound" by a secondary pick using the opposite lift.

Braid (plait)
The interlacement of threads to create a narrow structure. All the threads are used in turn to create the structure, there is no separately defined warp and weft.

Burling see Mending

Castle
The upright structure at the top of the loom from which the shafts are suspended.

Cone
Yarn wound onto a conical shape.

Cord
Two or more yarns or groups of yarns twisted together. (See Finishings, page 245.)

Count
The thickness of the yarn.

Crabbing
A finishing technique by which cloth is set by steam. (See Finishings, page 247.)

Crazing
Also known as "crows' feet." The distorted effect that can often occur after tabby weave is washed.

Dent
The space between two teeth in the reed or raddle.

Draft
The diagrammatic representation of the threading order, the weaving sequence and, by these, the cloth structure.

Dressing the loom
Placing the warp onto the loom—beaming, winding, threading, and sleying.

Drying Roller
A slatted or solid roller used to set and dry cloth.

End
A warp thread.

Fabric
Cloth, textile, or a woven piece.

Face of cloth
The top side of the fabric. Weaving may be done face down so that the face is on the underside of the weaving.

Fell
The position during weaving after the last pick.

Fiber
The small hairlike units that are spun into yarn. May be natural or man-made.

Filament
A continuous length of fiber such as silk or man-made. (See Fibers and Yarns, pages 12–15.)

Finishing
The work done to the woven piece after it has been removed from the loom.

Fish see Reed hook

Fringe
The ends of the warp either left loose or worked into a corded or braided structure. (See Finishings, pages 242–246.)

Fulling
A finishing technique—working the wet woven piece so that the structure melds together. (See Finishings, pages 242–246.)

Gray cloth
The cloth taken from the loom prior to finishing.

Ground cloth
The basic interlaced structure of a patterned cloth.

Harness see Shaft

Heading
A short series of ground cloth picks woven at the beginning and end of a piece to stabilize the structure and protect the woven edges when removed from the loom.

Heald see Heddle

Heddle
Wire or string loops attached to the shafts, with a central eye through which individual ends pass to maintain them in position during weaving.

Interlace
The interweaving of warp and weft.

Intersect
The movement from front to back and back to front of a warp end or weft pick.

Leash see Heddle

Lever
On a table loom and moved by hand. Controls movement of individual shafts.

Loom waste
That portion of the warp which cannot be woven. (See Warp Length Calculations, pages 20–21.)

Mending (Burling)
Darning in loose threads and broken ends, and replacing wrong picks prior to wet finishing. (See Finishings, pages 244–245.)

Milling see Fulling

Noiled yarns
Textured silk yarns.

Nubs
Tangled short silk fibers added during spinning to create textured silk yarns.

Pedals see Treadles

Pick (Shot)
A single inserted row of weft thread.

Plain weave see Tabby

Plait see Braid

Ply
The twisting together of two or more single strands of thread. (See Yarns, pages 14–15.)

Raddle
A frame, like an open comb, with teeth set at regular intervals into which the warp ends are placed to align them correctly during threading.

Reed
A frame, like a closed comb, positioned within the beater, with teeth set at regular intervals through which the warp ends are placed to align them correctly during weaving.

Reed hook (fish)
A thin, flat hook for drawing the ends through the reed.

Rice see Swift

Roller see Beam and Drying roller

Scouring
The process of removing oil and dirt from the cloth.

Selvedge
The closed woven edge on either side of the cloth.

Sett
The number of ends per measuring unit. Also the number of picks per unit.

Setting up see Dressing the loom

Shaft (Harness)
A frame holding heddles, suspended from the castle.

Shed
The opening between raised and lowered warp ends into which the weft is placed.

Shot see Pick

Shuttle
The stick or implement that holds the weft.

Singles
Fibers spun or twisted into a single strand.

Sleying
Threading the ends through the reed.

Spool
Yarn on a small tube.

Spool rack
Apparatus for holding several spools horizontally on a series of metal rods. Can be used as an aid when winding a warp.

Staple
The length of the individual fiber.

Sticks
• Apron: A loom-width stick attached to the front or back apron.

• Back: Tied onto the back apron rod to hold the warp ends.

• Cross: A pair of sticks, inserted into opposite sheds of the warp on either side of the cross (created when winding the warp), which maintain the alternating order for the warp ends to be threaded through the heddles.

• Front: Tied to the front apron rod to hold the warp ends.

• Heading stick: Can be inserted to provide a straight edge against which to beat the initial heading.

• Pick-up: Used to pick up warp ends not automatically raised by the shafts.

• Shed: Thin broad stick inserted into the warp that can be turned on edge to provide a shed.

• Tension: A stick, inserted under some of the warp ends behind the shafts, taken back to just under the back beam and hung with weights, to re-tension any loose threads.

• Warp: Inserted between the layers of warp threads when winding on the loom to keep the threads from embedding into the previous layer. Thick paper can be used instead of sticks.

Stretcher see Temple

Swift
A skein holder. It can be an umbrella, rotating with the skein held horizontally; or rice, where the skein is held vertically by two small revolving drums.

Tabby (plain weave)
The warp and weft interlace by moving over and under single threads.

Take-up
The reduction in length of the warp and width of the weft due to interlacement.

Tassel
A bound bunch of threads.

TAW
"Trompe as writ," woven as drawn in. The shedding draft follows the same pattern as the threading draft.

Teeth
The dividers in the raddle and reed.

Tension
The degree to which the warp is stretched during weaving. Also the degree to which the weft is stretched if using a temple.

Threading
Inserting the warp ends through the heddle eyes; also can be applied to inserting the warp ends through the reed (sleying).

Threading hook
A small narrow hook on a handle used to draw the warp ends through the heddles.

Thrums
The waste ends of the warp that cannot be woven.

Tie-up
The way in which the shafts are grouped for weaving. On a floor loom combinations of shafts are attached, or tied, to treadles.

Treadle (pedal)
The levers at the base of the loom to which the shafts are attached. Depressing the treadles automatically controls the movement of those shafts.

Twill
Weaving a set combination of adjacent ends together by sequential raising or lowering of those sets. (See Basic Threadings, pages 26–29.)

Twist
The spin given to a yarn to give it strength. Also the direction it is made: either S or Z. (See page 13.)

Tying on
Finally tying the ends onto the front (or back) stick at the completion of warping.

Warp
The threads stretching from the front to the back of the loom. Also the threads along the length of the cloth.

Warp-faced
Weaving in which only the warp threads show on the surface.

Warping see Dressing the loom

Warping board
A frame into which pegs are inserted and around which the warp is wound to provide the correct length before dressing the loom. (See page 11.)

Warping mill
A revolving drum or framework, either horizontal or vertical, around which the warp is wound in a spiral, to provide the correct length before dressing the loom. (See page 11.)

Weave
The systematic order of interlacements of warp and weft threads.

Web
An older term for the cloth on the loom.

Weft
The thread passing from side to side. Also the threads along the width of the cloth.

Weft-faced
Weaving in which only the weft threads show on the surface.

Whipping
Tight wrapping of a thread around a group of threads.

Winding
Placing the warp threads on the beam at the beginning of dressing the loom, and turning that beam so the warp threads are wound around it.

Winding on
Winding the section of just-woven cloth onto the front beam so the next section of warp can be woven.

Woolen
• Material: Woven using woolen yarn (see below).

• Yarn: Made from wool carded so that the fibers lie across the twist, thus entrapping more air.

Worsted
• Material: Woven using worsted yarn (see below).

• Yarn: Made from wool combed so that the fibers are straight and parallel before spinning. They are smoother and stronger than woolen yarns.

Woven as drawn in
see TAW

Yarn
Spun fibers. The type of thread used.

Index

Fold out this flap to find an at-a-glance guide explaining how to use the charts in this book.

Credits

In special memory of Vic Edwards: weaver and tutor.

My thanks to all those who have supported and encouraged me, especially my family, who have accustomed themselves to looms and yarns filling all available spaces in the house; the team at Quarto, who have guided me through the complexities of this book's production; and to all weavers past and present, who have set me on the pathway.

Thanks also to Nancy Lee Childs at Handweavers Studio (www.handweaversstudio.co.uk) for her unfailing wisdom and advice as to the yarns used.

Thanks to P&M Woolcraft (www.pmwoolcraft.co.uk) for supplying the selection of fibers.

Quarto would like to thank the following for supplying images for use in this book:
Pages 10–11 Fibrecrafts www.fibrecrafts.com
Old Portsmouth Road, Peasmarsh, Guildford, Surrey, GU3 1LZ, UK
Tel: 0 (+44) 1483565800